Clark Gable
in the 1930s

Clark Gable in the 1930s

The Films That Made Him King of Hollywood

JAMES L. NEIBAUR

McFarland & Company, Inc., Publishers
Jefferson, North Carolina

ISBN (print) 978-1-4766-8044-6
ISBN (ebook) 978-1-4766-4168-3

LIBRARY OF CONGRESS AND BRITISH LIBRARY
CATALOGUING DATA ARE AVAILABLE

Library of Congress Control Number 2021011603

Front cover: Clark Gable circa 1936

Printed in the United States of America

*McFarland & Company, Inc., Publishers
Box 611, Jefferson, North Carolina 28640
www.mcfarlandpub.com*

Acknowledgments

First and foremost, my thanks to my dear writing assistant Katie Carter, who has now been with me for about a dozen or so books. She truly lives every book with me, screening the films and offering valuable insights and observations, while also catching my errors. I wish I had her working with me from the very beginning, but she wasn't even born when I wrote my first two books!

Thanks also to John Gallagher. He shared with me his research on William Wellman, Loretta Young and Tay Garnett, which helped this project greatly.

Thanks to Peter Jackel, a friend for over 50 years, who allowed me to borrow freely from his massive DVD library so I could screen all the Gable movies I didn't already own myself.

Thanks also to Terri Lynch, Ted Okuda, Kelly Parmelee, Allie Schulz, Lea Stans, Kim Morgan, Farran Smith Nehme, Imogen Smith, Kat Ellinger, for providing encouragement and support with their work and their friendship.

Finally, to my late son Max Neibaur, who will forever inspire everything I do.

Table of Contents

Table of Contents

Introduction

Clark Gable is one of the true icons of American cinema, and in 1937 he was rightfully named the King of Hollywood films after consistent growth as a star during the 1930s. A careful study of his work during this decade is perhaps the best way to truly understand his lasting fame. The fact that our study of his 1930s movies will conclude with his most famous film, 1939's *Gone with the Wind*, makes this focus even more significant.

The 1930s is one of the most important decades in American cinema, ushering in the talking picture revolution, building its style with pre–Code classics, and exploring escapist musicals and anarchic comedies in response to the Great Depression. The decade culminated with what many believe to be the absolute greatest year in movies, 1939, the year that gave us such lasting screen classics as *The Wizard of Oz, Mr. Smith Goes to Washington, Dark Victory, Wuthering Heights, Gunga Din* and, of course, *Gone with the Wind*.

During this decade, Clark Gable represented the quintessential Hollywood actor. Tall, attractive and charismatic, he played heavy drama and light comedy with equal aplomb. His rugged image came to represent the quintessential male—tough, uncompromising, able to handle himself in any situation.

Early in his career, he was developing this image. It didn't take long, because its elements came naturally to him; they were already a part of his inherent personality. An oil rigger who found his way into theater, Gable scored in a stage performance of *The Last Mile*, which led to small parts in movies. There was always something about Gable's presence, his distinctive voice and his affable yet mysterious manner that attracted moviegoers, even if the role was quite small. Gable always managed to resonate when on screen.

He might have landed at Warner Brothers, nestled among Hollywood tough guys like Edward G. Robinson, James Cagney, Humphrey Bogart and George Raft. But he ended up at the glossy Metro-Goldwyn-Mayer studios, considered the major production company of the time. Right away he connected on-screen playing opposite the likes of Wallace Beery, Jean Harlow, Joan Crawford, Norma Shearer and Lionel Barrymore. By 1932, he was one of the biggest stars in Hollywood, and a film was already sold to exhibitors just because he was in it. Then in 1934, when his studio loaned him to the small studio Columbia Pictures as punishment, the result was *It Happened One Night*, one of the finest films of all time. Winning Academy Awards in every major category, *It Happened One Night* ensured that movie stardom would continue for Gable.

1

Introduction

In this book I will explore every one of Gable's 1930s movies, assessing each for its cinematic aesthetic. The text will discuss how well each of Gable's movies from this decade has held up over time and will provide as much background info that our research will allow. The goal is to have a book-length study that both investigates and celebrates Gable's timeless impact on movies of the 1930s.

Things didn't always work out. Sometimes Gable attempted roles that didn't jibe with his established screen persona. And although as an actor he was accepting of the challenge, his audience wasn't ready to accept him too far outside the norm. But we will discuss just why a historical drama like *Parnell* flopped, and how it almost cost him his biggest role, that of Rhett Butler in *Gone with the Wind*.

We will also see how his very early films, before he was a big star, also venture outside the screen persona he eventually established, which makes it interesting to reflect on those films knowing the type of roles in which he would later excel.

Gable remained active until his death, which occurred 12 days after completing his last film. Despite his life being shattered by the untimely death of his wife Carole Lombard in a 1942 plane crash, he had persevered. Even though he was no longer King of Hollywood, he continued to appear in good films like *The Hucksters, Command Decision, Teacher's Pet* and *The Misfits*. There will be a concluding chapter discussing these later films, but the body of the text will concern itself with each of the films Gable made in the 1930s, when he was at the height of his powers and did his best work.

This book is not a biography. It will not attempt to explore deeper issues in Gable's personal life unless they relate directly to the film being discussed. There are plenty of other books where one can read about Gable's personal life (see this book's bibliography). This text is concerned with examining his work—the films that remain his lasting legacy.

Adela Rogers St. Johns once wrote, "I've met, in my business, a lot of the great men of our time. I've met several presidents of the United States, and Colonel Lindbergh, and Jack London, and Captain Eddie Rickenbacker, and I knew Valentino. But I think Clark Gable is the only completely natural human being I have ever met in my life. And that's something to say about an actor."[1] As this book looks at the most significant decade in his film career, it will result in a better understanding and deeper appreciation of Clark Gable, the actor and the man.

1

The Early Years

Clark Gable was born William Clark Gable on February 1, 1901, in Cadiz, Ohio. His mother died when he was quite young. After his father remarried, his stepmother introduced him to music and literature, both of which he loved. Through his father, he developed interests in hunting and fishing. He also had a mechanical inclination, so he loved working on cars and engines.

Gable saw his first play, *The Bird of Paradise*, at the age of 17, and was drawn to the theater. He worked as an oil rigger in various towns while playing parts in small plays along the way. He was inspired by actress Laura Hope Crews, whom he met in Ohio; years later she would appear in some of his films. He was also connected with Josephine Dillon, a Portland, Oregon, theater manager. Josephine helped coach him as an actor, from getting his teeth fixed and hair styled to working on his vocal range. In 1924, they decided he should try a film career.

On the set of Gable's film *Manhattan Melodrama* (1934), he recalled for interviewer Wood Soanes[2]:

Dad was sure I was insane when I gave up a job in the Oklahoma fields at $12 a day to go with a traveling road company. We barnstormed through the Middle West and finally wound up in Portland. There the show collapsed and I joined another troupe, this time on a cooperative basis. It certainly was a stroke of genius on my part. One week we did 14 shows and my bit was exactly $1.30. Even then I was willing to go ahead, but the company collapsed and I got a job in the classified department at *The Oregonian*. I wasn't so hot as a solicitor, but I did earn enough as a collector for the telephone company to get my fare to Los Angeles.

Clark and Josephine Dillon traveled to Hollywood, where she both managed him and married him, despite being 17 years older.

Gable managed to secure some bit roles and extra work in a few major films, working with the likes of director Erich von Stroheim and actors Pola Negri, Clara Bow and Corinne Griffith. He had better success on stage. Lionel Barrymore encouraged him in the early days and became a dear friend.

In 1927, Gable was playing a newspaperman in *Chicago*, a play at the Lurie Theater in San Francisco. Adwal Jones wrote about his performance in the *San Francisco Examiner*[3]:

He gives the only three-dimension portrayal of a newspaperman that has ever been witnessed on the stage in San Francisco. He may not be a Sir Henry Irving but that achievement, in the eyes of critics, is glory enough. He is a large, genial and unabashed young fellow who might be a professional ball player, or something like that. "Well, the newspapermen seem to like it," he said. "I think it was Lionel Barrymore, with whom I acted in *The Copperhead*, that gave me the formula if there is a formula for acting. He told me that no matter how straight away the role was, to act it with a dash of character, to make real and not stagey. Oh, yes, I did once work on a newspaper. It was on a paper you never heard of, the *Akron Daily Journal*. I was dramatic editor on it. The town had one theater, and it was occupied by a semi-amateur stock company. Perhaps I wasn't very frank in my criticisms. You see, I was the Juvenile lead in the company." However, it is doubtful if any newspaperman in this city could act Jake in Chicago two-thirds as well. Gable moves with nonchalance, with the idea that a good murder is too precious to be wasted, and that if his tabloid doesn't put on a good show, the readers will be grievously disappointed.... His range has been wide, for a young player, and not the least of his merits is that his acting is curiously devoid of mechanical quality.

Gable's natural quality as an actor was noticed this early, but silent films couldn't capture that quality as well as stage productions.

In 1930, Gable appeared on stage in *The Last Mile*. He scored triumphantly and received more good notices. In an article for *The Los Angeles Times*, Alma Whitaker wrote[4]:

> It is still a tragically dramatic paradox that a young man of 29 in good standing can reach his highest attainment by depicting a condemned murderer leading a prison riot. Clark Gable, who enacts the role of John Mears in *The Last Mile* at the Majestic, radiates happy success when one greets him behind the scenes, without makeup, in the gray shirt and trousers of the prison garb. Yet before the curtain he depicts desperate wretchedness, ruthless vengeance, coldly savage brutality. "I wasn't intended for the stage," grins Gable. "I worked for a year with my father, who is an Oklahoma oil man. But I was unhappy and unsatisfactory and ran off with a little traveling show that played the northwest towns. Say, we felt like big time when we got into Portland, Oregon. Then I got ambitious and came to Los Angeles, intent on getting into the movies. When Miss Lillian Albertson sent for me for *The Last Mile*, I was in *Love, Honor and Betray*, with Alice Brady in New York. They telephoned me long distance on a Friday to be in Los Angeles by Monday! ... I saw the New York version. I want to tell you this part of John Mears draws something from all the experience I ever had. It is easily my best to date."

Gable mentioned that he failed in movies, and the reporter inquired about his perhaps trying them again, now that pictures could talk. Gable told her, "I'm so very American. I don't speak English as the Hollywood actors speak it. And I can't sing or croon or anything. So maybe my chances are not so good."

Gable divorced Josephine Dillon in April 1930. Their marriage had been one of convenience, for better opportunities in the theater. Gable and Dillon both later admitted that their marriage was never consummated.

Established on stage, Gable pondered the possibility of work in sound films. Theater actors were sought for their prowess in delivering dialogue, something many silent stars were not able to do. Also, foreign accents were often a hindrance, so Gable sounding American was actually a plus.

After finishing his run in *The Last Mile*, Gable felt that perhaps his American-sounding voice might work well in a Western that was being cast by independent producer E.B. Derr, president of the Pathe Exchange distribution company. He secured a supporting role, and thus began one of the most remarkable film careers in the history of motion pictures. Clark Gable was about to make his first talking picture.

2

The Films

The Painted Desert

Directed and Written by Howard Higgin, Tom Buckingham
Produced by E.B. Derr
Cinematographer: Edward Snyder
Editor: Clarence Kolster
Cast: William Boyd, Helen Twelvetrees, William Farnum, J. Farrell MacDonald,
    Clark Gable, Charles Sellon, Hugh Adams, Wade Boteler, Will Walling, Edmund
    Breese, Edward Hearn, William LeMaire, Richard Cramer, Al St. John, Edgar
    Dearing, G. Raymond Nye, James Donlan, George Burton, Jim Mason, Cliff
    Lyons, Clem Beauchamp, Cy Clegg, Brady Kline, Rose Plumer
Released January 18, 1931
Pathé Exchange
79 minutes

The Painted Desert has the distinction of being Clark Gable's first sound film, but
also an early vehicle for William Boyd who, a few years later, began his long run as
Hopalong Cassidy in movies (and then television). *The Painted Desert* benefits from
good cinematography that took advantage of the Arizona location. Despite the tentative dialogue delivery of many early talkies, it's a fairly good Western drama.

Traveling through the Arizona desert, cowboys Cash and Jeff (William Farnum
and J. Farrell MacDonald) find an abandoned baby in a covered wagon. They don't
want to leave it, so they take care of it, while arguing over which will become the
caregiver. Cash takes over the care of the child, causing animosity with Jeff. The baby
grows up to be Bill Holbrook (Boyd), who works on Cash's ranch. Jeff has his own
ranch and feuds with Cash over a water hole on Jeff's property. Bill attempts to solve
the rift when Cash tries to stampede his cattle onto Jeff's property. But he ends up
making things worse. Cash, feeling betrayed, asks Bill to leave. Bill goes to see Jeff,
who gives him permission to mine the property when tungsten ore is discovered.

Gable is Rance Brett, a drifter who lands a job with Jeff. Rance is smitten with
Jeff's daughter Mary Ellen (Helen Twelvetrees), which causes a conflict with Bill.
When Bill establishes a successful mine, it is sabotaged with explosions, and it is
feared that Cash has reacted. It turns out to be the work of Rance. In the end, the old
friends are brought together by the relationship of Mary Ellen and Bill.

As is often true of early talkies, the performances in *The Painted Desert* can
seem a bit melodramatic. Boyd's performance is central to the narrative and

effectively anchors the proceedings. This gives movie novice Gable a strong character to play off and respond to, allowing him to effectively explore the antagonist character he portrays. There are elements of Gable's acting that immediately establish factors that would continue to highlight future performances. The charisma is already evident. His voice and delivery are other factors—and, most significantly, the way he is able to subtly convey his feelings through expression. A lot of these factors are already evident from the first shot of him, before we have even gotten to know his character. There is something about the combination of his facial expressions and rather gruff delivery of dialogue that suggests someone with a roguish personality.

Because he had almost no experience in films, it is impressive that stage actor Gable was able to respond to the intimacy of the movie camera. He appears to already realize that the subtle nuance of his expressions would make a difference. One of his best scenes features him trading dialogue with Charles Sellon, an oldtimer who was in many Westerns. (Sellon might be best remembered as the blind Mr. Muckle in W.C. Fields' *It's a Gift*.) Sellon's drunken character wonders why Rance is not joining Mary Ellen's party, and he dismissively growls, "Nobody wants me there," with the classic Gable inflection. He is sitting on a nearby fence, smoking pensively. When he goes to the wagon to say goodbye, he smiles at Mary Ellen, and his expression turns to anger. When asked what's wrong, he growls, "Nothing!" without looking at Mary Ellen. With every moment of screen time, Gable's character resonates.

It has often been stated that Gable could not ride a horse when he got the job for this film and had to learn quickly. Other studies claim that Gable could indeed ride, but hadn't in years, so he arranged to take lessons in order to sharpen his skills. Gable recalled for interviewer Wood Soanes,[5] "They asked me if I could ride a horse and I said yes. But between the question and the ride there was some intensive practicing at a riding academy and a number of days when I preferred to stand. Since that time I've developed into a pretty proficient horseman."

The Painted Desert was co-directed by Howard Higgin, who was primarily a writer but dabbled in directing. Edward Snyder's cinematography benefits the film most. Because it was shot on location and not in a studio or on a backlot, the vastness of the negative space helps to enhance the narrative. When screening a sharp copy of the film, *The Painted Desert* is visually impressive.

It's obvious that to the moviemakers, dialogue was more important than action—no surprise since it's an early talkie—but to some extent this hampers the movie. The story concept and the fact that it was semi-epic, taking place over several years, is quite interesting but, as with many early talkies, the dialogue is often stilted.

There were some problems during the filming. Boyd and Gable were nearly killed during the filming of a sequence where an explosion caused falling rocks. Both men escaped serious injury, but several technicians were hospitalized, and director Higgin suffered a broken ankle. Even worse was that the baby who appeared in the earlier scenes, Thais Baer, died while on location. An article from Cameron, Arizona, stated[6]:

J. Farrell McDonald and Helen Twelvetrees flank Clark Gable in *The Painted Desert* (1931).

Thais Baer, 14-month-old movie star in the Pathe Film company's picture *The Painted Desert*, died out on the desert, it was learned here tonight, from an undetermined cause. The baby was portraying the infant life of William Boyd, playing the leading male role in the production. The company has been on location for the past week in the Painted Desert, approximately 50 miles from here. The child's death occurred Monday, but owing to lack of desert communication lines the demise was not learned until tonight. Mrs. Baer, wife of a Burbank, California, architect, was at the child's bedside when it died. The body, it was said, will be sent to the California city for burial. It was the fourth appearance of the baby in the movies. She portrayed an infant's part in *Eyes of the World*, and in two Educational pictures.

The Painted Desert was set to be released in the fall of 1930, but the financial situation at Pathé Exchange caused a series of delays. It finally premiered in January 1931 and was in wide release by that March. The *Picture Play* reviewer was not impressed[7]:

Perhaps, if you see this, you will tell me what it's all about or go further and explain the reason of its being. For a duller and more pointless picture I've never seen. Yet William Boyd is interesting and so is Helen Twelvetrees. So, too, is the Western scenery. But neither one nor the other can make a picture unaided by a story, or at least some general conception of what is in mind. Mr. Boyd, Miss Twelvetrees and Clark Gable act their respective roles with more

8

distinction than is usually found in a Western, but there is no denying their wasted efforts. So, too, are the activities of stampeding cattle who might just as well have been allowed to graze in peace, and dynamiting cliffs seem wasteful until the thought comes that perhaps the picture was written around the destruction for commercial purposes.

Despite this critic's misgivings, he appeared to be reasonably impressed with Gable's work.

Upon the release of *The Painted Desert*, the studio was inundated with letters from moviegoers who wanted to know more about this newcomer Clark Gable. Reviewers pointed out Gable, impressed with the stage actor's fine debut. The bigger studios took notice. Gable's friend from the theater, Lionel Barrymore, suggested that his studio, Metro-Goldwyn-Mayer, consider Gable. He was given a supporting role in the feature *The Easiest Way*.

The Easiest Way

Directed by Jack Conway
Screenplay: Edith Ellis
Based on the play by Eugene Walter
Produced by Hunt Stromberg
Cinematographer: John J. Mescall
Editor: Frank Sullivan
Cast: Constance Bennett, Adolphe Menjou, Robert Montgomery, Anita Page, Marjorie Rambeau, J. Farrell MacDonald, Clara Blandick, Clark Gable, Jack Hanlon, Dell Henderson, Andy Shuford, Hedda Hopper, Charles Judels, William H. O'Brien, Michael Stuart, Richard Bishop, Lynton Brent, Noel Francis, Francis Palmer Tilton
Released February 7, 1931
MGM
73 minutes

In his first MGM film after being put under contract, Gable truly resonates in a small role, just as he had in *The Painted Desert*. In this case, the character, and his surroundings, are much closer to the persona Gable would eventually develop and hone to perfection.

Constance Bennett is Laura, a young woman from a large, poor family during the Depression. She picks up a gig modeling for an ad agency and quickly attracts the attention of the head man, Mr. Brockton (Adolphe Menjou). She starts to see him for clandestine encounters, and soon is living in a swank apartment, riding in a chauffeured limo and wearing the best clothes. She then meets and falls in love with a newspaper reporter (Robert Montgomery), and tells Brockton she is leaving him. But while waiting for the newsman to finish a long assignment overseas, she runs out of money and returns to Brockton. When the newsman returns, she tries to go back to him, but Brockton tells him that she has been untrue, and he leaves her. Despondent, she goes to the home of her sister Peg (Anita Page), wife of honest, hardworking laundry truck driver Nick (Clark Gable). Nick comforts Laura and convinces her that the newsman will come back to her.

The Easiest Way was based on a 1909 play by Eugene Walter. In 1917, David O. Selznick produced the first film version, featuring Clara Kimball Young. First National was going to film it in 1927 with Henry King directing. There were moral objections about its content and the project was shelved. Subsequent attempts to film the play met with the same objections from the Hays Office. When the fearless Irving Thalberg decided to produce it, the Hays Office complained that Laura wasn't punished enough in the end for her lifestyle.

The Easiest Way is essentially a romantic melodrama. Adolphe Menjou functions just fine as the smarmy Brockton, Robert Montgomery has the sort of carefree dazzle that wealthy characters in early 1930s films always radiate, and Constance Bennett alternates between innocence and cunning savvy. Its content is quintessential pre–Code, and the performances are good. It is not difficult to see how the screen brightens up when Clark Gable appears. His character is pretty removed from the immediate narrative, but when he is on screen, he has a presence that is far more attractive and interesting than any of the three leads.

One of Gable's strongest scenes is when Laura visits Nick and Peg after she's established with Brockton. The film shows their modest but comfortable house, paid for by Nick's hard work, and their child. Peg is in the kitchen preparing dinner for her husband, who is arriving home soon. She is happy to see Laura and is delighted when her sister gives her a fancy dress as a gift. However, when Nick comes home, he will have no part of it. He realizes exactly how Laura obtained that dress and confronts her about her lifestyle. Proudly blue collar, Nick states, "I ain't stuck on havin' you drive up here in your fine cars and limousines. We ain't limousine people."

Gable's other impactful scene is when it all ends for Laura and she is back to her innocent, poor beginnings. She peers into the window of their home on Christmas night and is discovered by Nick as he arrives home. When she tries to run away, he stops her. She is invited in, and Nick levels with her:

> Listen, Laura. I wouldn't worry about that Madison guy. Y'know he'll come back one of these days and tear up this town 'til he finds you. He's no different than any other guy. And when he gets cool under the collar…well, you just watch and see.

With his deep, earthy delivery and the twinkle in his eye, this tough truck driver of infallible honesty is ready to offer both forgiveness and support.

The difference between the corrupt bad guy Gable played in *The Painted Desert*, and the honest man he plays in this one, showed how he could attract viewers in different roles. Interestingly, it was the bad guy character that more strongly attracted audiences and was most instrumental in helping him secure an MGM contract.

What is notable about these two roles is that in both, Gable offers up the same

Anita Page and Gable in *The Easiest Way* **(1931).**

tough guy persona. In *The Painted Desert*, he has bad intentions; in this film, his character may be a bit rough, but he is ultimately a good guy. This performance is more akin to his ultimate screen persona; his scene at the end is surprisingly sweet and memorable. The ending of this film is also interesting. It doesn't have a happy ending, but it also doesn't end in tragedy like so many pre–Codes do. Despite the despair that lingers on Laura's face, the movie ends on a note of hopefulness, and that hope is provided by Gable's character.

Because his role is small, period movie reviews didn't give Gable a great deal of attention, but some of the critics recognized him. *The New York Daily News* stated[8]:

We enjoyed *The Easiest Way*. We enjoyed it thoroughly, because Constance Bennett is a charming actress and so beautiful when she's dressed up; because Adolphe Menjou gives a convincing performance; because Robert Montgomery's work in this is far more ingratiating than it was in Garbo's *Inspiration*; because Anita Page, Marjorie Rambeau, and a newcomer to the screen named Clark Gable offer fine support; because the story is simple and logical; because there is plenty of tenement atmosphere and an abundance of beautiful scenery and stunning sets. The picture travels along without a let-up.

The way this review singled Gable out shows that the actor was being noticed right away as his career began.

Gable's ability to play a range of characters being exhibited with his first two talkie movie appearances only increased MGM's interest in the actor. While they were not completely sure how to best use his talents, Gable's performance in his first MGM movie was enough to warrant further investigation into his abilities.

Dance, Fools, Dance

Directed by Harry Beaumont
Screenplay: Aurania Rouverol, Richard Schayer
Story: Aurania Rouverol
Cinematographer: Charles Rosher
Editor: George Hively
Cast: Joan Crawford, Lester Vail, Cliff Edwards, William Bakewell, William Holden,[9] Clark Gable, Earle Foxe, Purnell Pratt, Hale Hamilton, Natalie Moorhead, Joan Marsh, Russell Hopton, Sidney Bracey, Tommy Shugrue, James Donlan, Harry Semels, Robert Livingston, Drew Demarest, Ernie Adams, Sherry Hall, Mortimer Snow, George Magrill, Sam McDaniel, Jack Trent, Ann Dvorak, Wilbur Mack
Released February 7, 1931
MGM
80 minutes

With each successive movie, Gable got a larger supporting role and made that much more of an impact. *Dance, Fools, Dance* is his first of several films with Joan Crawford, who was already an established star. While it is Crawford's film, Gable's impact is even more discernible than it was in his previous two movies. His scenes with Crawford resonate; moviegoers and producers noticed.

When a wealthy man dies soon after the 1929 stock market crash, his son and daughter are shocked to discover that he left them no money. While Bonnie (Joan Crawford) is upset, she is also willing to accept the circumstances and go to work. She prides herself on being a woman of independence and turns down a potential suitor who wants to marry her. Her brother Rodney (William Bakewell) responds more like a privileged rich boy believing that going to work is beneath him.

Bonnie finds a job as a cub reporter on a newspaper, while Rodney becomes involved with bootleggers. As Rodney gets himself into deeper trouble, Bonnie's reporter colleague, Bert Scranton (Cliff Edwards), is murdered by the gangsters for knowing too much. Bonnie decides to investigate the gang herself, taking up where Bert left off, and discovers her brother's involvement. She nearly gets herself killed when she goes undercover as a nightclub dancer to get closer to gang leader Jake Luva (Clark Gable).

One of the quintessential pre–Code melodramas from MGM, *Dance, Fools, Dance* is a Joan Crawford vehicle that allows Gable to truly own his scenes as a tough, snarling, no-nonsense gang leader. The way the Crawford character is developed is significant to how Gable is presented in this film. The opening scenes show Bonnie at a cheerful shipboard party of the privileged rich. She dances, she cavorts, she joins a bunch of the carefree young people diving into the ocean. Her wealthy father is incensed, stating, "I wish you were still young enough to spank!"

When Bonnie and Rodney are told by their late father's lawyer that the crash wiped him out, she is at first overcome—laughing crazily at the absurdity of going from socialite to pauper—and is then reduced to tears. It is a bravura scene for the young Ms. Crawford, and the type of thing she had already perfected. Bonnie had once lived a privileged life where everything came easily to her. She didn't have to worry about the Depression or its effects on the populace. She was in a bubble surrounded by luxury and convenience.

However, Bonnie also has wit and determination, and once she gets her cub reporter job, and is functioning as the only woman in a business filled with men, she gains a sense of self-respect beyond what she experienced as an entitled member of society. She becomes reflective:

> I'm not so sure that I'd like to run around with the old crowd again. I used to think that anything I did was all right. Society! Just a bunch of people who are all for you when you're on the up-and-up, but what would one of them do for you when it came to a showdown? Nothing, except grab your pet belongings at an auction. I'm not fooled about why we were in society, it was because Father had a lot of money. Was that any credit to us? We didn't make it. It isn't who you are, it's *what* you are that counts.

This exhibits not only her reaction to her circumstances (strength and pragmatism), it also reveals an area of women's power that defined a lot of the actress' roles at the time. This helps to also define the Gable character, a supporting role that connects directly to her.

While Bonnie is accepted as a reporter, she frequently writes more than necessary and is heavily edited, and has her stories relegated to the nether reaches of the paper. This isn't a case of the newspaper being dismissive of her, but of Bonnie's own learning process in developing her journalistic skills. She has a desk next to top level reporter Bert Scranton, who is sympathetic to her situation:

Gable and Joan Crawford in their first movie together, *Dance, Fools, Dance* **(1931).**

BERT: You'll learn, kid. Clearness, condensation. Where, what, when and why … that's the idea. Say, don't let those guys on the copy desk bother ya. They're just a lot of butchers at heart. Why, you know what they'd do if they got a chance?
BONNIE: What?
BERT: They'd cut the Lord's Prayer down to a one-line squib.

The film shows Bonnie connecting with Bert so that his murder at the hands of the gangsters hurts her more deeply. She is determined to find out who killed him. The paper is behind her.

Bonnie does not realize that her own brother who killed Bert. Rodney foolishly told Bert too much, so gang leader Jake Luva ordered him to kill the reporter or be killed himself. Rodney does as he's told, then goes into hiding. Bonnie goes undercover as a nightclub dancer, gets hired by Nick, and works to get closer to him. The fact that Bonnie is attractive and knows how to wittily handle men in power, works to her advantage. Jake is tough and commanding but not intelligent enough to figure out what Bonnie is up to. At one club performance, Bonnie's old society friends, including the man who once proposed to her, are in the audience. She can't blow her cover, so she lies to the old boyfriend when he goes back to her dressing room and asks pointedly, "Did you have to come to this?" Defiant, she replies, "Yes, I did."

Bonnie gets closer to Jake. When the phone rings and Bonnie answers, she recognizes Rodney's voice. She then sneaks out a bedroom window at Nick's and goes to her brother, but is spotted by a member of the gang. When she returns to her apartment, Nick and the other gangster are waiting for her. Rodney arrives, there is a shootout, and all three men are killed. Bonnie calls the newspaper and tearfully tells them what happened.

Gable was said to dislike playing bad guys, even though he did some of his best early work as characters on the wrong side of the law. On stage in *The Last Mile*, and in his film debut *The Painted Desert*, audiences connected with Gable in this type of role. However, the studio gave the actor the opportunity to play a good guy in *The Easiest Way*, so their experimenting as to how he was most effective continued. With this larger role, Gable is able to do more with the character. It is jarring when he suddenly slaps Rodney, who is exhibiting his inherent cowardice. He purrs his romantic lines to Bonnie, then snarls when he's at her apartment after finding her out. In their *Dance, Fools, Dance* review, the *Brooklyn Times Union* newspaper stated[10]:

> …Clark Gable figures as a worthy rival of the famous Edward G. Robinson as a portrayer of gunman roles. Gable has not, it may be said in his favor, attempted in the least to imitate Mr. Robinson. His acting in role of Jake Luva is honestly done and we imagine it is true to the life of such figures as Capone, *et al.*

Other reviewers also pointed out Gable's prominence in the film, and how his interpretation of the role was very genuine.

Cliff Edwards, aka Ukulele Ike, was a comic who played that instrument as part of his act. He had most recently done a typically silly comic role in the Buster Keaton MGM vehicle *Doughboys* (1930). He registers nicely as the ill-fated reporter Bert Scranton. When he was asked about playing a role without his ukulele, Edwards said that this was a much different part than he'd been known for playing. "I die at the end," he said.

Dance, Fools, Dance earned a profit of over half a million dollars, and MGM was pleased that Gable was part of the reason. The studio was slowly learning how much his presence could enhance a feature, even one headlined by a major star. In her autobiography, Joan Crawford recalled the effect Gable had on her as soon as he walked onto the set. She later stated that during the scene where he realizes her true identity and grabs her, "his nearness had such an impact, my knees buckled." She said if he hadn't been holding her shoulders, she would have fallen to the ground. "This magnetic man had more sheer animal magic than anyone in the world, and every woman knew it."[11]

The Finger Points

Produced and Directed by John Francis Dillon
Screenplay: W.R. Burnett, John Monk Saunders, Robert Lord
Cinematographer: Ernest Haller
Editor: LeRoy Stone
Cast: Richard Barthelmess, Fay Wray, Regis Toomey, Robert Elliott, Clark Gable, Oscar Apfel, Robert Gleckler, Mickey Bennett, Bob Perry, George Taylor, Adele Watson, James Burtis, Lew Harvey, Herman Krumpfel, Martin Cichy, Frank Marlowe, Bob Perry, Albert Petit, Frank McLure, Field Norton, J. Carrol Naish (voice only)
Released April 11, 1931
First National–Warner Brothers
85 minutes

Around the time that Gable was filming his scenes for *The Easiest Way*, he was loaned to First National–Warner Brothers to play a small role. Because of his background (he was best known for playing a killer in the hit play *The Last Mile*), Warners wanted him to play a similar part in *The Finger Points*.

The film stars Richard Barthelmess, who was quite a big star in silent movies but had trouble maintaining that level of impact in talkies. He later had some success in films like *Heroes for Sale* (1933) and *Only Angels Have Wings* (1939), then left show business to enlist in the Naval Reserve during World War II. Having invested wisely during his career, he lived comfortably until his death in 1963.

Barthelmess seems a bit miscast here as a newspaper reporter who not only makes a salary at his job, but also makes money being paid off by gangsters to keep certain stories *out* of the papers. He approaches the role in a soft and effete manner that doesn't jibe with a character who comfortably deals with underworld characters. Fay Wray, who plays his newspaper co-worker, sees that he lives beyond the means of a journalist and realizes that he is on the take. The film also features Regis Toomey as a hotshot reporter type and Gable as the gangster who arranges for Barthelmess to get hush money payments (and takes a sizable percentage himself each time).

It is hard to believe that Wray's character would be romantically interested in Barthelmess. She, Barthelmess and Toomey all have decent chemistry as a group of friends, but she comes off as a lot tougher than both of them. It is hard to sympathize with Barthelmess, especially as the film progresses and he continues to take money from the gangsters. In his own way, he is as crooked as the Gable character.

During Gable's first big scene, he sets up the initial payment to Barthelmess. Gable easily steals the scene from Barthelmess. Exhibiting his cool assurance and tough-but-calm demeanor, he plays a man who is completely in control. He sits behind his desk and picks up his phone, and in just minutes, a deal is struck for $20,000. The reporter doesn't like splitting the money with the gangster, so he starts making the deals himself. The gangster doesn't like being cut out of the action, so he confronts the reporter at his home. Suddenly, the naiveté previously exhibited by the reporter turns to smugness, which further angers the gangster. In this scene, director John Francis Dillon shows how Gable towers over Barthelmess in height, which adds further effect to the scene. It's also interesting that the gangster sees that the reporter is walking into real trouble with his next situation. Eventually the reporter's continued smugness frustrates him, and he realizes that arrangements must be made to rub him out.

Made before *Dance, Fools, Dance* but released later, *The Finger Points* didn't amount to much in Gable's career; in studies of the actor's career, it is often overlooked. In a review printed in the October 5, 1931, *Honolulu Star Bulletin*, critic

Henry E. Daughtery stated,[12] "There has been a lot of publicity distributed about Clark Gable in recent months, and he may be an actor of superlative worth but he is not a prodigy in this film." Irene Thirer of the *New York Daily News* was more positive, stating,[13] "We enjoyed Regis Toomey's work, thought Fay Wray pretty but stilted, and admired Clark Gable's performance tremendously. In fact, the cast does a great deal for an only fair program picture." According to the critic for the periodical *Silver Screen*, "Most exciting gangster film seen since *Little Caesar*.... The picture isn't plausible all the

A young Gable was building his career in 1931, playing both good guys and bad guys. In *The Finger Points*, he's a bad guy.

way through, but it's thrilling. Richard Barthelmess, Clark Gable and Regis Toomey are grand."

Gable being singled out along with the film's two bigger male stars as "grand" would further influence MGM's continued interest in his work.

The Secret Six

Directed by George W. Hill
Screenplay: Frances Marion
Produced by George W. Hill, Irving Thalberg
Cinematographer: Harold Wenstrom
Editor: Blanche Sewell
Cast: Wallace Beery, Lewis Stone, Johnny Mack Brown, Jean Harlow, Marjorie Rambeau, Paul Hurst, Clark Gable, Ralph Bellamy, John Miljan, DeWitt Jennings, Murray Kinnell, Fletcher Norton, Louts Natheaux, Frank McGlynn, Theodore von Eltz, Charles Giblyn, Lee Phelps, Oscar Rudolph, Hector Sarno, Tom London, George Magrill, Lynton Brent, Arthur Thalasso, Carol Tevis, Joseph Girard, Buddy Roosevelt, Walter Walker, S.D. Wilcox, Mary Carlisle, Betty Lawson
Released April 18, 1931
MGM
83 minutes

Clark Gable alternated between playing good guys and bad guys in his first few MGM films, including a stopover at Warner Brothers. In *The Secret Six*, Gable has another supporting role, this time as a reporter who is going after gangsters, not unlike Richard Barthelmess had done in *The Finger Points*. It is interesting that *The Finger Points* was released at around the same time as this one (they came out within a week of each other, although they were made months apart). In the previous film, Gable was the gangster. This time he is the reporter and Wallace Beery is the racketeer.

The origin of *The Secret Six* can be traced to one of MGM's biggest hits of the previous year, the gritty prison drama *The Big House*. That film had a screenplay by Frances Marion, direction by George Hill, and featured both Wallace Beery and Lewis Stone. *The Secret Six* casts both Beery and Stone, has a screenplay by Marion and is directed by Hill in the hope that cinematic lightning would strike twice.

Bootlegger Johnny Franks (Ralph Bellamy) works out of a steakhouse he owns. One of his regular customers is Louie Scorpio (Wallace Beery). Franks gives Scorpio the opportunity to do a dangerous job for him, realizing he likely will be killed. Franks needs someone expendable and the slow-witted lout Scorpio seems to be the best choice. After Scorpio manages to survive the rival gang's gunshots, he returns to confront and kill Franks. Scorpio then takes over the steak joint *and* the bootlegging operation. Working closely with crooked lawyer Newton (Lewis Stone), he soon rules the city's underworld.

Jean Harlow and Gable in *The Secret Six* (1931), their first film together. They quickly became friends.

Scorpio pays a steakhouse cashier, Anne Courtland (Jean Harlow), to romantically entice newspaperman Hank (Johnny Mack Brown), in an attempt to keep him from reporting on the bootlegging and racketeering going on at the steakhouse. Clark Gable plays Hank's rival Carl. Despite their being on competing newspapers, Carl and Hank are friends. Carl reveals to Hank that Anne was paid off, so Hank drops her. But Anne has started to actually fall for Hank and wants to pursue their romance. She tries to tell him, but he won't believe her.

Hank and Carl enlist the cooperation of a vigilante group called the Secret Six and attempt to get Scorpio charged with Franks' murder. Scorpio orders his men to kill Hank. Anne goes to warn him, but she's too late: He is gunned down in a subway car before her eyes. At a trial, Anne and Carl testify against Scorpio, but lawyer Newton has selected the jury and Scorpio is found not guilty. Carl and Anne are kidnapped by Scorpio's men, but police arrive at the steakhouse where they are being held. In the ensuing shootout, Newton is killed. Scorpio goes to the electric chair while Carl and Anne end up together.

Clark Gable in the 1930s

The year 1931 was a big one for gangster movies, but previous studies that claim Irving Thalberg was inspired by the success of *Little Caesar* and *The Public Enemy* are inaccurate. This film was in production before *Little Caesar* was released. *The Public Enemy* also features Jean Harlow in the cast and was not released until a month after *The Secret Six* was in theaters.

Gable gets his first chance to play opposite Jean Harlow, with whom he would co-star frequently during her short life. Their dialogue was edgily flirtatious in the best pre–Code manner:

> CARL: Oh, baby, you got a pair of the most beautiful blue eyes I've ever seen. You know, I'd sure like to take you around and introduce you to my Aunt Emma.
> ANNE: What a break for Aunt Emma!

Harlow is a bit tentative with her dialogue this early in her career, but her beauty and presence still resonate.

Gable recalled in an interview years later, "We were darned lucky we had jobs and our only hope was that there would be another job when we finished. I thought she was a nice kid but a rotten actress." In the same interview, Harlow admitted, "I thought he was a lot of fun, but I thought he was just another actor and not a very hot one at that."[14] Still, they were friendly on this project and, as each grew in the industry, they played opposite each other in several more films, and eventually became dear friends. In *The Secret Six*, Harlow was billed fourth, Gable seventh.

Gable's scenes with Harlow truly resonate. The murder of Hank separates Anne from Scorpio, and she connects with Carl to put Louie away. Harlow recalled in an article[15]:

> I had the unique experience of having three lovers at once. I've heard girls boast about being engaged to two or three men at one time, but I'll bet that none of them ever had such lovers as I had in *The Secret Six*: big handsome Johnny Mack Brown, big handsome Clark Gable, and Wally Beery, whom all superlatives fail to describe. Clark was like a boy; laughing and joking, making a frolic of his work.

Producer Thalberg noticed while watching the rushes how Gable stood out among the veterans in the cast and, quite impressed, ordered writers to add more scenes featuring Gable. *Motion Picture Herald's* Secret Six review mentioned Gable alongside Beery and Lewis Stone as one of three great performances in the movie. The review in *New Movie Magazine* stated[16]:

> Gangster pictures are a long way from dead; in fact, they are not even ailing, if this may be taken as a sample of what to expect. For concentrated excitement, *The Secret Six* breaks some sort of a record; it does not matter just what. Wallace Beery, as a gangster fresh from a slaughterhouse, his boots still smeared with blood, is tremendous, terrible, frightful, anything you may wish to call him. And Lewis Stone, especially in the first part of the picture, as a drunken, soiled gang leader, well, you never saw Stone like that. Then there are others just as good. You must see *The Secret Six*. It will keep you awake.

The Secret Six was popular enough to inspire a group of boys at an Oceanside, New York, high school to form a six-man vigilante team. Reports like this resulted in the tabloids complaining that such films had a negative influence on American youth. This incident did not stop a police chief in New York from scheduling a screening of *The Secret Six* at a police benefit.

With each successive film, Gable was continuing to make an impact and build a successful film career. Being under contract with the biggest studio in Hollywood, scoring with moviegoers, and having the opportunity to play a range of characters, Gable was kept very busy during his first year in movies. It's impressive to see how he was alternate from villains to heroes in his early Hollywood years. He used the same charismatic tough guy persona for both—they are all undeniably Clark Gable characters—but he was able to fine-tune it to suit the character he's playing. As a result of his hard work, he would soon define actors in Hollywood cinema for the decade of the 1930s.

Laughing Sinners

Directed by Harry Beaumont
Screenplay: Edith Fitzgerald, Bess Meredyth, Martin Flavin
Based on the play *Torch Song* by Kenyon Nicholson
Cinematographer: Charles Rosher
Editor: George Hively
Cast: Joan Crawford, Neil Hamilton, Clark Gable, Marjorie Rambeau, Guy Kibbee, Cliff Edwards, Roscoe Karns, Gertrude Short, George Cooper, George F. Marion, Bert Woodruff, Henry Armetta, Karen Morley, Mary Ann Jackson, Henry Armetta, Suzanne Wood, Jack Baxley, Clara Blandick, Tenen Holtz, Lee Phelps, Sherry Hall, Henry Rocquemore
Songs: "(What Can I Do?) I Love That Man," Music: Martin Broones, Lyrics: Arthur Freed; "Brighten the Corner Where You Are," Music: Charles Gabriel, Words by Ina Duley Ogden; "Oh, My Sombrero" ("Cielito Lindo"), Written by Quirino Mendoza, Sung by Joan Crawford
Released May 30, 1931
MGM
72 minutes

A Joan Crawford star vehicle based on the play *Torch Song*, *Laughing Sinners* wasn't supposed to feature Clark Gable at all. John Mack Brown, who had appeared opposite Crawford in *Montana Moon* (1930), was being groomed by MGM as a leading man when cast opposite her in this film. Brown had actually shot most of the movie when the powers-that-be, including Crawford herself, felt they didn't have the necessary chemistry. Clark Gable was substituted for Brown. The footage that had been shot was scrapped and re-shot with Gable in Brown's role. This ended Brown's

Joan Crawford and Gable were co-stars again in *Laughing Sinners* (1931).

leading man push, as MGM instead decided to groom Gable, a better actor with more charisma. Under the name Johnny Mack Brown, Brown began a career as the star of B Westerns and enjoyed a very prolific and successful career in that subgenre through the 1950s.

Laughing Sinners features Crawford as Ivy Stevens, a café singer in love with salesman Howard Palmer (Neil Hamilton). When he deserts her, she attempts suicide, but is rescued by Salvation Army officer Carl Loomis (Clark Gable). Ivy reads in the newspaper that Palmer is engaged to be married, so she attends a Salvation Army picnic at the park to find Carl. She connects with him out of desperation and gratitude and finds a new life upon joining the Salvation Army and using her pain to help others. Palmer re-enters her life and she again succumbs to his charms. Carl attempts to change her mind, and Ivy realizes her life is better with the Salvation Army. She leaves Palmer and remains with Carl.

Crawford turned in an exhilarating tour de force performance as Ivy, a positively giddy young woman, deeply in love, and putting on her dance routine at the night-club with oodles of positive energy. Crawford's background in dance was put on great display during this cheerful scene, showing another area of her vast talent. This scene is followed by Palmer's attempt to tell Ivy that he's leaving, and this time isn't coming back. But he can't bring himself to do so. She finishes her break and goes back out to sing a song especially for him. When she returns, she finds a note that causes her to faint.

The way director Harry Beaumont films her attempted suicide is visually impressive. He shoots her feet walking along the pavement and toward a bridge, which she attempts to climb. We hear Carl's voice stopping her, and Ivy tearfully insists he leave her alone. The camera then pans up and shows them both. Their scene continues from that point.

Because his innate charisma exudes from his screen characters, Gable likely does better than John Mack Brown had in the original footage. But a Salvation Army officer isn't quite the type of role best suited for the actor. Even the movie trade magazines felt he was miscast. It was due to the chemistry that Gable and Crawford exhibited in *Dance, Fools, Dance* that he was given the role, and Clark was at a point in his career where it was too early for him to balk at the roles he was given. He's a big hunky presence with his distinctive verbal delivery but clad in a Salvation Army uniform and playing someone of the religious order seems like an incongruity.

However, Gable still exudes a warmth and sweetness that feels very sincere, and is something of a preview of his Rhett Butler responding to daughter Bonnie years later in *Gone with the Wind*—especially when he first meets Ivy and tries to do everything possible to make sure she is okay. We don't get to see that side of him too often, but he does play it well. Crawford also seems out of place in a Salvation Army outfit, but Ivy isn't supposed to be an organic part of the experience. She is there in desperation because of a broken heart. In this case, the incongruity works in context.

Neil Hamilton does nicely as the foppish cad Howard Palmer. A leading man in romantic dramas, Hamilton completely redefined his career over 30 years later as Commissioner Gordon on TV's popular *Batman* TV series (1966–1968). *Laughing Sinners* is bolstered by the appearance of welcome character actors Roscoe Karns, Cliff Edwards and Guy Kibbee. Kibbee is repeating his role from Broadway's *Torch Song*. Later that same year, he signed with Warner Brothers and became a fixture in many of their pre–Code films.

Crawford does a good job showing that Ivy has changed after she succumbs and

spends a night with Palmer. She feels guilty about it, and her demeanor is far different than the giddiness she exhibited earlier. Ivy appears to fall more heavily for Carl,
as the charisma exuding from Gable is irresistible, and also for a way of life that is
cleaner and more forthright. The tears in Ivy's eyes, which Crawford is able to call up
so effortlessly, tell her true feelings

There is an offbeat scene featuring some of the other salesmen, and a showgirl
acquaintance of Ivy's unable to be revived after some drunken partying. That scene
goes nowhere and is never resolved. But it extends to one where Ivy runs into one
of the salesmen (Kibbee) and starts doing a bit of drinking herself. Soon they are
dancing about and carrying on, joined by the other salesmen and Palmer. The liquor
removes Ivy's inhibitions, and she accepts her situation. She believes that since she
spent the night in Palmer's room, she has ruined her status with the Salvation Army.
It is then when Carl confronts Palmer and tries to talk sense to Ivy:

> If you love him, and you want to go back to him, I'm not the one to set myself up as a guide.
> I just want you to be happy, whatever you do. But if you're going back because of what you've
> done, you don't need to, Ivy. We all stumble. All we can do is pick ourselves up again and go
> on and on and on until we find ourselves through our own mistakes. It won't make any differ-
> ence to me, Ivy. I want you to know that. I guess you know where I'll be if you want me.

Scenes like this kept Gable's name in conversations among moviegoers, and
MGM remained interested in grooming him.

Throughout 1931, MGM experimented with Gable in different roles, wondering
if he registered best as a hero or a gangster. Initially the public responded better to his
bad guy characters. As he made more films, it was evident that his presence was having a consistently greater impact with each successive role.

In her Gable biography *Long Live the King*,[17] writer Lyn Tornabene stated that
MGM behaved as though Gable might melt if left outside the gates overnight, and
quickly cast him in *A Free Soul* immediately after he finished his scenes in *Laughing
Sinners*. Having played the ultimate good guy as an officer of a religious order, Gable
was now being cast again as a bad guy.

A Free Soul

Produced and Directed by Clarence Brown
Screenplay: John Meehan
Based on the play by Willard Mack and the book by Adela Rogers St. Johns
Executive Producer: Irving Thalberg
Cinematographer: William H. Daniels
Editor: Hugh Wynn
Cast: Norma Shearer, Leslie Howard, Lionel Barrymore, Clark Gable, James Glea-
    son, Lucy Beaumont, Roscoe Ates, Edward Brophy, Larry Steers, George Irving,

James Donlan, Francis Ford, Ann Brody, William Stack, Carl Stockdale, Henry
Hall, Edward LeSaint, Sam McDaniel, Phillips Smalley, Beth Flowers, Lee Phelps
Released June 20, 1931
MGM
93 minutes

Gable appears very early in *A Free Soul*, unlike his previous films where the plot
is set up before his character is introduced. It is also his first film with his mentor
Lionel Barrymore, the man who had suggested that Gable try his luck at acting in
movies.

The story deals with an alcoholic lawyer (Barrymore) who successfully defends a
murderous gangster. The gangster (Gable) then falls for the lawyer's daughter (Norma
Shearer), much to the attorney's chagrin. The elitist lifestyle that the daughter is used
to living, is challenged by a new lifestyle surrounded by the aggressive behavior and
ruggedness of the gangster's world. The wealthy young man (Leslie Howard), whom
the daughter left for the gangster, decides to kill the new beau, and is then himself
defended in court by her drunken lawyer father.

Gable was becoming quite comfortable with his developing screen persona. In
his first scene, the gangster (on trial for murder) enters the lawyer's quarters during
a trial recess. The lawyer's daughter is visiting, and when she first sets her eyes on the
gangster, she is transfixed. Gable plays the role securely and with an unflappable presence, even when Shearer says the line, "You're on trial for your life, aren't you?"

Shearer, playing a character who is bored with the dull sameness of her privileged life, is attractive enough to begin joking and flirting with the forbidden fruit
that the gangster represents. When she goes out with him for the first time, rival gang
members drive by and riddle their car with bullets, forcing them to race to a hideout.
She finds this exhilarating. He finds it commonplace.

A Free Soul is a film filled with alcoholism, premarital sex, revealing negligees,
kidnapping, gambling and murder. It was also a censor's nightmare, even during the
pre–Code era. However, by 1931 MGM wielded enough power to override the censorship of the pre–Code era (something that would be much more difficult after the
Hays Code was more strictly enforced after 1934). Thus, a scene where the lawyer's
daughter lies back on the couch, reaches out and says, "Come on, put 'em around
me!" was kept in the film, despite the censors' recommendations that it be removed.

Gable's snarling charisma is central to the film's dramatic power, as he bullies
and slaps his way through the narrative as the sort of gangster who alternates from a
frighteningly grim racketeer to an attractive presence. Lionel Barrymore wavers from
introspection to bewilderment as a shrewd lawyer whose alcoholism is out of control. Norma Shearer is spunky and rebellious as the lawyer's daughter. Leslie Howard
is appropriately charmless as her elitist beau. Backing all of this up is James Glea-
son in a small role as the lawyer's partner, enacted in his wry manner and with that
memorable voice. He doesn't have the classy oratory skill of a Claude Rains or James
Mason, but his inimitable dees-dems-dose delivery is every bit as distinctive.

Gable once again gets to tap into the pure evil of a character, something he did often during this part of his film career. His scenes with Shearer are passionate and sometimes brutal. His conflict with Howard is made more interesting via the fact that they would famously be involved in another onscreen love triangle eight years later in *Gone with the Wind*.

Barrymore won his only Oscar for this film. Amazingly, it would be the only time he'd be nominated as an actor in his long, illustrious career. (He was also nominated for directing the 1930 version of *Madame X*.) Barrymore is actually a supporting player in this movie, but there was no category for supporting actors at this time so he got a Best Actor Oscar for a supporting role (the only time that has ever happened). He is also the Best Actor Oscar winner with the least amount of screen time in the movie for which he won. (This is often credited to Anthony Hopkins for *The Silence of the Lambs*, but in this film Barrymore has even less screen time.) Barrymore's tragic lawyer is able to muster up courageous defiance when confronting Gable about his romance with Shearer, letting him know that his status as a free man does not elevate him to the elite level of his betters. It is real Depression-era class-system stuff when Barrymore tells Gable, "The only time I hate democracy is when one of you mongrels forgets where you belong. A few illegal dollars and a clean shirt, and you move across the railroad tracks."

Shearer got the part for this film over Joan Crawford, whom original writer Adela Rogers St. Johns had selected for the role (the movie was loosely based on St. Johns' account of her own life). Shearer's status as wife of studio head Irving Thalberg likely made a difference as to who was cast. She was adept at playing good girls who liked playing bad, and rich women who were attracted to the lower class. She always maintains a certain uppity manner even when she realizes her attraction to Gable is difficult to harness. When he insists they get married, she realizes that her attraction to him is only sexual. She uses the situation as a bargaining tool, promising her father she will leave the gangster if Dad sobers up. Her father agrees, but his alcoholism has too strong a hold. There is an interesting reversal of gender roles here, in that typically the woman wants marriage, and the man doesn't. It's too bad the film doesn't explore this further.

The highlight of *A Free Soul* involves Barrymore, not Gable. During the climactic courtroom scene, he makes an impassioned plea for the life of the Leslie Howard character. The impressive monologue was shot in a 14-minute take. It is a screen triumph that has a place in the *Guinness Book of World Records* for the longest take in a Hollywood film shot in 35mm. Barrymore's soliloquy shows his character depleted of all resources, struggling with his words, but ultimately making his point before collapsing. It is likely the scene that cinched his Oscar win. This was something of a comeback for Barrymore, who had just decided to leave directing and return to acting.

Director Clarence Brown had a real knack for establishing shots, sometimes opening with a medium shot, and other times reeling back for a long shot with an elevated camera. He keeps everything in the frame, closing in when he wants to present

Director Clarence Brown, Leslie Howard, Gable and Norma Shearer look over a miniature on the set of *A Free Soul* (1931).

the subtle nuances that each of these actors had. Brown had a long and successful career at MGM.

A *Free Soul* does not have quite the unrelenting grittiness that Warner Brothers or Paramount were offering during this same period, but even the gloss of MGM cannot overshadow the seamier elements in the narrative. Toss in great direction and fine acting from some of Golden Age Hollywood's icons, and *A Free Soul* deserves its status as a pre–Code classic.

A *Free Soul* was important to Gable's screen career. At one point, Shearer tells him, "You're just a new kind of man in a new kind of world." And that is exactly what was happening to the moviegoing culture. The leading men who were popular during the silent era—the John Gilbert type, the Rudolph Valentino type, the Douglas Fairbanks type—had bled into early talkies. In *A Free Soul*, it isn't the Gable character that is supposed to be the standout attractive leading man, it is the effete Leslie Howard. But the moviegoing public, especially women, were far more attracted to Gable's character. His rugged bad guy demeanor, promising danger and excitement, was far more interesting than the vanilla Leslie Howard with all of his wealth and refinement. Shearer's character is duly smitten in the same manner, stating, "The rest of my life can't wash the filthy mark of you out of my soul!"

Gable asserts his masculine authority in his confrontations with Howard when he and Shearer plan to marry. "When I get through, you won't have the guts to marry her," Gable insists. "Let me lay it on the line for you: She tossed all her ritz overboard months ago. She came to my place and she stayed there. You get that? She's mine, she belongs to me." In pre–Code cinema, Clark is able to claim his woman by alluding to their sexual encounter.

The New York Times' stodgy old Mordaunt Hall, unimpressed with *A Free Soul*, stated in his review:

> Talking pictures are by no means elevated by the presentation of *A Free Soul*.... Nevertheless, it should be stated that Lionel Barrymore does all that is possible with his role. In fact, his is the only characterization that rings true, the other players being handicapped either through miscasting, the false conception of human psychology or poorly written lines. Norma Shearer may be the star of this film, but Mr. Barrymore steals whatever honors there may be.... Miss Shearer, who looks as captivating as ever, is called upon to act a part which is quite unsuited to her intelligent type of beauty. Leslie Howard is lost in the shuffle for some time, but he finally turns up as the hero in this lurid, implausible affair. Clark Gable is all very well as a gangster, but it is problematical whether a young woman of Miss Shearer's type would ever become enamored of an individual who behaves as he does here. Not only are the natures of the persons involved frightfully strained, but also the incidents.

This didn't hamper the movie's success. *A Free Soul* was the fifth most popular film at the box office in 1931. According to *Photoplay*[18]:

> Lionel Barrymore's performance in the role of a brilliant but heavy-drinking criminal lawyer is magnificent. Norma Shearer is excellent and handles the part of his daughter perfectly. Her clothes are breathtaking in their daring. But you couldn't get away with them in your drawing room. Clark Gable and Leslie Howard are both grand. The story concerns a modern girl, brought up by her clever but erratic father to do exactly as she pleases—to be "a free soul." She pleases to have a sordid affair with a gambler, whom she discovers to be a cad. By all means, see it!

Shearer was also Oscar-nominated, as was director Brown. It was the first film to be Oscar-nominated for Best Actor and Best Actress but not Best Picture. Also, it is the first film to be nominated for both lead acting categories and Best Director, without a Best Picture nomination.

Night Nurse

Directed by William Wellman
Screenplay: Oliver H.P. Garrett, Charles Kenyon
Based on the novel by Dora Macy (aka Grace Perkins)
Cinematographer: Barney McGill
Editor: Edward M. McDermott
Cast: Barbara Stanwyck, Ben Lyon, Joan Blondell, Clark Gable, Blanche Frederici, Charlotte Merriam, Charles Winninger, Edward J. Nugent, Vera Lewis, Ralf

Night Nurse (1931)

Harolde, Walter McGrail, Betty Jane Graham, Marcia Mae Jones, Allan Lane, Willie Fung, Robert Allen, Jim Farley, James Bradbury, Jr., Lucille Ward, Jed Prouty, Bob Perry, Betty May
Released August 8, 1931
Warner Brothers
72 minutes

Gable made *Night Nurse* while on loan to Warner Brothers, playing a role that some sources claim was originally intended for Warners contractee James Cagney. It was directed by William Wellman, who had helmed Cagney's *The Public Enemy*. In fact, Wellman was assigned to *Night Nurse* before he directed *The Public Enemy*, but when he replaced Archie Mayo on the Cagney film, *Night Nurse* was postponed. Cagney was not considered for the role Gable played in *Night Nurse*: He and Gable were hired for the movie together, according to a *Film Daily* article[19]:

James Cagney and Clark Gable have been added to *Night Nurse* which is almost ready to start production at Warner Brothers studios. It is almost certain that Barbara Stanwyck will play the title role. Ben Lyon will be leading man, and prominent roles have been assigned to Joan Blondell and Charles Winninger.

The reason frequently given for Cagney not participating was the success of *The Public Enemy*: It became a sensation, and he was now considered a star actor who would no longer be playing supporting roles. *Night Nurse* began production in April 1931, roughly two weeks before *The Public Enemy* was released. The smaller role Cagney was to play in *Night Nurse* was assigned to Allan Lane.

Gable had been carving a niche for himself playing bad guys, some with redeeming qualities but often despicable characters. In *Night Nurse* he portrays his most heinous screen role thus far: a chauffeur who helps a creepy doctor keep a woman intoxicated while slowly starving her two children in order to collect money in their trust fund, left to them by their late father. This is certainly a situation that could not have been produced after the Production Code was more sternly enforced in 1934.

Gable is fourth-billed but doesn't show up until halfway through the 72-minute running time. He has perhaps the least screen time in any movie since *The Painted Desert*. Even though the gangsters Gable had previously played were bad men, there was still something charming about them. But there is no appeal to his *Night Nurse* character—he is pure evil.

The narrative concentrates on the top-billed star, Stanwyck, who secures a job as a nurse despite not even having a high school diploma. She is initially rebuffed by the head nurse, but a chance meeting with the hospital's top surgeon, and his rather creepy attraction to her, results in her hiring. With her street smarts, she responds well in situations that are familiar to her, from dealing with gangsters with bullet wounds, to being accosted by a drunk whose girlfriend (the children's mother) is unconscious. It is during the latter scene where we first see Gable, his entrance shown

Gable was loaned to Warner Brothers to play one of the "baddest" of his bad guy roles in *Night Nurse* (1931) with Barbara Stanwyck.

with the camera pointing downward as his feet walk into the room. It pans up as he slaps around the drunk who has attacked nurse Stanwyck.

Gable moves to Stanwyck and insists she help out the drunken woman without consulting with the doctor first. When she insists on calling the doctor, he squeezes her wrist until she agrees. It is as this point that Stanwyck realizes that the children are undernourishment. When she goes to the doctor on the case, he angrily rebuffs her. She consults with the doctor who got her the job, and he suggests she continue working with the children in order to learn more.

MGM loaned Gable to Warners, who were pleased with his performance in *The Finger Points* and wanted to use him again. They were starting to cultivate a coterie of gangster actors with Edward G. Robinson and Cagney, and wondered if actors like Gable (and Ben Lyon, who also appears) might contribute similarly. Gable's popularity and general interest was growing pretty quickly but it hadn't quite reached the level of the studio realizing that he'd be a major star by the following year.

The narrative's dynamic includes Lyon as the bootlegger whose bullet wound is treated by nurse Stanwyck, after which he feels loyal to her. It is he who saves the day by contacting the doctor who is Stanwyck's benefactor, who rushes to the baby and plans a transfusion. Gable knocks him out to stop him. After Gable shoves Stanwyck aside, he is confronted by the bootlegger. When the doctor comes to, a blood transfusion saves the child. Meanwhile, the bootlegger arranges for the chauffeur to be taken for a ride.

Night Nurse is very much Stanwyck's film, and she turns in one of her finest pre–Code performances. She is ably assisted by wise-cracking, gum-chewing Joan Blondell at her snappiest. Charles Winniger anchors his scenes as the kindly older doctor, and Ben Lyon completes the ensemble as the bootlegger.

Gable's character is part of the group that are the outsiders, the ones committing the crimes. We never find out if unscrupulous doctor Ralf Harolde is disbarred, but we assume so based on the dialogue that indicates those in the know are ready to expose him. With the chauffeur conveniently out of the picture, it is presumably much easier to do so.

One of the interesting aspects of *Night Nurse* is that even though the bad guys are very bad, the good guys are also kind of bad. The hero is a bootlegger, and he resolves the situation not by bringing in the police, but by arranging a hit on the chauffeur. Stanwyck's character seems to accept this. There is this sense of lawlessness throughout the film that gives greater emphasis to its pre–Code status.

The character Gable plays allows him to be at his most eerily unsettling, starving children while beating up young girls and old men and old ladies, but backing down when confronted by a man of his own stature. Had this role been played by a character actor who did not later rise to superstardom as Gable would, it might not register so strongly. But because it is Clark Gable playing the role, his later stardom gives it greater significance in retrospect. We are aware of what he would become, and can therefore be fascinated by the smaller, edgier roles that he essayed during his first year in talkies.

Gable didn't get a lot of attention in the *Night Nurse* reviews. *Variety* stated that he goes through socking everybody, including Stanwyck, and is finally done away with by inference. *Modern Screen* stated that Gable played a character so ridiculously villainous that it's silly.[20] Stanwyck once said,[21] "It was Gable who brought the crowds to see *Night Nurse*. He became a rage when *A Free Soul* came out … the public couldn't get enough of him. Joan Blondell and I were in awe, he was just the kind of guy who made you look at him all the time."[22] It didn't seem to matter how small the parts were, Gable was attracting moviegoers (and co-stars) by his very presence.

According to Frank Thompson and John Gallagher in their book *Nothing Sacred: The Cinema of William Wellman*[23]:

> Wellman kept costs down by usually making only one or two takes. The production reports note various half-hour delays caused by malfunction of the Vitaphone recording equipment; and on April 30, Ben Lyon arrived a half-hour late for his 9:30 a.m. call when he reported to the First National lot instead of Warners Burbank. The Brothers Warner knew from whence its bread was buttered—as technical adviser they hired Dr. Harry Martin, husband of powerful Hearst newspaper columnist Louella Parsons. The sordid proceedings were too much for the Maryland censors, however, and on July 3, 1931, they banned the picture in their state.

Sporting Blood

Directed by Charles Brabin
Screenplay: Charles Brabin, Willard Mack, Wanda Tuchock
Based on the story "Horseflesh" by Fredrick Hazlitt Brennan
Cinematographer: Harold Rosson
Editor: William S. Gray
Cast: Clark Gable, Ernest Torrence, Madge Evans, Lew Cody, Marie Prevost, Hallam Cooley, J. Farrell MacDonald, John Larkin, Eugene Jackson, Harry Holman, Eddie Frazier, Richard Cramer, James Donlan, Bradley Page, Gertrude Howard, Edward Brophy, Tenen Holz, Sidney Bracey, Lynton Brent, Phillips Smalley, Buddy Roosevelt, Lee Phelps
Released August 8, 1931
MGM
82 minutes

Sporting Blood is notable as Gable's first starring role, and the first time he received top billing. But the actor doesn't show up until the feature is nearly half over. *Sporting Blood* was released on the same day as *Night Nurse* and was included in double features at many theaters. And, according to actress Madge Evans in an issue of *Film Fan Monthly*, she and Gable were active on other projects and made this film on weekends, shooting their scenes while doubles were used for the long shots.

The story deals with horse breeder Jim Rellence (Ernest Torrence), whose most prized and beloved horse falls into a large puddle and breaks her leg while running from a storm. While there, she gives birth to a foal, whom they name Tommy Boy. Dwindling finances force Rellence to sell Tommy Boy and the horse passes through several owners, each of whom use him for personal gain. He eventually enters high stakes horse racing and becomes very successful. In the end he wins the Kentucky Derby.

Sporting Blood has two halves that seem like two different movies. The first involves Rellence and the stable workers on his horse farm. Black actors who are often relegated to mere bit roles in most mainstream films of this period, are given larger roles and more layered characters to play. We see their families, and the respect they get from their employers. It is a relaxed, pleasant film that is filled with stirring emotional scenes.

In one of the strongest early scenes, the rainstorm suddenly occurs while the brood mares are grazing. Director Charles Brabin does a nice job of showing the galloping horses in a long shot, while cutting back to the horse who slips in the mud and falls in the puddle. Rellence and his workers discover the baby colt and see that the mother horse has broken her leg. This shocking, emotional scene is perfectly shot. We hear the gunshot offscreen while the camera is fixed on Rellence walking toward the wagon. He stops as he hears the shot. There is a closeup of his teary-eyed face. Then he resumes slowly walking to the wagon. He sits, stares back at the dead horse, pauses for a few beats, and the wagon slowly pulls away. The falling rain, the

Gable, top-billed in *Sporting Blood* (1931), doesn't appear until halfway through the movie. Here he is with co-star Madge Evans.

forlorn expressions, and how Brabin frames each shot makes this sequence a high-light, despite it showing up very early in the movie.

The next scene has Uncle Ben, a stable hand played by veteran black charac-ter actor John Larkin, bringing the new colt home, putting it in blankets and feed-ing it with a bottle of milk like a baby. We are introduced to his wife and children, who scurry to help him as he tells them what to do. His wife puts milk in a pan on the stove, stating, "I know what to do!" Rellence comes in and slowly walks over to Sam (Eugene Jackson), who was partially responsible for the mare's death, as it was his duty to round up the horses when it stormed. Rellence approaches the crying young man with understanding and forgiveness. The next scene shows Sam introducing

Tommy Boy to a mare who lost her foal. The two connect. This is followed by a series of scenes showing the development of Tommy Boy as a racehorse, with Sam riding him. Rellence has an affection for Tommy Boy and avoids selling him. There is a scene where Rellence downplays Tommy Boy's prowess to a potential buyer as Uncle Ben tries to stifle his own laughter. However, the buyer is impressed with Tommy Boy and offers $3000—an outrageous price—because he sees through the ruse. He raises the price to $6000, reminding Rellence that he's been buying horses from him for some time. Rellence relents and Tommy Boy is sold and put in a truck. There is a powerful scene were Sam runs alongside the truck, shouting instructions and tips on how to take care of the horse. The vehicle pulls away and Sam stands there crying. Jackson recalled in a 1985 interview with the author, "*Sporting Blood* was one of the best pictures I did. I had a lot of good scenes in that, and got to work with some great actors and a great director. I was proud of my work in that picture."

Sporting Blood shifts gears and Tommy Boy is a racehorse in a world of wealth and gangsters. The man who bought him races him successfully until Ludeking, a wealthy man, buys him for a whopping $40,000 because his frivolous wife wants him. When they attempt to run him in a race that he isn't ready for, he loses, and Mrs. Ludeking is so incensed she wants him shot! Tommy Boy is next sold to crooked gambler Tip Scanlon (Lew Cody). One of Tip's accomplices is Rid Riddell (Gable).

Gable is first seen at a roulette wheel surrounded by wealthy women who are attracted to his charm. The shot composition effectively emphasizes his tall, imposing presence. He is obviously attracted to Tip's girl Ruby (Madge Evans), and the feeling is mutual, but both are reticent about breaking from Tip. Rip is optimistic, stating, "Tip is going to be taking me off the tables and introduce me to the racing game." When Ruby takes a drink out of a flask, this dialogue is heard:

> RID: Aw, don't do that, Ruby!
> RUBY: Why not?
> RID: I hate to see anyone hit the hootch the way you do.
> RUBY: You don't know how bad I need this drink.
> RID: It's not good medicine.
> RUBY: It is for what ails me.
> RID: What's that?
> RUBY: You.

Tommy Boy wins a series of races, both legitimate and fixed. It gets to the point where the horse is ragged and loses a race that he was supposed to win. Several gamblers bet on him due to Tip's assurances. Tip is murdered by the mob. Tip's murder is another highlight, occurring off screen as he leaves a room also occupied by Ruby and Rid. Once they hear the shot, Rid and Ruby run out. The camera shoots upward, showing their faces looking down, presumably at Tip's corpse, as the smoke from the gun whisks past them.

Ruby ends up with Tommy Boy, and the film's two halves are joined when Ruby decides to rehabilitate him. She brings him back to Rellence's horse ranch, explaining how he was doped and overworked. The reunion of Tommy Boy with Rellence, Sam and the mare that acted as his mother is another emotional scene. Rellence tells Ruby that there are 14 spare rooms in the house and they are all empty. So Ruby rehabilitates on the ranch as Tommy Boy does. In another emotionally charged moment, Ruby is watching Tommy Boy practice sprinting through binoculars and fixes on Rid, who has come to see her. They reconnect and a newly rehabilitated Tommy Boy is entered in the Kentucky Derby.

Sporting Blood was another box office success and Gable's name was the draw, even though he doesn't appear until the second half. Arguably, Ernest Torrence steals the movie. A veteran of such films as *The Covered Wagon* (1923) and *Peter Pan* (1924), and memorable as Buster Keaton's disappointed father in *Steamboat Bill, Jr.* (1928), Torrence is just right as the big-hearted breeder. Lew Cody, at the end of his long career (he died in 1934), also stands out as desperate gangster Tip Scanlon. But Gable was considered the big name of the feature even though he had rather limited screen time.

Moviegoers loved the emotional pull of *Sporting Blood* as described by a *San Francisco Examiner* critic:[24]

> *Sporting Blood*, a picture which ranks with *The Big Parade* for heart tugs and with *Ben-Hur* for thrills, [stars] Clark Gable, MGM's new film sensation. Any other company would have road-showed *Sporting Blood*. However, it will play at the Fox Oakland at popular prices. Coast reviewers who previewed it first gave a hint of its importance. "Brought forth a panic of applause at the conclusion," stated the *Hollywood Herald*. "It will be loved and cheered and wept over 'til it takes a top-notch place in this season's record," said the *Motion Picture Daily*. Then it came to San Francisco and played at the magnificent Fox Theater. Ada Hanifin, newspaper critic of that city, saw it and said: "*Sporting Blood* is an achievement Metro-Goldwyn-Mayer may well be proud of! Time will place it among the great films of the sound screen."

The box office success of *Sporting Blood* pleased MGM executives and Gable's career continued to rise. Gable just felt that he was enjoying a string of luck.

Right around the time *Sporting Blood* was released, there was further interest in Gable when reporters located Josephine Dillon. Gable was now married to Maria Langham, but it wasn't known publicly. The MGM publicity department did not advertise that Gable was a bachelor, but also didn't mention his marriage. Josephine was now an acting teacher and didn't want to disparage Gable in the press, despite threats from reporters who printed stories about the lavish lifestyle of Clark and his current wife, while presenting Josephine as his first wife who was now living in poverty. Josephine saw a way to get money, so she privately wrote to Louis B. Mayer of MGM and stated that she believed she should be getting something for all the coaching and teaching she gave to Gable during their years together. To keep her quiet, MGM gave her some money each month for a while but finally stopped payments when she broke their pact by giving an interview. Once the payments stopped, she told the press that basically she was the reason behind Gable's success as an actor. Columnist Adela Rogers St. Johns, a friend of Clark's, wrote a column that stated that

Josephine was no more responsible for his success than an elocution teacher in high school.

MGM countered this by turning Gable over to the press so they could see how normal and unaffected he was. This backfired. Gable was so down to earth, he would make disparaging wisecracks about his projects and dismissive comments about his looks. That didn't sit well with MGM publicity. So, after every movie was wrapped, MGM had Gable the outdoorsman go on a fishing trip. It was while he was fishing that he read in the newspaper that he was to star opposite Greta Garbo in her next movie.

Susan Lenox (Her Fall and Rise)

Produced and Directed by Robert Z. Leonard
Screenplay: Wanda Tuchock, Zelda Sears, Leon Gordon
Based on the novel by David Graham Phillips
Cinematographer: William H. Daniels
Editor: Margaret Booth
Cast: Greta Garbo, Clark Gable, Jean Hersholt, John Miljan, Alan Hale, Hale Hamilton, Hilda Vaughn, Russell Simpson, Cecil Cunningham, Ian Keith, Marjorie King, Eddie Kane, Jack Baxley, Carl Leviness, Pat Moriarty, Larry Steers, Charles Sullivan, Walter Walker, Nella Walker, Bess Flowers, Rose Dione
Released October 10, 1931
MGM
76 minutes

Upon hearing that Greta Garbo requested Gable as her leading man in her next movie, he balked at the assignment. He realized that a star of Garbo's magnitude would be the draw and he'd be relegated to mere support, and that was something he thought he had risen above at this point. But he took the role, realizing that a request from Garbo was really a demand.

Garbo came to America from Sweden in 1925. Soon she was a top film star playing opposite John Gilbert in such hits as *Flesh and the Devil* (1926), *Love* (1927) and *A Woman of Affairs* (1928). It was feared that her accent would ruin her career once talkies arrived, but her first sound film, *Anna Christie* (1930), was a huge hit. By the time of *Susan Lenox (Her Fall and Rise)*, she was one of the biggest stars in Hollywood.

Rumors circulated that Gilbert was to be her *Susan Lenox* co-star, and that King Vidor was slated to direct. Then, according to Louella Parsons' syndicated column[25]:

> All the trouble over Greta Garbo's picture, *The Fall and Rise of Susan Lenox* [sic], has been straightened out with some changes. King Vidor will not direct Miss Garbo. I understand King asked to be released from the picture since he and Miss Garbo did not agree on certain phases of the story. Robert Z. Leonard, who has done nobly by Marion Davies and Norma Shearer, will direct the Swedish favorite. But the thing about this story is that neither Jack

Greta Garbo was a longtime movie star when she appeared opposite Gable in *Susan Lenox (Her Fall and Rise)* (1931).

Gilbert nor Nils Asther will play opposite Garbo. Both were considered, but none other than Clark Gable has been given this delectable role. Clark Gable a year ago was unknown on the screen. Today he is considered one of the greatest bets on the Metro-Goldwyn-Mayer lot. Again I say you can never tell from day to day what is going to happen in these movies of ours.

Parsons again reported on the production of the film a few days later, stating:[26]

Clark Gable in the 1930s

Garbo was much annoyed over the constant reports that Jack Gilbert or Nils Asther would play opposite her. Both men had been attentive to her in the past and Garbo is sensitive when it concerns any hint of a romance. She welcomed Clark Gable, therefore, as her leading man. He has one of the brightest futures of any newcomer to the screen. She also approved of Robert Leonard as her director.

This sort of publicity generated further interest in a film that featured a major movie star and an up-and-coming leading man who was currently making his mark.

The film was "born" the day MGM chief Irving Thalberg overheard three secretaries discussing the 1917 novel, even though it had been long unavailable in bookstores by then. He purchased the screen rights with the intention of putting Garbo in the title role. The novel's author David Graham Phillips was murdered shortly after completing it, and the novel was not published until six years after his death.

In the movie, Helga (Garbo) is promised by her abusive uncle (Jean Hersholt) to Jeb, an uncouth, aggressive man, who tries to rape her. Amidst a violent storm, Helga runs away through the woods and hides out in a barn. There she meets Rodney (Gable), an architect who lives in a cabin on the property. He takes her in and treats her kindly, and they quickly fall in love. After he leaves to sell his drawings in town, Helga is found by her uncle and Jeb. They try to take her back, but she escapes and hops a train. Getting involved with circus people, she changes her name to Susan Lenox and becomes a dancer in the troupe. She writes to Rodney, who comes for her. Police, sent by the uncle, search for her at the circus. She is hidden by the circus owner (John Miljan), who rapes her. She meets up with Rodney, but he leaves her when he finds out about the circus owner. Helga ends up the mistress of a New York politician (Hale Hamilton). She sends for Rodney, lying that it is about an architectural job. When he arrives, he is upset at the ruse and leaves. Susan goes to his home, but he has left. She vows to search for him, traveling all the way to South America and getting a job as a dancer. She meets wealthy American Robert Lane (Ian Keith), who is interested in her, but Susan still longs for Rodney. She and Rodney finally meet up when by chance he visits the dance hall where she works, and their relationship is rekindled.

Director Leonard frames some of the scenes with a real artistry, especially early ones in the remote home where Helga is abused and nearly raped. She braves the elements when she escapes, the rain and wind beating at her as she trudges through the darkness. The fact that the film opens with a montage where we see Helga grow from a small child to a young woman, and all the abuse she suffers, is also effective on more than one level. These clips are presented as shadows on the wall, a creative, efficient and effective way to give the viewer an understanding of her background before getting into the meat of the story. When she meets Rodney, the film changes rhythm, going from a dark and creepy nature to light and relaxed.

This was the only film in which Garbo and Gable co-starred, and it is said that they didn't get along well during the production. Their approaches to acting were far different, and so were their offscreen personalities. Garbo dismissed Gable as crude and common. Gable found Garbo to be uppity and aloof. It isn't that they both aren't good in the movie, but Gable and Garbo do not have great chemistry.

One of the most interesting aspects of *Susan Lenox* is the difference between Garbo and Gable's approach to acting. Garbo's silent film stardom gave her the experience of understanding nuance. There are several moments where she conveyed her character's thoughts with the subtlest facial expressions. Her performance is very much steeped in "classical" film acting. Gable, on the other hand, is bursting with earthy charisma; the sort of screen character that was becoming quite popular in 1931 with actors like James Cagney and Edward G. Robinson. An actor like John Gilbert would have approached the Rodney role much like Garbo's playing of the title character. But Gilbert would never smolder as effectively as Gable during the scenes where he is brooding: His skill as an architect is diminished to the point where one of his buildings collapses, injuring workers.

As effective as he was, Gable was correct in assuming that he'd likely be overlooked in a film starring Garbo. In his column "Piping the Plays," critic Boyd Martin stated[27]: "It is unnecessary to add that Clark Gable is Miss Garbo's leading man, for the advertising has made that clear."

For the entire length of his *Pittsburgh Press* review, Karl Krug praised Garbo, and gave Gable only one sentence: "The screen's First Lady has discovered a leading man who can match her step for step in her acting, a leading man in the personable Mr. Clark Gable, who, far from being awed by the Regal Presence, sails in for the best performance of his meteoric career in Hollywood."[28] Irene Thirer of *The New York Daily News* believed that Gable and Garbo recalled the Garbo-Gilbert screen romances of the silent era.[29]

Screening it as late as the 21st century, *Susan Lenox (Her Fall and Rise)* is interesting as the only pairing of the iconic Greta Garbo and the equally iconic Clark Gable. But in a study of either actor's films, it doesn't resonate as among the best from Garbo or from Gable. Even when one dismisses the melodramatic narrative that was very much of its time, and accepts the historical significance, the film remains a rather standard romantic outing, and each actor offers that which is appropriate to his or her particular style. Gable and Garbo's characters come together and break up too many times, and the characters grow tiresome. However, it is impressive how Gable handles his role and the transition from an upstanding guy to a gruff and troubled man as the story progresses.

Hell Divers

Produced and Directed by George W. Hill
Screenplay: Harvey Gates, Malcolm Stuart Boylan
Additional Dialogue: James K. McGuiness, Ralph Graves
Cinematographer: Harold Wenstrom
Editor: Blanche Sewell

Clark Gable in the 1930s

Cast: Wallace Beery, Clark Gable, Conrad Nagel, Dorothy Jordan, Marjorie Rambeau, Marie Prevost, Cliff Edwards, John Miljan, Landers Stevens, Reed Howes, Alan Roscoe, Frank Conroy, Robert Young, Eric Alden, Sherry Hall, John George, Pat O'Malley, Buddy Roosevelt, Charles Sullivan, Niles Welch, Jack Trent, Jack Pennick
Premiered October 29, 1931. Released January 16, 1932
MGM
109 minutes

Hell Divers is sometimes listed as a 1932 release because while its premiere was held in October 1931, its general release was not until January 1932. Because its wide release didn't happen until January 1932, the film Wallace Beery shot after *Hell Divers*, *The Champ*, had already been in release for a few months. *The Champ* was a huge hit and eventually netted an Oscar for Beery.[30] In fact, *Hell Divers* was the very next production Beery filmed after *The Secret Six*. That shows his level of stardom and his clout. Up-and-coming Gable had appeared in five movies since *The Secret Six*.

Gable's star had been rising steadily, so the studio felt that pairing him with a notorious scene-stealer like Beery, then one of the screen's biggest stars, would be a real test for the actor. When Gable had appeared in a Beery film earlier that year, his being seventh billed didn't allow him to combat any of the leading man's scene-stealing. He was just another actor in a Beery movie. Having now risen to a level where he could co-star with Beery, it was presumed that casting him in *Hell Divers* would help to capitalize on the momentum of his career.

Hell Divers features Beery as Chief Petty Officer "Windy" Riker, an aerial gunner of long standing. For the past five years he's held the title of "champion machine gunner"—but then a young upstart named Steve Nelson (Gable) joins the squadron. Windy is a troublesome character who is quick to use his fists, but because his work with the squadron is so good, he is constantly protected by the Skipper (John Miljan).

The conflict between Windy and Steve occurs early in the film, when the younger man refutes his superior's reasoning for an air accident. This escalates when Steve's fiancée visits and Windy arranges for a woman friend to approach Steve as if she's a sweetheart. The upset fiancée leaves, despite Steve's protests and his attempts to explain.

When the Skipper loses an arm in a collision and must leave the force, he is replaced by Duke Johnson (Conrad Nagel). Windy's carelessness results in his forgetting his code book during a bombing exercise, delaying his craft's takeoff. He is restricted from liberty. Windy's girlfriend Mame is waiting for him and is told by Steve that he won't be meeting her. They leave together for a drink. Windy finds out and leaves his detail, flouting his "no liberty" restriction. He confronts Steve, but Mame insists they shake hands and make up. The two men have a drink, but end up fighting. Steve avoids the MPs, but Windy is put in jail and eventually demoted.

Steve suffers a broken leg when his aircraft crashes during a mock battle exercise,

Advertising material for *Hell Divers* (1931) gives us a good idea as to how the film was promoted.

Wallace Beery and Gable in *Hell Divers* (1931). They weren't particularly fond of each other.

killing the pilot. Windy and Duke come to save them. When Duke is injured, it is up to Windy to rescue both men. In a few days, Steve and Duke are worse, so Windy arranges a daring rescue using Steve's crashed bomber to find an aircraft carrier. They do, but crash upon landing, injuring Windy. With his last words, he asks to be buried at sea.

Steve and Windy are in constant conflict in *Hell Divers* so the fact that Gable and Beery were not fond of each other works well for their characters. Beery was a notoriously jealous actor and a scene-stealer and was generally not well liked. Gable's talent was solid and uncompromising, so he had no trouble holding his own in scenes with Beery. Both men are tough and come across effectively. Gable once again balances forceful with playful and maintains his character's focus while allowing his charm to carry a lot of his scenes. Beery is able to convey growling toughness with an "aw shucks" amiability. The two of them are impactful onscreen, despite their offscreen misgivings about each other. As a result, they would be paired again in other films.

The fact that *Hell Divers* was a big box office hit, almost tripling its production

Dorothy Jordan with Gable in *Hell Divers* (1931).

costs, was great for Gable, whose stardom was soon to reach its zenith; he maintained that status for the remainder of the decade. Along with the acting, writing and direction, one of the most impressive aspects of *Hell Divers* was the effective aerial footage which added to the action. It was made with Navy cooperation.

The character of Windy was based on Frank Wead, who co-wrote the script. Wead was later portrayed by John Wayne in the biopic *The Wings of Eagles* (1957). The Gable-Beery conflict had some similarities to the Quirt-Flagg relationship in the silent 1926 military drama *What Price Glory*.

For the most part, critics praised *Hell Divers* and it was well received by audiences. Irene Thirer of *The New York Daily News* reported[31]:

> The gentlemen in the audience at the Astor Theatre cheered themselves hoarse throughout *Hell Divers*, a male's movie if ever there was one. It's built against a background of Panama Canal zone maneuvers. And there are countless thrilling shots of planes in formation; airplane gun action; difficult and breath-taking landings of planes aboard ship after amazing nose dives down through the air. Superb scenes, these; credit to Camermen Harold Wenstrom, Reginald Lanning and Charles Marshall. More than a hundred vessels of the United States fleet participated in these Panama battles, besides sixty planes and the dirigible *Los Angeles*. Our boyfriends will simply love this stuff, even if we find the grand and glorious sky shots a bit monotonous after the sixth reel. However, let's count ourselves out. *Hell Divers* was

not made to pleasure us gals. Why, we're hardly allowed any footage. Dorothy Jordan, Marie Prevost and Marjorie Rambeau are briefly seen and heard from. And Dorothy is Gable's girl. Marie is Cliff Edwards' sweetie. And Marjorie is the dame who's been waiting down in Panama sixteen years for Wally Beery. From the names we've just mentioned, you'll note the slick cast. And there are others John Miljan, Conrad Nagel, Alan Roscoe, for instance, all of whom give estimable performances. The picture earns applause for its entire cast. Also for George Hill's capable direction. Send the men in the family to see it. They'll be completely satisfied.

Other film critics considered *Hell Divers* to be one of the big hits of its time, praising all who were involved.

In its December 29, 1931, issue, the *Motion Picture Times* trade publication had a boxed review by Ben Shylen which gave a brief nod to Gable but saved most of its praise for Wllace Beery[32]:

Metro-Goldwyn-Mayer scores a smashing hit with *Hell Divers* which opened at a $2 top at the Astor theater last Tuesday night. *Hell Divers* is the *Big Parade* of the current season and will undoubtedly register in a great big way at the box offices around the country. Exhibitors can put this down as a definite hit and one that will send Wallace Beery's star into further ascendancy.... There is a touch of romance—just enough to attract the women fans—and, while Gable will also draw them in, they'll idolize Beery for his exceptional and natural performance. George Hill deserves credit for a fine directorial effort.

Audiences were said to laugh and applaud throughout the film at screenings across the country. Meanwhile, Gable's star status continued to rise.

Possessed

Produced and Directed by Clarence Brown
Screenplay: Lenore Coffee
Based on the play *Mirage* by Edgar Selwyn
Cinematographer: Oliver T. Marsh
Editor: William LeVanway
Cast: Joan Crawford, Clark Gable, Wallace Ford, Richard "Skeets" Gallagher, Frank Conroy, Marjorie White, John Miljan, Clara Blandick, Norman Ainsley, Joan Standing, Wilfred Noy, Jean Del Val, Gino Corrado, Andre Cheron, Bess Flowers, Francis Ford, Fred Malatesta, Mary Gordon, Jack Pennick, Walter Walker, Wilhelm von Brincken, Larry Steers
Released November 21, 1931
MGM
76 minutes

Possessed doesn't give Clark Gable much opportunity in the role of a wealthy attorney, but it was still one of the best films in which he had appeared thus far. He offers a solid and committed performance, but it is Joan Crawford's film, and it is she that most benefited from it. Director Clarence Brown responds well to Lenore

Coffee's script and connects with his stars. *Possessed* is gripping, well-acted and visually impressive.

Crawford plays Marian Martin, a factory worker who lives with her mother in a very poor section of town. Her boyfriend Al Manning, another factory worker, hopes to marry her. Marion sees a train slow down and stop near her home. She looks in its windows, seeing the wealth that exists in a world she cannot fathom. After the train comes to a full stop, she meets a passenger outside the train. He is a wealthy, pleasantly drunken man named Wally Stuart (Skeets Gallagher) who shares his champagne with Marian and gives her his address. When she returns home, tipsy from drinking, she is confronted by Al, who tears up the address.

Marian, determined to find a better life, goes to New York, but Wally doesn't remember her. But in the process, she is introduced to attorney Mark Whitney, and the two form an attraction. Marian becomes Whitney's kept woman, enjoying romance and wealth but no real commitment. She is presented to others as a wealthy divorced socialite but most close to Whitney know the truth. Three years go by and Al comes to New York with big ideas, finds Marian and attempts to rekindle their relationship. He believes Whitney is merely a friend and uses Whitney's influence to get an important contract. When Marian admits to Al what her relationship to Whitney is, he loses interest in her, but still wants the contract. When Whitney runs for governor, his political rivals reveal his situation with Marian. She confronts a hostile crowd and claims that he no longer belongs to her, but now belongs to the people. They cheer, she runs away sobbing. Whitney goes after her and proposes marriage.

Possessed is another film that likely could not have been made after the Code was more strictly enforced. While the film was not blatant, it still featured a wealthy attorney who supported a woman with whom he was carrying on a romantic (sexual) relationship with no intention of marrying her. Still, this plot element never seems exploitative. Gable's performance as the attorney shows us a man for whom most things come easily, and who takes Crawford's character for granted. Marian is a dreamer from the outset. Early in the film, there is the great shot of a train coming to a stop while Marian watches. She sees in each window an indication of privilege: servants preparing dinner, a woman dressing up, etc. It is an artful, effective shot and helps us to understand the basis of Crawford's character.

Gable's performance is strong, despite the role's limitations. He didn't want to do this film. His star was ascending rapidly, he had acquired a following, and he felt the character was a bit too foppish and sophisticated for him. However, he did like the idea of working with Crawford again, and he liked that Brown was directing. (Brown had directed him in *A Free Soul*, which is usually cited as the film that put the name Clark Gable on the map.)

Crawford plays a layered character whose evolution from a poor working girl to a lady of entitlement is brilliantly played. She never lets Marian's original status get buried too deeply. Although Whitney arranges for her to have a makeover and carry herself in more sophisticated circles, she is understanding when a fellow tycoon brings his crude and earthy mistress to a gathering. This character is played

Gable teamed again with Joan Crawford in *Possessed* (1931). It was the 12th feature film featuring Gable that was released in 1931.

by Marjorie White, perhaps best known for appearing with the Three Stooges in their first Columbia short *Woman Haters* (1934). A pretty blonde, she exhibits a lower-class demeanor as she loudly carries on and displays no discretion. Whitney is embarrassed by her and tells the man who brought her, "If you weren't drunk, I'd wipe up the floor with you." He tells them to leave. Marian intervenes with compassion, stating, "She can't help who she is." She tells the woman to call her any time, indicating, "I'm in the book."

Director Brown worked well with cinematographer Oliver T. Marsh, who was quite adept at showing Crawford to her best advantage. Although he only lived to be 49, Marsh managed to rack up over 130 films as a cinematographer, dating as far back as 1918. Brown and Marsh collaborated on some strong visuals, including a very subtle background that comes early in the film. Crawford and Wallace Ford are walking toward the camera in a tracking shot, and Brown shows, soft focused in the background, a drunken man confronting what appears to be his wife, in front of their home. It is off to the side, merely part of the negative space, but it offers another layer to the situation in which Marian and beau Al Manning discuss how tired they are.

The scene with Wally and Marian sets up the basis for the film's continued narrative. He is rich, carefree, pleasantly sloshed, and while he might not be physically attractive to Marian, she responds quite positively because of his position. When she comes home drunk, her long-suffering mother is ashamed, and Al is livid. He proclaims that he realizes his place in society and implies that she is foolish to hope for more. The fact that he himself becomes a successful businessman later in the film adds a touch of irony.

Possessed was based on a play that dated back to the teens and was produced on Broadway in 1920. There was a 1924 silent version; MGM studio mogul Irving Thalberg wanted to make it as a talkie. He hired Lenore Coffee to adapt the play as a vehicle for Crawford, promising her $800 per week while she worked on the adaptation. Coffee worked hard but was chagrined to discover that her first paycheck was for only $500. She enlisted the aid of her agent and attempted to protest this double-cross but was unsuccessful. Thalberg and MGM were too powerful. Coffee's bitterness seeped into the script, but later drafts softened the character Crawford was assigned to play. Coffee got along well with Clarence Brown but didn't believe Crawford was a particularly good actress.

Possessed flips expectations around. Instead of the typical scenario of Gable still refusing to marry Crawford and choosing his career, prompting her to go back to her small town life and sweetheart, it ends up being the small town guy who spurns her and Gable who accepts her. This was a good character for Gable in that he got to be noble without being too soft, despite not having much of significance to do in this film.

At the time she filmed *Possessed*, Crawford's marriage to Douglas Fairbanks Jr. was ending, resulting in a romantic involvement with the still-married Gable. Joan recalled, "In the picture we were madly in love. When the scenes ended, the emotion didn't." Because of Gable's marriage, and the studio anxious to avoid negative publicity about its rising stars, Joan and Clark could only see each other on the set. Crawford later wrote that she realized it was not to be as a long-term thing, but the attraction, and subsequent romance, were not denied.

Possessed was another box office hit for MGM and continued to boost Gable's career despite the limitations of his role. He was still able to infuse some of his trademark style to the character, and the fact that the film ends with him doing the right thing made a difference. The critics like *Possessed*, Ada Hanifin stating in *The San Francisco Examiner*[33]:

> *Possessed* Is superbly directed, beautifully and sincerely acted by Clark Gable and Joan Crawford. There are moments when tears dance on the edge of the heart, and in those moments Joan and Clark Gable convey a sincere expression of emotion that is all too rare on the screen. Clark Gable gives the most artistic and romantically sincere performance of his screen career. In no other picture has he had the opportunity to bring to his characterization, finesse, poise, manner, and to read his lines with shaded meaning. He is an excellent actor apart from the glamour that haloes him as the film idol of the hour. He is charming. There are few actresses on the screen who have made the rapid strides toward artistic achievement as has Joan Crawford.

Other critics responded similarly and *Possessed* became one of the most profitable films in which Gable had thus far appeared. Crawford made another movie by this title, in 1947, but it has nothing to do with this movie.

At this point, Gable was getting restless. He had appeared in many movies throughout 1931 and had proven himself. He had fans and admirers, and his movies made money. He was beginning to feel a bit perturbed by how much more money the established stars like Wallace Beery were making. He was making one movie after another and wanted a rest.

Polly of the Circus

Directed by Alfred Santell
Produced by Marion Davies
Screenplay: Carey Wilson
Dialogue: Laurence Johnson
Based on the play by Margaret Mayo
Cinematographer: George Barnes
Editor: George Hively
Cast: Clark Gable, Marion Davies, C. Aubrey Smith, Raymond Hatton, David Landau, Ruth Selwyn, Maude Eburne, Little Billy Rhodes, Guinn "Big Boy" Williams, Clark Marshall, Lillian Elliot, Edward LeSaint, John Roche, Jack Baxley, Phillip Crane, Frank McGlynn Sr., Ray Milland, Tiny Sandford, Florence Wix, Frank Rice, Florence Wix, Seessel Anne Johnson, Carmencita Johnson; aerial stunts performed by Alfredo Codona and Vera Bruce
Released February 27, 1932
Cosmopolitan Productions for MGM
69 minutes

Polly of the Circus was the worst film Gable had appeared in up to this point. It is a slow, meandering drama and Gable is miscast. William Randolph Hearst made the film via his Cosmopolitan Productions, and it starred his mistress Marion Davies,

Marion Davies insisted that Gable be her co-star in *Polly of the Circus* (1932).

who also produced. Davies wanted the new star Clark Gable to be her leading man. Cosmopolitan Pictures operated out of MGM. Gable had no choice. Hearst was that powerful.

Hearst was already a publishing magnate in 1918 when he decided that he wanted to branch off into motion pictures. He formed Cosmopolitan, first in conjunction with Adolph Zukor of Paramount. The studio saw it as an opportunity to secure the film rights to stories that had appeared in the wide variety of Hearst's magazines, including *Cosmopolitan*, hence the name of the production company. Hearst also owned *Harper's Bazaar* and *Good Housekeeping*, which were equally popular and had wide distribution. Much of the reason behind Hearst's getting into movie production was to promote Davies' acting career. After a falling out with Zukor in 1923, Hearst moved his production company to MGM where it remained until 1934. So it was at

MGM where Hearst decided to star Davies in *Polly of the Circus*. It was a movie adaptation of Margaret Mayo's 1907 play, which had been filmed before, as a silent, in 1917.

The story deals with a traveling circus whose star attraction is trapeze artist Polly Fisher (Davies), who loftily flaunts her stardom to the other performers. As their train comes into a small town, Polly finds that her attractive figure has been covered up on the city's billboards advertising her appearance at the circus. Appalled at the censorship, she visits the local minister she believes is responsible. The Rev. John Hartley (Gable) denies that it was his idea, indicates that he is a fan of the circus and says he is looking forward to attending. Polly, still angry, leaves in a huff. At her performance, a heckler yells out "Where's your pants?" which distracts Polly enough to cause her to fall and suffer serious injuries. She is brought to the minister's nearby home, and the local doctor instructs that she is not to be moved.

While she is convalescing at the reverend's home, the two fall in love, and when she recovers, they plan to marry. Because of her sordid past, their marriage causes John to be exiled from the church. He is so unhappy that Polly believes he'd be better off without her. She is told that divorce is out of the question, so she plans to return to the circus and have a fatal accident in order to rescue her husband from her stigma.

Polly of the Circus was already old-fashioned hokum when it was filmed back in the 1910s. It creaked even more in the early 1930s. But Hearst wanted to film this stage melodrama with Marion in the title role. Gable met with Hearst and Louis B. Mayer in Mayer's office and made some demands before he would even walk on the set. The priest was changed to a minister, for instance. But the film was still a wrongheaded project for him, and he knew it. After only one day of shooting, he walked off the set and headed to Palm Springs. Even after Mayer threatened to suspend him, Gable still refused to return to Hollywood.

While Mayer was quite angry with Gable, Davies was not. She realized that Gable was not quite right for the role, but also knew that playing opposite the biggest up-and-coming star in movies would only make this project, and her own performance, that much better. She had faith in Gable's ability as an actor to pull it off and knew his name would generate moviegoer interest. She went to Hearst and asked him to fix things somehow.

Hearst admired Gable's strength in standing up to someone as powerful as Mayer, even though Clark was quite new to stardom. Hearst met with Mayer and worked out a new two-year contract for Gable at MGM where he'd be receiving far more money per week.[34] Gable, content with this outcome, agreed to come back to the studio and do the movie.

Polly of the Circus can't be saved by Davies' appealing performance as Polly or by Gable's hard work to seem earnest as a minister. Davies comes off best when she is pushy and wisecracking, but once she settles into the role of a minister's wife, reading the Bible and focusing on domestic issues, the results are quite dull. Gable settles into the minister role with that certain level of calm security that is projected by all great actors who play clergymen. It is effective and charming. Gable's rascally nature never bleeds through: He maintains the calm, collected demeanor that a minister might have.

But it is a very limited role, one that Gable couldn't do much with, and he never really owns it.

Polly of the Circus is strongest during its first half as it focuses on the developing relationship between Gable and Davies. But after they admit their love for each other and get married, the film becomes increasingly dull and predictable. Davies doesn't get much to do as she settles into domesticity; neither does Gable. He does his best but since his character never changes or has anything other than pleasant things to say or do, it's sort of a one-note performance. He's good at playing nice guys, but this one just wasn't a very interesting one. It also seemed kind of silly that Davies' character would be so ostracized for being a former circus member—she gets the same treatment that women of the street do in other pre–Code movies. But the covering up of the billboards does establish that this is a particularly conservative town, and thus its reaction by clergy to "show folk" from the circus.

The critics were not kind to *Polly of the Circus*. John McNulty of *The Pittsburgh Press* stated[35]:

> To see this film is to realize how much progress the American stage has made toward naturalness and away from wooden, incredible patterns. Once *Polly of the Circus* was considered quite a play. If memory serves, it has been translated accurately enough to the screen, and embellished with modern dialogue. It remains, nevertheless, a very ordinary picture, overly sentimental, and a poor selection for either Miss Davies or Gable. Not for a second could anyone conceive the cave-man Gable being a minister. He looks constantly as if he is just wearing the garb of the clergy as a masquerade. Choice of such a role for Gable, excellent in his proper sphere, is pure stupidity. Miss Davies does not succeed either in being anything like the good comedienne that she has frequently proved herself to be. She seems stilted; her comedy forced, and obviously cares no great shakes for the part she's playing. *Polly of the Circus*, in a word, is one of the lesser pictures, and the sooner the Clark Gable and Marion Davies fans can forget about it, the better.

Other critics were equally unimpressed. Kate Cameron of *The New York Daily News* stated,[36] "Both the star, and her chief prop, Clark Gable, seem to fit uneasily into their roles, neither of which is made convincing. The direction is smooth enough and the backgrounds are suitable, but the production as a whole lacks that vitality necessary to put a picture over successfully. It sums up to moderate entertainment."

Polly of the Circus did turn a profit, but only $20,000—a pittance compared to the $600,000-plus that *Possessed* made for the studio. Thus, moviegoers were also unimpressed with *Polly of the Circus* and the film was quickly forgotten. Gable, however, remained friends with both Davies and William Randolph Hearst, not forgetting Hearst's intervening and helping him secure a better contract at MGM.

Around this same time, Gable was one of the MGM stars appearing in the short subject *The Christmas Party*, which came out around the holidays in 1931. The premise has Jackie Cooper asking his mother to throw a Christmas party for his football team. Their house is too small, so they get permission from Louis B. Mayer to hold the party on one of MGM's sound stages. This results in the children being served dinner by the studio's top stars.

Strange Interlude

Produced and Directed by Robert Z. Leonard
Screenplay: Eugene O'Neill (from his play)
Cinematographer: George Barnes
Editor: George Hively
Cast: Clark Gable, Norma Shearer, Alexander Kirkland, Ralph Morgan, Robert Young, May Robson, Maureen O'Sullivan, Henry B. Walthall, Mary Alden, Tad Alexander
Released June 14, 1932
MGM
109 minutes

Eugene O'Neill's play *Strange Interlude* was an epic five-hour production, sometimes run over two nights, in other situations offering a one-hour intermission.

MGM's Irving Thalberg secured the rights with the intention of casting stage stars Alfred Lunt and Lynn Fontanne in the leads. Lunt and Fontanne turned the offer down; they had made the movie *The Guardsman* the previous year and didn't particularly care for the experience of film production. Thalberg then cast his wife Norma Shearer along with Clark Gable, and the lengthy play was abridged to the usual movie running time (in this case, just under two hours).

While he had experience on stage, Gable never took on such lofty material as an actor, O'Neill being one of the 20th century's great playwrights. The actor was a bit intimidated by the opportunity, but also eager to take it. Despite his misgivings, he actually does quite a good job in the role of a man who has an affair with an errant woman, that produces a child. It's pretty heavy material, even for pre–Code Hollywood.

The film spans a 30-year period. During World War I, Nina (Shearer) was in love with a flyer and wanted to marry him, but her father refused to give his consent. The flyer was later shot down and killed in action. Charlie (Ralph Morgan) is smitten with Nina, but too shy to tell her. And she does not love him. Nina marries Sam (Alexander Kirkland) but discovers that she cannot have a family with him, due to mental illness in his heritage. Gable plays Ned, a man with whom Nina has an affair in order to have the child she wanted to have with Sam but cannot. Robert Young plays Gordon, the result of that affair, who does not realize that Ned is actually his father.

There are a lot of layers to the narrative and to each character. Ned is a doctor who is Sam's best friend. It is decided that Sam must have an emotional balance, and it is believed that a child will provide that. But because of the insanity in Sam's family (revealed to Nina by Sam's mother), the child cannot be Sam's. Ned's agreeing to the affair is to help out his friend. It is considered by the doctor to be a clinical thing, but he ends up falling in love with Nina. However, she realizes her purpose, and that her leaving Sam would destroy him. As the child grows to manhood, he has great respect for Sam, whom he believes to be his father, but dislikes Ned, who actually *is* his father.

This causes further emotional trouble for Ned. Gable rises to the challenge of playing perhaps the most complex character he'd had to portray thus far in his career.

This could have been a very conventional story, but the outcome is more interesting. Rather than making the second half of the film about how the affair affects Gordon, it's about how the affair and the lie affects Ned and Nina. There also seems to be some underlying criticism about the upper class. Sam is wealthy and lazy, and Gordon grows up to be just like him, to the dismay of Nina and Ned, who want to see him make something of himself.

The play was an unusual presentation at the time. In it, the actors spoke their characters' innermost thoughts to the audience. In the film, voiceovers are employed to present the thoughts of each character. It is a novel approach, but ultimately unsatisfying and, nowadays, it makes the movie seem creakier and more dated.

There are a lot of ideas that work well in theater, but not on film, and vice versa. This is one of those ideas. The voiceovers frequently hinder the action, and the long pauses that result are awkward—especially when there isn't dialogue for a long time because the film flips between multiple characters' thoughts. The film will stop in the middle of a conversation and a character will seemingly (and awkwardly) stare into the distance. The disclaimer about this at the top of the film is also very interesting; apparently the filmmakers didn't trust the audience to figure out that the characters were voicing their thoughts.

This failed concept is not helped by Shearer's overtly melodramatic performance, which has not aged well over time. It is Gable who comes off best. He may have the most challenging role among the male cast, and he manages to convey the doctor's conflicting personality traits quite effectively. At the time of the film's release, the May 1932 issue of *Silver Screen* magazine ran a story in which the writer stated[37]:

> Few actors have had greater scope in emotional roles than Clark Gable, who has risen in a brief two years from comparative obscurity to enormous popularity. In *Strange Interlude*, Clark Gable has his first heavy dramatic role. As Doctor Ned Darrell, he is neither romantic nor brutal, he is neither a hero nor a villain. He is a man tragically thwarted by life.

Critics were generally impressed with *Strange Interlude*. The *New York Times'* Mordaunt Hall gave it a rave review[38]:

> From Eugene O'Neill's melodrama, *Strange Interlude*, which on the stage was in nine acts and ran for five hours, Metro-Goldwyn-Mayer have produced a shining example of a motion picture that runs for one hour and fifty minutes. It was presented last night at the Astor before an audience which listened intently to every word uttered. The famous asides spoken by the characters are extremely effective, although at times they are delivered somewhat too hastily. In its compact screen form it is an engrossing piece of work, one that has been brilliantly directed by Robert Z. Leonard and beautifully photographed. It is one of those very rare pictures in which the intelligent dialogue never elicited so much as a murmur of disapproval, which on a first-night is exceptional.

Critics in other cities were also impressed.

Eugene O'Neill considered the play to be one of his most satisfying creations,

Gable played opposite Norma Shearer again in *Strange Interlude* (1932).

and he was not pleased with this film, despite providing the screenplay himself. He claimed that the story was edited down to the point where it was imbecilic. The *New York Daily News* critic appears to have agreed with O'Neill, stating in an article discussing books and plays adapted to film[39]:

In the case of *Strange Interlude* the plot is retained almost intact, as is the point. Here again, though, a sentimentalizing process has gone on, and while it is seemingly O'Neill's *Strange Interlude* it isn't. In other words, the mood has been lightened and softened. Now if, as the complaints have it, *Strange Interlude* is interesting and holding to an audience unacquainted with the play, then there is still no use or good in asserting it is O'Neill's *Strange Interlude* because it isn't. It is just the framework of *Strange Interlude* with the very individualistic style, feeling and mood of the original in other words, the certain things that made *Strange Interlude* an original, and I believe, a lasting dramatic work removed.

MGM released publicity stories in the trades claiming standing room only showings where police had to control the crowds. In fact, those who did attend found the movie unintentionally funny, at least according to this Illinois exhibitor[40]:

Not the kind [of audience] that assembles in New York to see a Eugene O'Neill play, but the most heterogeneous crowd that assembles in a semi-provincial semi-cosmopolitan place like Metropolis, Illinois, on a family night. By some fatuity of the booker, the family night had been dated for this select production, therefore it was a well-filled house with many children. For two weeks there had been a notice on the screen of the innovation of MGM that in this play an invisible speaker would deliver the "innermost thoughts" of so much that was expected of the action from this stroke of genius. But, as to the audience, the movie had barely begun when there was a misplaced titter of merriment. The effect was most ludicrous … and now broke out a theater phenomenon which grew to such proportions … first a titter, next a laugh, then a loud guffaw. As for this stroke of genius of MGM, I consider it a clumsy expedient and would express hope that it will not be followed up were it not for the feeling of assurance that there is no danger of any such innovation.

Strange Interlude was only a fair success at the box office. While its returns were not as poor as *Polly of the Circus*, it netted less than $90,000, which is unimpressive even as far back as 1932. Still, the film was a success for Gable's continually building career. He showed that he could be cast against type and succeed in a role that was different than the screen persona he'd established.

Red Dust

Director: Victor Fleming
Screenplay: John Lee Mahin, Donald Ogden Stewart
Based on the play by Wilson Collison
Producers: Victor Fleming, Hunt Stromberg
Cinematographer: Harold Rosson
Editor: Blanche Sewell
Cast: Clark Gable, Jean Harlow, Gene Raymond, Mary Astor, Donald Crisp, Tully Marshall, Forrester Harvey, Willie Fung
Released October 22, 1932
MGM
83 minutes

Clark Gable in the 1930s

John Gilbert, a great star of silent films who was struggling with talking pictures, was originally set to play the *Red Dust* lead opposite his longtime co-star Greta Garbo. When Garbo dropped out of the project, it was decided to pair Gilbert with Jean Harlow, whose career was rising much the same way Gable's was. *The Los Angeles Times* reported in July 1932[41]:

> Jean Harlow, recently so red hot in *Red Headed Woman*, will alter her style muchly in *Red Dust*. She is to do a role invested with much more sympathy, albeit there will be plenty of spice in the portrayal. The picture brings Harlow and John Gilbert together on screen. It is John's last film under his present contract.

A month later, it was announced in the trades that Gilbert was no longer attached to the project, having been replaced by Gable. Gilbert's last film under his MGM contract turned out to be Tod Browning's *Fast Workers*, although he returned to the studio to appear opposite Garbo in *Queen Christina* at her insistence. Gilbert made one more film, Columbia's *The Captain Hates the Sea* (1934). He died two years later.

Gable and Harlow became friendly as novice actors when they appeared together in *The Secret Six*. In the year since that movie came out, both were attaining stardom, and *Red Dust* was a project that advanced both of their careers. It is also further cemented their friendship.

Red Dust is set in Indochina where Gable plays Dennis Carson, who struggles to manage his rubber plantation during monsoon season. Harlow is Vantine, a prostitute hiding out on the plantation due to charges in Saigon. Her carefree, wisecracking, sometimes flamboyant personality attracts the rugged Carson, and they have an affair. Their romance is interrupted when engineer Gary Willis (Gene Raymond) arrives on the plantation with his wife Barbara (Mary Astor). Carson and Mrs. Willis develop an attraction to each other, and Carson plans to take Barbara away from Willis. However, Willis looks up to Carson with great respect. Carson just can't bring himself to do such a thing to the young man. In an effort to make Barbara dislike him, Carson arranges to be caught romancing Vantine, and claims he could never be loyal to only one woman. Barbara shoots Carson, and Gary rushes in. Carson covers up for Barbara by telling Gary, "I made a pass at her and she shot me." Vantine realizes what Carson is doing and plays along. Gary is upset by the betrayal of a man he respects and admires, and leaves the plantation with his wife, never catching on about the affair.

This was Gable's first time working with director Victor Fleming, who understood Gable's more rugged "man's man" qualities and emphasized them in the Dennis Carson role. While it is filled with romantic conflicts, *Red Dust* is still something of a male-dominated, or perhaps male-centric, movie. However, its female characters are far from one-dimensional. Harlow plays Vantine with a pride and an understanding. Vantine is beyond the hot, sticky elements on the plantation, she is toughened by her experiences and can stand up to Carson, which makes her more attractive to him.

Gable does a good job playing a character conflicted between what Vantine's beauty and personality have to offer, and the more refined Barbara, played with

Gable teamed with Jean Harlow in *Red Dust* (1932), and became a true friend when Jean's husband died while the movie was in production.

understated brilliance by Mary Astor. And the conflict extends to Gary Willis, with Gene Raymond's youthful enthusiasm being somewhat the opposite of Gable's manly authority. That is presented as the catalyst for Astor's attraction. Another reason for Gable's attraction to Astor: She is the opposite of what he is used to. He isn't in a situation where he is often exposed to the company of refined ladies. She's also a harder conquest, because she's less likely to throw herself at him than someone like the openly flirtatious Vantine.

There were some strange and interesting methods used to add authenticity to the plantation surroundings for *Red Dust*. A syndicated article released to the press during filming stated[42]:

> The peculiar odor of boiling sap from rubber trees recently brought many curious citizens in nearby districts to the high fence surrounding the MGM backlot. Those who had the ambition to climb on boxes, were startled to see a complete jungle rubber factory in operation. This elaborate installation was made to provide authentic scenes for *Red Dust*, a picture of life on rubber plantations near Cochin, China…. Large sealed containers full of the natural white sap from trees in the jungles of Africa and South America were brought to the set. Just before the cameras were to operate, the milky substance was poured into large kettles. As action began in the scene, the sap was poured from one kettle through a strainer into another, as is actually done in the jungle. Then the substance was placed in wooden trays where workmen performed the miracle of creating raw rubber from the "milk." Acetic acid was poured in and immediate coagulation took place before the camera lens. The white glutinous mass was then run through a large iron "wringer" which spread it out in narrow strips to be hung up for drying. After the drying was complete, a scene showing the packing into bales was photographed with Gable as plantation foreman overseeing the work. A technical expert from one of the world's largest rubber companies checked up on every part of the action to ensure absolute authenticity.

Newspapers also revealed how dust storms were simulated to look effective on screen, allowing fascinated moviegoers to read about how special effects were created.

Red Dust was a fun project for all involved. The actors got along offscreen and responded well to each other in character. Everything was going well until the mood changed with the death of Jean Harlow's husband Paul Bern. This tragic event has been discussed in many other studies, some inaccurate, others speculative. The fact remains that it overwhelmed Harlow emotionally. Production on *Red Dust* was suspended to allow Jean Harlow time to recover. A syndicated article stated,[43] "For 10 days or so the cameras will grind without her, the "shooting around the star" expedient often used when stars become ill or for another reason cannot work. And at the studio they insist she will be back before the cameras, health permitting, to finish the picture."

After a week, Harlow returned to the *Red Dust* set, but her eyes were so weary-looking from crying that her scenes often had to be re-shot. Fortunately, she received emotional support from the cast and crew. Mary Astor kept her busy by running lines and chatting about things unrelated to the tragedy. Gable wrapped his arms around her and maintained a strong, supportive attachment to her for the duration of the movie. Because of this, their friendship deepened, and would continue over ensuing film projects and to the end of Jean's life.

Red Dust was a huge hit. Gable and Harlow both received billing above the title and benefited strongly from its success. It is perhaps the first of Gable's films in which he plays the "man's man" type of character that would continue to define his work.

Red Dust almost tripled its production costs at the box office, becoming a huge hit and helping make MGM the only studio that turned a profit at the end of 1932. The Depression was having an impact even on the movie industry.

No Man of Her Own

Director: Wesley Ruggles
Screenplay: Maurine Watkins, Milton H. Groper
Story: Edmund Goulding, Benjamin Glazer
Based on the novel by Val Lewton
Producer: Albert Lewis
Cinematographer: Leo Tover
Editor: Otho Lovering
Cast: Clark Gable, Carole Lombard, Dorothy Mackaill, Grant Mitchell, Elizabeth Patterson, George Barbier, J. Farrell MacDonald, Tommy Conlon, Walter Walker, Paul Ellis, Charley Grapewin, Lillian Harmer, Wallis Clark, Margaret Marquis, Ferdinand Munier, Clinton Rosemond, Oscar Smith, Jerry Tucker, Dixie Lee Hall
Released December 30, 1932
Paramount
85 minutes

No Man of Her Own turned out to be a significant entry during this portion of Gable's filmography.

Its pre-production was not without incident. Paramount bought the movie rights to Val Lewton's novel *No Bed of Her Own* for $7500. The intention was to make the film with George Raft and Adrienne Ames in the lead roles. Believing neither had enough star power, the woman's role was then cast with Miriam Hopkins, and for the male lead the studio borrowed Gable from MGM.

In a roundabout way, the casting of Gable was due to Marion Davies, who wanted Bing Crosby to appear opposite her in her next film *Anything Goes*. The power of William Randolph Hearst at MGM has already been noted in the *Polly of the Circus* chapter. Thus, MGM agreed to let Paramount make a movie with Gable in order to obtain the services of Crosby.

Hopkins then left the project, ostensibly because she was told that Gable would be given top billing. Hopkins was under contract to Paramount and an up-and-coming star in her own right, so she took umbrage at an actor being borrowed from another studio and given a bigger role and better billing. She claimed that the role didn't suit her, so she took advantage of a clause in her contract that stated that she may do a stage play whenever she wished. She flew to Palm Springs to relax for a weekend and then was determined to carry out her original intention of going to New York for a play.

Paramount then sought Joan Bennett to take the role that Hopkins vacated. But

Bennett was under contract with Fox and they refused to loan her out. They then decided to give the role to Carole Lombard, an actress they had under contract. Lombard was currently off salary, the studio having suspended her for refusing to be loaned out to Warner Brothers to play opposite James Cagney in *Hard to Handle*.

One would think that Gable and Lombard meeting and working together for the first time would be an especially significant event in both of their lives. However, they really didn't connect well on this project, personally or professionally. At the time Gable was still married, while Lombard was married to actor William Powell. It would be four years later when Gable and Lombard would meet again and fall in love.

The story has Gable playing New York card sharp Babe Stewart. A conflict with his girlfriend Kay (Dorothy Mackaill) results in her threatening to expose his cheating in a recent poker game. Babe leaves New York and ends up in the small town of Glendale, where he meets Connie (Lombard), a librarian who feels confined by her small-town existence. They connect, eventually marry, and relocate to New York. Connie believes Babe has a legitimate job, but he is back to his card sharp exploits. To cover his tracks, Babe does get a job as a stockbroker, and ends up excelling at this position. Connie sees Babe hide a deck of cards. The deck is stacked in order to cheat at poker, but Connie secretly shuffles the deck, ruining the game and costing Babe a lot of money. Babe plans to take a trip to South America with two accomplices but before boarding the ship, he changes his mind and asks a cop acquaintance to charge him with something so that can spend 90 days in jail. Connie, now pregnant, is confronted by Kay while Babe is away. Kay tries to reveal Babe's past and is surprised to discover that Connie is aware of it. She realizes she has lost Babe forever, so she gives Connie her blessing and leaves. When Babe gets out of jail, he returns home and tells Connie all about the South American trip he took as the film ends.

Now that *Red Dust* established a screen persona for Gable that used his tough guy qualities as part of his charm, the actor built upon that for this role. Babe's response to Kate's longing for him to stay with her offers dialogue like, "I'm a hit-and-run guy. Never gonna have to comb any gal out of my hair" and "Listen, kid. That thing you've got on is pretty thin but I've got tough skin, see—and I don't feel it." Thus, the incongruity of Babe in a dull small town matches Connie's restlessness. Their connection is inevitable. Then, when Connie and Babe ignite their attraction, it is the polar opposite of the tough guy detachment he shows Kay. Now his dialogue includes sappy pickup lines like "Do your eyes bother you? Because they bother me" and "What do you do with all the hearts you break?" Small town Connie eats it up.

Lombard shows the essence of the romantic comedy star she would later become via *My Man Godfrey* (1936), *Nothing Sacred* (1937) and *To Be or Not to Be* (1942), but at the time she was not a particularly big star. She had been in films since the silent era (her 1928 Mack Sennett short *Run Girl Run* is a minor classic). But at this point she was just starting to make an impact. Despite not being nearly as madcap as in her best movies, Lombard still shows a toughness and a wit that keeps up with Gable's occasionally snappy dialogue.

Carole Lombard and Gable first met when they co-starred in *No Man of Her Own* (1932), but their romance didn't happen until years later.

No Man of Her Own is only fair. It has some highlights, and the historical interest of future Hollywood couple Gable and Lombard in their only movie together, but for the most part it moves very slowly and has none of the verve of *Red Dust*. Gable still has a lot of rugged charisma, and he maintains a rhythm that keeps one's interest, but there isn't a great deal of strength to the screenplay or the dialogue. The culmination is gratifying, with Babe making the right decision for both him and Connie; and his affectionately reference to buddy Grant Mitchell as "Pie Face" is pleasantly amusing.

Theater exhibitors reported that it was well received by moviegoers. Exhibitors went on record with these comments[44]: "Metro never gave us as good a picture as with Gable," "This is the kind of picture the public likes" and "Gable is a popular star and this picture is one of his best." Critics were also pleased. *Film Daily* called it "Just a nice little piece of entertainment," *Variety* stated it was "an audience picture of better than average appeal," and the *New York Daily News* called it "a snappy, always entertaining program picture, mixing small-town placidity with big city swindling."

Originally, Marion Gering was announced as director. Then there was talk of Lowell Sherman behind the camera before Wesley Ruggles was brought over from RKO to direct. Paramount was so pleased with his work that they bought out the rest of his contract and hired him.

Paramount made some effort in making the film seem authentic. In fact, a local gambler was hired to give Gable some tips on how to deal the cards, and other nuances. One morning the gambler failed to show up at the studio, so director Ruggles ordered a search started for him. He was finally located—in jail! Filming went smoothly at first, until a flu bug affected crew members and actors alike. Both Lombard and Gable were out a different times recovering from the illness.

Although she was not a star at Gable's level, Lombard was being built up by the studio. Gable found her to be a prima donna and, at the end of the shoot, gave her a pair of ballet slippers. Lombard responded by giving Gable what she thought of him: a ham with his photo on it.

The White Sister

Director: Victor Fleming
Screenplay: Donald Ogden Stewart
Based on the novel by F. Marion Crawford
Cinematographer: William H. Daniels
Editor: Margaret Booth
Cast: Clark Gable, Helen Hayes, Lewis Stone, Louise Closser Hale, May Robson, Edward Arnold, Alan Edwards, Gino Corrado, Nat Pendleton, William Stack, Nora Cecil, Lumsden Hare, Greta Mayer, Gene O'Brien, Sarah Padden, Mary Jo Ellis, Anthony Jowitt, Inez Palange, Carolyn Spahn
Released April 4, 1933
MGM
105 minutes

In the summer of 1932, it was announced that MGM had purchased the film rights to F. Marion Crawford's 1909 novel *The White Sister*. By that July, another announcement indicated that Helen Hayes, the First Lady of the American theater, would star. *The White Sister* had been a Broadway play and a successful 1923 silent film with Lillian Gish and Ronald Colman. It was felt that the MGM production would not only benefit by the addition of sound dialogue, it would be given a much more lavish production.

From a syndicated article by Hubbard Keavy[45]:

[Can] a silent picture be remade as a talkie and only slightly resemble the original? The question is answered in the affirmative by Victor Fleming. Fleming, who soon will begin directing *The White Sister*, believes that however well and favorably remembered a silent film may be, the new version can (and should) be made sufficiently different to avoid obvious and odious comparison. Somewhat of a classic in movie annals, *The White Sister*, which starred Lillian Gish, can still be quite vividly recalled after these eight years by many who saw it. "Helen Hayes, who will star in the talkie, is as unlike Miss Gish as any two actresses could be," Fleming pointed out. "That gives us a great advantage to start with. The hero, whom we have yet to select, will not be remindful of Ronald Colman, nor will any of the other players resemble their predecessors. We will change the locale of the scenes also. For example, if a love sequence in the old picture was played in a garden, we'll do it in a ballroom or in a café."

Despite Fleming's insistence that the leading man be nothing like Ronald Colman, Colman was one of the actors MGM considered for the role. Others rumored to be in the running included Charles Farrell, Robert Montgomery and John Gilbert.

Gable was chosen to be the leading man and his participation was announced in December. Edwin Schallert stated in the December 15 *Los Angeles Times*[46]:

The White Sister will begin filming today. The Clark Gable choice is set, and there will be much curiosity as to his performance in the leading role originally played by Ronald Colman, although the selection resulted from numerous tests.

The White Sister features Hayes as Angela Chiaromonte, a high-level Italian aristocrat. Her father (Lewis Stone) has chosen a husband for her as is their custom, but she falls for Lieutenant Giovanni Severi (Gable). When he is reported missing in action during the First World War, Angela is so overcome with grief that she becomes a nun. Giovanni is discovered alive, but she has taken her vows and refuses to leave her duties as a nun. She has made a commitment. Giovanni is later mortally injured and dies with Angela grieving beside him.

While this romantic melodrama comes off as pretty creaky today, it was a big hit in Depression-era America, its box office almost tripling its production costs. Critics were generally favorable toward the film, with *Variety* stating[47]: "Helen Hayes is the sorrowing Angela, as solid and satisfying a bit of acting as comes to the screen in a blue moon. Clark Gable is a gallant soldier hero and leaves nothing to be desired."

Theater owners announced in the trades that their audiences were quite pleased. Their comments included[48]:

"This is a splendid picture. Hayes gives a fine performance, and Gable is very good. It is well directed. It is a beautiful story and well played."

"Far superior to the old silent. Metro director and stars all deserve the highest praise for giving us a great picture."

"Story and acting are just about perfect ... will rank well up among the ten best pictures of the year."

"Fine cast and good performances. A good drawing card, especially with feminine patrons."

Lavish sets, romance, a religious angle and top-level stars from a major movie studio were all the ingredients moviegoers of the day needed.

The White Sister is significant as being the first time Gable worked with Helen Hayes. (They again appeared as a couple in the star-laden *Night Flight* later this same

Gable starred opposite theater great Helen Hayes in *White Sister* (1932).

year but shared no scenes.) Hayes much preferred the theater to film but she acted in a number of movies, from the silent era to nearly the end of the 1970s (she lived until 1993). Hayes won a Best Actress Oscar for the 1928 film *The Sin of Madelon Claudet*, and later won Best Supporting Actress for *Airport* (1970).

And while Gable often balked at playing in drippy romantic melodramas, he had, by now, established a certain persona in movies and was able to tap into his rascally screen character as an underlying basis for his performance as Giovanni.

Perhaps *The White Sister*'s main problem is that Gable and Hayes do not have particularly good chemistry. One can conclude that Hayes' acting in the theater did not translate as well to the screen. Sometimes her performance seems over the top. However, this was not only acceptable in its time, it was applauded. Hayes was quite popular with moviegoers, especially for her appearance in the movie adaptation of Ernest Hemingway's *A Farewell to Arms*. But her approach does not quite translate well over 90 years. When she won the Oscar for *Airport*, she had adapted and refined her performances for the movies and television. She progressed as acting itself evolved into a more intimate approach. Gable does a good job, especially making that transition from desperately trying to force Hayes to leave the convent to finally accepting that that wasn't the right thing to do.

Hold Your Man

Produced and Directed by Sam Wood
Screenplay: Anita Loos, Howard Emmett Rogers
Story: Anita Loos
Cinematographer: Harold Rosson
Editor: Frank Sullivan
Cast: Clark Gable, Jean Harlow, Stuart Erwin, Dorothy Burgess, Muriel Kirkland, Garry Owen, Barbara Barondess, Paul Hurst, Elizabeth Patterson, Inez Courtney, Blanche Frederici, Helen Freeman, G. Pat Collins, Nell Craig, Lillian Harmer, Theresa Harris, Vera Lewis, George Reed, Wade Boteler, Bobby Caldwell, Sam McDaniel, Dorothy Vernon, Eva McKenzie, Nora Cecil, Phillip Sleeman, Louise Beavers, Joe Sawyer, Ben Taggart, Jack Cheatham, Frank Hagney
Released July 7, 1933
MGM
87 minutes

Since Gable had last teamed with Jean Harlow in *Red Dust*, he had reached the level where his name was all that was needed to draw in customers. Harlow had gone from her stiff and tentative performance in *The Public Enemy* to her commanding presence in *Red Dust*. Each of them was box office dynamite, so their re-teaming for *Hold Your Man* was hotly anticipated.

Scripted by Anita Loos, *Hold Your Man* is a solid pre–Code drama that benefits from good witty banter between Gable and Harlow. Loos' screenplay also offers good dramatic scenes that allow the two stars to exhibit their range. However, unlike the grittiness seen in movies from Warner Brothers and Paramount, *Hold Your Man* has a good dose of MGM moralizing. Con men become altruistic, female

65

rivals become supportive friends, and prisoners sacrifice their freedom for religious reasons.

This film seems to belong to Gable for the first half, then in the second half it concentrates on Jean. Both were major stars, but it is Harlow who commands the most attention.

Small-time crook Eddie Hall (Gable) and his accomplice Slim cons a man on the street out of his money. The man alerts the police, who give chase. Eddie ducks into an apartment building and enters a room to hide out. He opens a door and discovers Ruby Adams (Harlow) taking a bath. She is more bemused than upset, and appears to be attracted to him, so Eddie asks her to throw the police off his track.

As enacted by Harlow, Ruby is a Depression-era woman who has been through a lot. She has become so weary after battling life's basic struggles, she wants no more than to just settle down with a man. This approach plays well off of Gable's portrayal of Eddie as a con man looking for that one big score. Gable's established screen persona fits the character perfectly as he fast-talks his way into Ruby's life, but he is eventually conflicted by her more conventional desire for comfortable domesticity.

There are a couple of scenes that give more depth to Harlow's character: first, an early scene with a good guy named Al (Stuart Erwin) who could certainly provide her with what she wants, and is willing to do so. She, however, believes he is too nice a guy for a woman like her (or as she perceives herself to be). The other is a confrontation with Gypsy, a former girlfriend of Eddie's. This scene shows another layer to Ruby's personality. Gypsy demands to know who Ruby is. There is some back and forth dialogue between the two women, when Ruby says, "You wouldn't be a bad-lookin' dame if it wasn't for your face." Gypsy slaps Ruby. Ruby punches Gypsy. Eddie is suitably impressed.

Ruby eventually gets involved with one of Eddie's schemes, and it ends up with him knocking a man out and accidentally killing him. Eddie takes off, leaving Ruby to be accused of the crime and sent to a reformatory. Ruby discovers that one of her cellmates is Gypsy and their conflict continues. Ruby soon finds that she is pregnant with Eddie's child. When Gypsy leaves prison, she tells Eddie. Gypsy then visits Ruby in prison and tells her that the pregnancy has changed things and they become friends.

Although the cops are looking for him, Eddie takes a chance and visits the reformatory, pretending to visit another girl. The other inmates set up a scheme where Eddie and Ruby are taken to the chapel where a visiting minister is praying with his imprisoned daughter. Eddie pleads with the clergyman to marry the two of them so the child will not be illegitimate. After the ceremony is performed, the police close in and arrest Eddie. When he gets out of prison, he is reunited with Ruby and their child. He plans to get a job and thereafter go straight.

It was typical of MGM to end their films with a shallow wrap-up that tried to be earnest and convincing, but Gable and Harlow are strong enough actors to make it work. Loos' script offered roles that both actors were able to make their own, and each was good at the tough, often witty, dialogue.

Gable and Jean Harlow were successfully reteamed in *Hold Your Man* (1933).

What is most interesting is how *Hold Your Man* is two different movies in one. The first half was grittier and more earthy in its presentation of a world-weary woman and a crook. The second half deals with imprisonment, renewed responsibility and the central characters paying for their sins. The film claims that neither will return to the lives they once knew, and that Ruby's dream of domesticity was about to come true with the unlikeliest of suitors. To drive this point home, the little family plans to move to midwestern Cincinnati and not back to New York.

The role of Eddie was perfect for Gable during this period. He is the quintessential man's man, with dazzling charisma and a playful naughtiness. But Gable is also allowed to extend beyond these parameters and be more dramatically emotional. Eddie's tearful pleading with the preacher to marry him and Ruby for the sake of their unborn child is some of Gable's finest dramatic work.

As for the supporting cast, Dorothy Burgess stands out as Gypsy. With little screen time, she must show Gypsy as being drunk and carefree, bitterly jealous, angry and defiant, and, finally, kind and understanding. Another fine performance comes from black actress Theresa Harris, who plays the wise prisoner Lily Mae. Harris appeared in 90 films, usually in small, uncredited roles. When she appeared in an all-black movie for Million Dollar Productions, a studio that specialized in race films, she told the press[49]:

> I never had the chance to rise above the role of maid in Hollywood movies. My color was against me any way you looked at it. The fact that I was not "hot" stamped me either as uppity or relegated me to the eternal role of stooge or servant. My ambition is to be an actress. Hollywood had no parts for me.

Lily Mae's preacher father is played by black actor George Reed (he played Jim in the 1920 film version of *Huckleberry Finn*). Remarkably, MGM filmed Reed's scenes with a white actor playing the role for release of *Hold Your Man* in Southern states. It is pure cinematic irony that the actor who played the preacher in these edits was Henry B. Walthall, who is noted for portraying the confederate colonel in D.W. Griffith's *The Birth of a Nation* (1915).

Director Sam Wood might be best known for directing the Marx Brothers in *A Night at the Opera* (1935) and *A Day at the Races* (1937). Wood had a good visual sense; the darkness that surrounds the central characters during the church scenes in which Eddie and Ruby are being married adds nuance and enhances the scene.

Gable and Harlow were lauded by reviewers, and audiences also responded favorably. *Hold Your Man* was one of the top grossers of 1933, its box office more than tripling its production costs. Phillip Scheuer stated in *The Los Angeles Times*[50]:

> "Give him love and you'll hold your man," hums Jean Harlow.... Similarly the presence of Miss Harlow with Clark Gable as her man is assurance that a picture will hold its audience. Yesterday it seemed that Loew's State would scarcely hold its audiences, which jammed the lobbies and overflowed onto the sidewalks. Those who got in saw a shrewdly contrived co-starring vehicle which moved them to both laughter and tears.

Night Flight

Produced and Directed by Clarence Brown
Executive Producer: David O. Selznick

Night Flight (1933)

Screenplay: Oliver H.P. Garrett
Based on the novel by Antoine de Saint-Exupéry
Cinematographer: Oliver T. Marsh
Editor: Hal C. Kern
Cast: Clark Gable, Helen Hayes, John Barrymore, Lionel Barrymore, Robert Montgomery, Myrna Loy, William Gargan, C. Henry Gordon, Leslie Fenton, Harry Beresford, Frank Conroy, Dorothy Burgess, Irving Pichel, Helen Jerome Eddy, Buster Phelps, Ralf Harolde, Marcia Ralson, Ed Peil, Sr., Ed Brady, Francis McDonald, Louis Natheaux, Wallace McDonald, Sherry Hall, Otto Hoffman, Sidney D'Albrook, Evelyn Selbie, Inez Palange, Michael Mark, George Irving, Claire DuBrey
Released October 6, 1933
MGM
84 minutes

Night Flight is not much of a Clark Gable movie, his part (broken up throughout the film) so small it could be considered a cameo. He is again romantically partnered with Helen Hayes, but they share no scenes. Gable is a pilot who spends all of his footage in the confines of a plane, while his wife anxiously awaits his return home. He has only two lines of dialogue.

Riviére (John Barrymore), a hardened airline director stationed in South America, sends his pilots out on missions despite the weather and conditions. Inspector Robineau (Lionel Barrymore) works carefully with Riviére and is forced to carry out orders, despite his misgivings. When a pilot (Robert Montgomery) is late bringing a serum to Rio de Janeiro to battle an outbreak of polio, Riviére sends out another pilot and radio operator. The pilot, Jules Fabian (Gable), gets caught in a rainstorm without fuel, so he and his radio operator (Leslie Fenton) parachute from the plane and drowned in the waters below. Riviére continues to send men on such missions: A young pilot (William Gargan) is next, sent out over the objections of his fearful wife (Myrna Loy). He is successful despite conditions and the serum is delivered in time to save a little boy's life.

David O. Selznick was the idea man behind *Night Flight*, eager to bring the Antoine de Saint-Exupéry

Gable was the star, but he had less screen time than usual in *Night Flight* (1933).

novel to the screen. *Night Flight* was set to be filmed with an all-star ensemble cast *à la* the popular *Grand Hotel* and *Dinner at Eight*. John and Lionel Barrymore had both appeared in the other two all-star-cast features. Clarence Brown was set to direct due to his background in aviation. Columnist Louella Parsons wrote[51]:

> Who better than Clarence Brown who flies his own plane and is an air enthusiast if I ever saw one. He will direct this air mail tale which carried off the French literary award. The principal role is that of a ground officer, who sends his planes over the Andes in South America, rain or shine. Oliver H.P. Garrett, who did such fine job on *A Farewell to Arms*, is getting the story in readiness to shoot.

John Barrymore was announced for the film by March 1933, Lionel not long afterward. The next month, both Gable and Hayes were announced, with Loy and Gargan cast the month after that.

Production was pretty rocky. Brown as able to keep Selznick's interference to a minimum, but John and Lionel were a different problem. According to Gwenda Young's book on Brown[52]:

> Lionel did his best to steal every scene from John. Brown knew how to handle the older Barrymore, but dealing with John pushed him to the breaking point. A chronic alcoholic, John was often erratic, but he was going through a particularly bad bout of drinking, frequently arrived late to the set and struggled with his lines. Brown later recalled that the actor was "almost imbecilic" and impossible to manage. The director tried to get him fired from the production. MGM refused, which was just as well because in his moments of lucidity, Barrymore gave an impressive performance as the megalomaniacal boss who displays a reckless disregard for the safety of his pilots

The newspapers announced that John was taking up flying in preparation for his role. This is unlikely, as John never plays an active pilot in the movie.

The film was not a box office success, mostly because third-billed Gable was barely in it, and had only a couple lines of dialogue. Gable was quite a big star now and had a strong following. He was prominently advertised, so many moviegoers went to see the movie due to his being in it. The movie critic for the *Brooklyn Daily Eagle* stated[53]:

> *Night Flight* doesn't make much use of its stars, or rather the stars haven't much to do in this film at the Capitol. The production is composed almost entirely of scenes of the perilous flights of the mail carriers over the snow-covered, fog-bound Andes, and in the radiophone stations along the line. The flight scenes, although obviously most of them were filmed in the studio, are thrilling enough, but one comes away from the Capitol with the impression that fewer airplane shots and more of Miss Hayes, Mr. Gable, Mr. Montgomery and the Barrymores might have resulted in a more absorbing drama. Actually, John Barrymore never moves away from his desk in the office of the air line. Miss Hayes has but a few brief scenes in her home and in the airport's radiophone room, and only the head and shoulders of Mr. Gable are visible in the periodic scenes showing him in the cockpit of his plane. With all this talent on hand it seems a shame that so little has been done with it.

Night Flight was a step back for Gable. This is the sort of role that should have been given to an up-and-comer rather than a leading star. Gable was a big enough star at this point to warrant bigger roles. We don't even really get a sense of his character at all, since he just sits in a cockpit and doesn't interact with the other characters for the entire movie.

Saint-Exupéry, author of the original book, was unhappy with the movie, and especially chagrined at its being a box office flop and dismissed by the critics. As a result, he refused to renew his author's rights, which he had granted to MGM for a ten-year period. *Night Flight* was therefore withdrawn from circulation in 1942. The author died in 1944, but the conflict with his estate was not resolved, and *Night Flight* remained out of circulation until 2011. It was then shown at the TCM Film Festival and released on DVD. Its world television premiere happened the following year.

Latter-day audiences were, on average, disappointed when they finally saw *Night Flight* after having read about it for decades. Many expected the same type of winning ensemble dramatics found in *Grand Hotel* and *Dinner at Eight*. While both Barrymores are good, and Robert Montgomery has a standout scene dealing with his fears, Gable and Loy barely register, while Hayes played her character a bit too over-the-top. One could glibly make the excuse that she was better suited for the stage, but by the time she acted in *Night Flight*, Hayes was a movie veteran.

Gable was not at all pleased with his nothing part and complained to the MGM brass about how he was being used, now that he was a popular leading man whose presence in a movie ensured good box office. The studio responded by putting him in yet another unlikely project: a musical!

Dancing Lady

Directed by Robert Z. Leonard
Producer: David O. Selznick
Screenplay: Allen Rivkin, P.J. Wolfson
Based on the novel by James Warner Bellah
Cinematographer: Oliver T. Marsh
Editor: Margaret Booth
Cast: Clark Gable, Joan Crawford, Franchot Tone, May Robson, Winnie Lightner, Fred Astaire, Robert Benchley, Ted Healy, The Three Stooges (Moe Howard, Larry Fine, Jerome "Curly" Howard), Arthur Jarrett, Grant Mitchell, Nelson Eddy, Maynard Holmes, Sterling Holloway, Gloria Foy, Eve Arden, Max Barwyn, Stanley Blystone, Ferdinand Gottschalk, Frank Hagney, Jack Baxley, Jean Howard, Matt McHugh, Lee Phelps, Charles Sullivan, John Sheehan, C. Montague Shoaw, Victor Potel, Pat Somerset, Charles Williams, Charles C. Wilson, Mary Wilbur, Ardelle Unger, Marion Weldon, Anita Thompson, Irene Thompson, Zelda Webber, Frances Sawyer, Geneva Sawyer, Jackie Page, Wilburn Riviere, Jackie Page, Linda Parker, Jean Malin, Patsy O'Dea, Linda Parker, Chicquita Marcia, Iris Nicholson,

May Packer, Lester Ostrander, Miriam Marlin, Jess Mendelson, Margaret McConnell, Patsy Lee, Mary Halsey, Edith Haskins, Robert Lees, Peaches Jackson, Louis Delgado, Alan DeAstray, Lynn Bari, Edna Callahan, Shirley Deane, Bonita Baker
Released November 24, 1933
MGM
92 minutes
Songs: "Hold Your Man," Music: Nacio Herb Brown, Lyrics: Arthur Freed; "Alabama Swing," Written by James P. Johnson, "Everything I Have Is Yours," Music: Burton Lane, Lyrics: Harold Adamson; "My Dancing Lady," Music: Jimmy McHugh, Lyrics: Dorothy Fields, Performed by Arthur Jarrett; "Heigh-Ho, the Gang's All Here," Music: Burton Lane, Lyrics: Harold Adamson; "Let's Go Bavarian," Music: Burton Lane, Lyrics: Harold Adamson; "(That's The) Rhythm of the Day," Music: Richard Rodgers, Lyrics: Lorenz Hart; "Hey! Young Fella," Music: Jimmy McHugh, Lyrics: Dorothy Fields

Clark Gable wasn't particularly fond of being what he felt was a supporting actor in a film that featured Joan Crawford as the star. He didn't like his name being used to attract moviegoers for the sake of newcomers like Fred Astaire and Nelson Eddy. However, despite his misgivings, *Dancing Lady* was a box office smash and remains a delightful pre–Code movie musical.

Crawford plays Janie Barlow, a talented dancer who can't find work in legitimate theater so she works in burlesque as a stripper. One night, playboy Tod Newton (Franchot Tone) and his society friends attend the show while slumming, an activity they apparently do frequently in order to be derisively amused at the proceedings. When the show is closed and Janie is hauled into night court for indecent exposure, Tod posts her bail in an attempt at receiving sexual favors in response. Janie, no stranger to such advances, keeps him at bay, but doesn't remain friendly toward him. The entitled playboy believes it's just a matter of time before she succumbs. He finds a way to connect with her when he discovers she has been trying to get a part dancing in a Broadway musical's chorus. Tod agrees to put his money in the show if Janie gets a role. The show's director, the tough-minded Patch Gallagher (Gable), is chagrined at first, but discovers Janie is quite talented. Janie works hard and her talent gets her a starring role. Fearing her success would keep her from him, Tod backs out of the production and it is forced to shut down. Janie, not realizing this, goes away with Tod. When she realizes what he did, she returns to the show, which Patch is now putting on with his own money, taking a real gamble. The show is a success.

MGM purchased the property in January 1933 and planned to have Clarence Brown direct. Later in the month, Louella Parsons announced her in column that because *Dancing Lady* wasn't ready to roll, Crawford would star opposite Wallace Beery, with Clark Gable, in a drama about modern Russia. Parsons said it was two years in preparation and that six writers crafted the screenplay. None of these actors appeared in such a film.

On February 18, 1933, *Los Angeles Times* columnist Edwin Schallert wrote of *Dancing Lady*[54]:

Dancing Lady (1933)

> Joan will be shown first as a poor girl, later as working in a dry goods store (she did work in a department store once) and then as a beauty and fascinator of men. She doesn't want to be the temptress, just wants to follow out a career, but the men are intrigued just the same. Joan will dance in the picture and may also sing a number. Lee Tracy plays a hoofer.

This is not the plot of the movie, and Lee Tracy is not in it. A March column by Len G. Shaw stated that Tracy "has been devoting himself assiduously to daily dance lessons" to prepare for *Dancing Lady*. Days later, it was announced that Tracy would instead star in a movie called *The Chaser* (which was released as *The Nuisance*).

In late March it was announced that Crawford would appear opposite Gable in *The Prizefighter and the Lady*, which ended up featuring actual prizefighter Max Baer and Myrna Loy. Then in April, newspapers reported that Fred Astaire would make his movie debut dancing with Joan in *Dancing Lady*, and her leading man would be Robert Montgomery. Robert Z. Leonard was set to direct because Clarence Brown was busy doing *Night Flight* retakes.

Gable was finally announced as starring with Crawford in *Dancing Lady* in June, but Robert Montgomery's name was still attached to the project as well. At about the same time, MGM put an ad in the California newspapers that it was conducting screen tests for dancing girls to appear in the film. The applicants were expected to be 18 to 21 years old, from 5'5" to 5'8" in their stocking feet, beauty of face was "imperative," and the girls were to report with bathing suits.

Only days later, it was announced that Montgomery was too busy filming *Another Language* and could not take the *Dancing Lady* role, so he was then replaced with Franchot Tone. By June 10, the newspapers announced the correct cast, including Ted Healy, claiming it was his feature film debut (which is incorrect—Healy was in the Fox feature *Soup to Nuts* with the Three Stooges in 1930). *Dancing Lady* began production in June. Backstage musicals were popular in the 1930s and Warner Brothers had scored big earlier in the year with the hit *42nd Street*. MGM probably produced their best musicals in the 1940s and '50s, but they were responsible for *Broadway Melody* (1929), the first sound film to win an Oscar, and a backstage Broadway musical that set the tone for those that came afterward. *Dancing Lady* was a pretty typical backstage musical for the period with the blustery director, desperate, hard-working performer, problems with money and backing, and romantic drama.

Despite his balking at playing "just another gigolo" in Crawford's movie, Gable is great as director Patch Gallagher. The passion of a theater director allows Gable to bank on his natural charisma, and he is ably supported by tough assistant Ted Healy and the Three Stooges. The Stooges started out working with Healy on stage and in some films. They broke with Healy the year after this movie and embarked on their now-iconic series of short comedies at Columbia. Because of their timeless popularity, the Stooges' small part in this movie makes it a curio, even for people not especially interested in movies of this era.

Franchot Tone had been attracting moviegoers for the past year in films like *Midnight Mary* and *Gabriel Over the White House*. As the sly, entitled, unscrupulous playboy, Tone brings a real sense of purpose to his role as Tod, believing his

Gable and Joan Crawford were re-teamed for the musical comedy *Dancing Lady* (1933).

money gives him the power to manipulate Janie's life so that he is the one who benefits.

Crawford is at her most attractive and vulnerable as Janie. She has the strength and street smarts to stand up to tough-talking Healy, who fiercely bars her attempts to see Patch and get a role. But she also can be demure when confronting either the ruggedly attractive Gallagher or the smarmy, entitled Tod.

In one of Gable's strongest scenes, he confronts Tod and Janie after realizing it was Tod who pulled his financial support. Gable exhibits angry passion as he drunkenly yells at Tod for throwing actors, dancers and stagehands out of work. When the owner of the nightclub sympathetically asks him to calm down, Gable shifts to a quieter demeanor, and calmly tells the proprietor, "It's okay. I won't bust up your joint." The volume of his voice is way down; it is calm and controlled. Gable plays this scene brilliantly.

Fred Astaire was an internationally known stage star when he debuted in this film. He has two scenes with Joan, one in which he rehearses a dance with her, and another where they put on a big musical number in the closing show. Astaire's dancing is characteristically brilliant, but we are reminded of Crawford's dancing background, as she keeps up with her partner. Their dances are two more highlights. This movie is often referred to as Nelson Eddy's film debut, but he appeared in MGM's *Broadway to Hollywood* which was released a couple of months earlier. Winnie Lightner is amusing and fun as Janie's gal pal Rosette. And Eve Arden, then little-known, has a small part as an actress trying to pull off a Southern accent in order to get hired, and provides an amusing few moments.

While it is Crawford's movie, Gable strongly registers in one of his more appealing roles from this period. He makes his character compelling and admirable simply by giving him the qualities of Clark Gable's nicely honed screen persona. Gable was every bit as much the reason for the film's success as Crawford. They made a mutually complimentary team. According to available records, *Dancing Lady* enjoyed a profit of nearly three-quarters of a million dollars—quite impressive for 1933.

After finishing his work on *Dancing Lady*, Clark Gable was out sick for several weeks. His teeth had rotted, and he was suffering from gum disease that was so advanced, it was almost malignant. He had to have all his teeth pulled, and then wait until his gums healed before he could be fitted for dentures. Once he was ready to get back to work, he complained to MGM brass about the roles he'd been getting. This got back to studio head Louis B. Mayer, who became livid. Mayer believed that his studio was responsible for Gable's stardom, building him up with their publicity and cultivating his transition from stage actor to movie star.

Mayer decided that Gable needed to be punished. So he worked something out with Harry Cohn, head of Columbia Pictures. So Gable was banished to Columbia to appear in a movie to be directed by Frank Capra. Paramount was having similar difficulty with Claudette Colbert, so she was banished to the same project. Gable and Colbert felt during the entire filming that they were making one of the worst movies of their careers and it would quietly go away and be forgotten. The film was from a story called "Night Bus." Its title was changed to *It Happened One Night*.

It Happened One Night

Produced and Directed by Frank Capra
Screenplay: Robert Riskin
Story: Samuel Hopkins Adams
Cinematographer: Joseph Walker
Editor: Gene Havlick
Cast: Clark Gable, Claudette Colbert, Walter Connolly, Roscoe Karns, Jameson Thomas, Alan Hale, Arthur Hoyt, Blanche Friderici, Charles C. Wilson, Ward Bond, William Bailey, Wallis Clark, Oliver Eckhardt, Bess Flowers, Harry Holman, Frank Yaconelli, Joseph Crehan, Harry C. Bradley, Wallis Clark, Jessie Arnold, George Breakston, Claire McDowell, Irving Bacon, Milton Kibbee, Maidel Turner, Marvin Loback, Fred Walton, Jane Talent, John Wallace, Bert Starkey, Charles Wilroy, Harry Schultz, Blanche Rose, Patsy O'Byrne, William

McCall, Mimi Lidell, Kate Morgan, Sam Josephsen, Mimi Lindell, Joaquin Garay, Ken Carson, Jessie Arnold, Ernie Adams, James Burke, Ray Cooke, Mickey Daniels, Dolores Fuller, Sherry Hall, Hal Price, Harry Todd, Linda Lee Solomon, Billy West, Kit Guard, Jack Evans, Frank Holliday, Eva Dennison, Jack Curtis, Neal Dodd
Released February 22, 1934
Columbia
105 minutes

There are some films that achieve the level of timeless classic because they are essentially flawless. *It Happened One Night* is one of those films. Its beginnings were so inauspicious, its pre-production so slipshod, and its filming so challenging and volatile, the fact that it came off so well is remarkable. It featured a top director, a great writer, and excellent actors who all performed at somewhere near their best. Even Claudette Colbert, who felt the entire time that she was making a bad movie, turned in what might be a career-high performance.

It Happened One Night was based on the Samuel Hopkins Adams story "Night Bus." The movie rights were purchased by Columbia in the summer of 1933; as early as August, they were already announcing it as a Frank Capra project which would feature Robert Montgomery on loan from MGM[55]:

Columbia has one called *Night Bus* ... which will be made fairly soon ... a job for the cinematographers, meaning the boys with the camera, who will be hard put to it to squeeze out angles in the restricted space of the bus interior, and you can't photograph them from the outside and get anything interesting over a long period. Robert Riskin is writing *Night Bus*, which will be directed by Frank Capra, with Robert Montgomery, borrowed from MGM, to star.

By the Fall, the press was indicating that Montgomery would instead be appearing at his own studio, MGM, in *Transcontinental Bus*, while Gable would be in *Night Bus*[56]:

Clark Gable and Robert Montgomery will become rival bus travelers. Gable goes into the lead of *Night Bus* (title to be changed) at Columbia, while Robert Montgomery is in *Transcontinental Bus* at MGM. The Gable assignment is new, and eases that difficulty which occurred when Montgomery was proposed as the featured player in both pictures. It was owing to this situation that Columbia was able to secure Gable, who is not often lent to other studios. There is a fair possibility that Elissa Landi will play the lead with Gable. The Gable role is in a very breezy comedy vein, and the heroine of the picture is seeking to avoid a marriage at the time she meets the hero. Experiences that the two have on a trip from Florida to New York are depicted. Among other things, they run out of money. The bus part of the film is to be made secondary; much of it transpires in auto camps. The same director and writer, Frank Capra and Robert Riskin, who were responsible for the highly successful *Lady for a Day*, are joined in *Night Bus*....[57]

As stated in the previous chapter, Gable was being punished by Louis B. Mayer, who contacted Columbia's Harry Cohn and arranged that Gable appear in a movie

Gable, Claudette Colbert and Roscoe Karns in *It Happened One Night* (1934), one of the most successful films of its time.

at that studio. At the time, MGM was considered the greatest of movie studios, while Columbia was looked upon as one that did low budget second features. A filmmaker the caliber of Frank Capra was slowly beginning to change that, but "banished to Columbia" was indeed a step down for a major studio's top star.

In November 1933, columnist Louella Parsons announced that Paramount's Claudette Colbert would be loaned to Columbia for this film. Colbert was not happy about this assignment and demanded double her salary and a briefer shooting schedule. While Gable eventually settled into the project and got along well with Capra, Colbert remained difficult and angry throughout. Capra later admitted that Colbert threw tantrums on the set rather regularly, but "was wonderful in the part."[58]

Gable plays newspaper reporter Peter Warne, who is on the outs with his boss and quits his job during a drunken phone call. Colbert is Ellie Andrews, an heiress who has run away from her wealthy father because he is against her marriage to foppish King Westley, whom her father believes is a phony. Peter runs into Ellie when they are both on the same bus, realizes who she is, and agrees to protect her identity if she allows him to stay with her and get an exclusive story. Of course, through circumstances, they go from bickering to falling in love.

Considered the very first screwball comedy, *It Happened One Night* has all of the basic foundational elements of this subgenre. The two main characters are well drawn and are opposites at every level. They learn from each other as they become more and more attracted to one another. The dialogue is sharp and witty. The supporting characters are charismatic and appealing. The bad people are merely misguided. The plutocratic father has a sense of altruism. There is little distinction between the privileged and the poor, despite the backdrop being the Great Depression. This is among the elements that make this film so appealing. It brings someone of Ellie's status down to the level of normal folk, making it easier to relate to her problems even though we still realize that she's the privileged rich. It is likely this dynamic also made the characters more real and appealing, to Depression-era audiences.

It Happened One Night is filled with highlights from the very start of the film. The opening scene establishes heiress Ellie's conflict with her father (a delightfully blustery Walter Connolly), resulting in her dramatically diving off a ship and swimming to shore. Reporter Peter Warne is then shown on the phone in a drunken call to his managing editor, telling him off. His tirade attracts a crowd of fellow reporters and citizens, celebrating Peter's triumphant moment. One says to the other, "There's a man biting a dog in there," offering an old saying that represents journalistic interest.

Each character is established with their first scene. Ellie is pretty, headstrong and entitled. Peter is a brash upstart, connected to the city as a working journalist. He has the gumption to confront his boss and dazzle the Depression-era onlookers who'd love to do the same, but haven't the security to do so. Peter realizes he's a great reporter; his harried editor even begrudgingly admits it, and knows that his work is sought despite his brash individualism and rebellious manner.

Once Peter and Ellie meet on the bus, and are forced into the same seat together, their connection becomes tense during a 15-minute stop. Ellie's bag is stolen, leaving her with only a few dollars, Peter tries to intervene and help, but because of her secrecy she has to angrily brush him off, which he finds insulting. However, after traveling overnight, they come to a 30-minute breakfast stop and Ellie tells the driver

Gable and Claudette Colbert in the Walls of Jericho scene from *It Happened One Night* (1934).

to wait while she takes care of a few things. Of course, when she returns 20 minutes late, the bus has departed. Peter is there waiting for her.

This establishes how helpless Ellie is. Her privileged perspective makes her think a bus driver who must adhere to a schedule will wait for her while she takes an extra 20 minutes. When she returns to discover that she isn't quite so important as that, she also finds that a waiting Peter has her ticket, which he found on the seat. Furthermore, he reveals that he knows who she is. This establishes the narrative where Peter wants his scoop while Ellie, recognizing that Peter is fully aware of his surroundings and far more experienced and responsible, decides to connect with him purely out of necessity.

Peter is dismissive of Ellie and her privileged attitude. He is very clear with his disdain, stating:

> You know, I had you pegged right from the jump. Just a spoiled brat of a rich father. The
> only way you get anything is to buy it, isn't it? You're in a jam and all you can think of is your

money. It never fails, does it? Ever hear of the word *humility*? No, you wouldn't. I guess it would never occur to you to just say, "Please, mister, I'm in trouble. Will you help me?" No, that would bring you down off your high horse for a minute. Well, let me tell you something, maybe it will take a load off your mind. You don't have to worry about me. I'm not interested in your money or your problem. You, King Westley, your father. You're all a lot of hooey to me!

This establishes Peter as more than the cynical reporter as first established. He also has a dollop of Depression-era idealism that gives his character more depth.

Ellie eventually fesses up as to who she is and what she stands for, revealing to Peter that she understands herself better than he realizes:

You think I'm a fool and a spoiled brat. Well, perhaps I am, although I don't see how I can be. People who are spoiled are accustomed to having their own way. I never have. On the contrary. I've always been told what to do, and how to do it, and when, and with whom. Would you believe it? This is the first time I've ever been alone with a man!

At one point, Ellie bluntly insists, "I'd change places with a plumber's daughter any day."

In another highlight, Ellie changes places on the bus to avoid Peter. She ends up with fast-talking salesman Shapeley (a wonderfully amusing Roscoe Karns), who tries to pick her up. "Fun-on-the-side Shapeley, they call me," he loftily claims. He eventually sees a report about Ellie in the newspaper and naturally plans to turn her in and collect the reward. When the bus breaks down, Peter plays that he is a gangster who has kidnapped Ellie for ransom and frightens Shapeley into running off into the woods.

One of the most noted scenes features Peter and Ellie stopping overnight at a trailer camp while the bus is repaired. Peter puts up a rope between the two beds and drapes a blanket over it and refers to the barrier as "the Walls of Jericho": "I like privacy when I retire. I'm very delicate in that respect. Prying eyes annoy me." He then explains a man's method of undressing. stating:

Perhaps you're interested in how a man undresses. You know, it's a funny thing about that. Quite a study in psychology. No two men do it alike. I once knew a man who kept his hat on until he was completely undressed. Now he made a picture. Years later, his secret came out. He wore a toupee. I have a method all my own. If you notice, the coat came first, then the tie, then the shirt. Now, according after that, the pants should be next. There's where I'm different. I go for the shoes next. First the right, then the left. After that it's every man for himself.

Because Gable wore no undershirt in this scene, men decided to likewise go bare-chested under their shirts, and sales of undershirts plummeted to the point where some clothing manufacturers complained to Columbia. They wanted the scene removed!

Another highlight occurs a few scenes later in the same trailer camp. A couple of detectives, among the many hired by Ellie's father to find her, are at the door. Suddenly Peter and Ellie lapse into the type of characters that stay in places like this:

Gable and Claudette Colbert were sent to Columbia as punishment, but they helped make *It Happened One Night* (1934) an enduring classic. The hitchhiking scene was one of its highlights.

CAMP OWNER: These men are detectives, Mr. Warne.

PETER: I don't care if they're the whole police department. They can't come busting in here, shooting questions at my wife.

ELLIE: Now, don't get so excited, Peter. The man just asked a civil question.

PETER: Oh, is that so? Say, how many times have I told you to stop butting in when I'm having an argument?

ELLIE: Well, you don't have to lose your temper!

PETER [MOCKINGLY]: "You don't have to lose your temper." That's what you said the other time, too. Every time I try to protect you. The other night, at the Elks Dance, when that big Swede made a pass at you!

ELLIE: He didn't make a pass at me! I told you a million times!

PETER: Aw, nuts! You're just like your old man! Once a plumber's daughter, always a plumber's daughter! There isn't an ounce of brains in your whole family!

CAMP OWNER: Now, you see what you've done?

DETECTIVE: Sorry, but we've got to check up on everybody.

Gable and Colbert play the scene brilliantly, lapsing into different characters in order to distract the detective. The timing and their delivery make the scene both funny and important to the development of their characters. They really do become different people in that moment; Ellie assumes a totally different accent. It's funny but also a great way to show how in-sync they are with each other.

Peter and Ellie resume their journey on the bus. Also aboard are some musicians who are entertaining the riders with songs. By request, they perform "Man on the Flying Trapeze," and everyone on the bus joins in the chorus. Then different passengers take turns doing various verses. The scene might be the strongest in the film, as well as one of the best in all of 1930s American cinema.

This may seem like hyperbole, but this sequence truly resonates. The way Capra films the cheerful passengers singing in the cramped quarters of the bus, framing the shots with the singer of the verse standing in the aisle, surrounded by the others, and how the passengers start dancing in the aisle as they sing the chorus is layered with more than the superficial entertainment it exudes. Suddenly, there is no Depression. The different people who come from various downtrodden situations, are now as one, enjoying each other as they sing and dance together. The scene is both uplifting and moving.

This happy moment ends very suddenly with a little boy crying that his mother has fainted. Now the passengers are united in concern for a fellow traveler. The boy reveals they have not eaten in several days. The Depression is now back into the forefront. Peter and Ellie give the child the last of their money. "I've got millions," Peter brags. The altruism that concludes this scene makes it even more impactful.

The film's next highlight is the noted hitchhiking scene where Peter loftily claims he knows so much about it, he may write a book. However his attempts to flag down cars fail, and so Ellie walks out, lifts her skirt and reveals her shapely leg. This results in the very next car coming to a stop. It is a delightful scene that was later parodied hilariously by Laurel and Hardy when Stan Laurel did the same thing in the duo's classic feature *Way Out West* (1937).

Colbert didn't want to do the scene. She didn't like the idea of showing her bare leg in a closeup. So Capra hired a chorus girl to act as a double. When they got ready to shoot the scene, Colbert had it stopped. She stated that her own leg was much better looking, and agreed to do the scene.

Peter's altruism continues to the very end, when he goes to send a telegram, causing Ellie to think she's been deserted and resulting in her contacting her father with the provision that she be allowed to marry Westley. As Peter is returning, he sees the motorcade going in the other direction with Ellie in one of the cars. He now believes it is *he* who has been deserted. He contacts Ellie's father and arranges to see him in person to collect money. Mr. Andrews believes it is the reward Peter is after, but he only wants to be reimbursed for the paltry expenses he laid out during the journey. Impressed with his pure, unselfish candor, the father talks Ellie into bolting from the wedding and going to Peter. (He does this as she is literally walking down the aisle to marry Westley.)

In the final scene, which takes place after Ellie and Peter are married, they reenact the Walls of Jericho situation, but this time the wall between them comes down. The closeup of the Walls falling is a great final shot in that it ties back to what came before and shows how far Peter and Ellie's relationship has come. Also, with this film being released at the tail end of the pre–Code era, it manages to imply a lot more by showing a lot less.

It Happened One Night was an enormous hit, but not right away. Columbia had little faith in the movie and quietly released it to neighborhood theaters. Word of mouth made it a sensation and in a matter of days, it was being presented in the top movie houses and in the major cities, leading to massive success.

It Happened One Night was the first film to win Academy Awards in all the major categories: Best Picture, Best Actor, Best Actress, Best Director and Best Screenplay. This was not matched until *One Flew Over the Cuckoo's Nest* (1975). Gable reportedly gave his Oscar to a child who admired it, telling him it was the winning of the statue that had mattered, not owning it. The child returned the Oscar to the Gable family after Clark's death. Claudette Colbert spent 1934 appearing in three popular movies that were nominated for Best Picture Oscars: this one, *Cleopatra* and *Imitation of Life*.

Reviews were strong, with major newspapers and the movie trade magazines raving. Lenore M. Tobias of *Photoplay* stated[59]:

> It was consoling indeed to this pessimist to see the effect a picture like *It Happened One Night* had upon an average audience. Every girl pictured herself as the charming younger heiress (Claudette Colbert) in love with that lovable scamp of a newspaper man (Clark Gable) in whose shoes every man would like to have been. It seems to me that if a movie can put so many people in a good mood, it has been of service in promoting a new optimistic outlook among American people.

Theater owners and exhibitors made their pleasure known to the *Motion Picture Herald*, saying such things as[60]:

> Marvelous Entertainment! Did a grand business! First picture to ever run five days in my town! It will surely bring them in! One of the best pictures this year! Has mass appeal! Nothing can be added to the praise of this picture from what has already been said by other exhibitors!

MGM sent Gable to Columbia as punishment, and the result was a movie that elevated the studio to the level of the majors. And the romantic leads don't even kiss once in the entire movie!

Animator Friz Freleng later admitted that the Bugs Bunny character, which debuted six years later, was inspired by *It Happened One Night*. First, the Shapeley character calls Peter Warne "Doc" in their scene together. When Peter is pretending to be a gangster to intimidate Shapeley, he refers to a gangster named "Bugs" Dooley. Peter later chomps on a carrot and wisecracks with a full mouth, something that was a character trait for the cartoon rabbit.

There were a couple of interesting radio adaptations of the film. On the March 20, 1939, *Lux Radio Theater*, Gable and Colbert reprised their movie roles. Even more intriguing, a January 28, 1940, *Campbell Playhouse* broadcast featured William Powell as Peter, Miriam Hopkins as Ellie and Orson Welles as Ellie's father. There are a couple of movie remakes as well. *Eve Knew Her Apples* (1945) features Ann Miller as a radio singer on the run from her management, hooking up with a reporter who wants the scoop. Director Dick Powell's *You Can't Run Away from It* (1956) is a scene-for-scene remake featuring Jack Lemmon and June Allyson.

It Happened One Night has lived on as the quintessential Depression-era comedy, continuing to be just as entertaining in the 21st century. When Frank Capra was honored by the American Film Institute, a retired Claudette Colbert flew in from her Barbados home to be one of the people honoring him. Despite her misgivings throughout the movie, Colbert, looking great at age 79, took to the stage and thanked Capra for "making magic out of a simple story." She added, "Flying from Barbados, I kept thinking, if only Clark could be standing there with me."

While Gable had already risen to the level of leading man, and movie star, with his performance in *Red Dust*, *It Happened One Night* was still a game changer for the actor. It established his screen character in such a way that the attitude he projected in this movie permeated every subsequent role. Capra explained to Merv Griffin[61]:

> *It Happened One Night* is the real Gable. He was never able to play that kind of character except in that one film. They had him playing these big, huff-and-puff he-man lovers, but he was not that kind of guy. He was a down-to-earth guy, he loved everything, he got down with the common people.

Some believe this film to be Capra's best movie, as well as the top film from Gable and Colbert.

Men in White

Directed by Richard Boleslavsky
Screenplay: Waldemar Young
Based on the play by Sidney Kingsley
Produced by Monta Bell
Cinematographer: George J. Folsey
Editor: Frank Sullivan
Cast: Clark Gable, Myrna Loy, Jean Hersholt, Elizabeth Allan, C. Henry Gordon, Wallace Ford, Russell Hardie, Russell Hopton, Samuel S. Hinds, Berton Churchill, Henry B. Walthall, Frank Puglia, Leo Chalzel, Donald Douglas, Dorothy Gray, Sarah Padden, Wallis Clark, Ray Cooke, Purnell Pratt, Perry Ivins, Ruth Channing, Neil Craig, Jill Dennett, Harry C. Bradley, Frank Burke, Eulalie Jensen, Ann Gillis, Isabel La Mal, Mary MacLaren, Treva Lawler, Dorothy Peterson, Lee Phelps, Larry Steers, Frank Reicher, Isabelle Keith

Men in White (1934)

Released April 6, 1934
MGM
80 minutes

As soon as he finished shooting *It Happened One Night*, Gable was almost immediately cast in the medical drama *Men in White*. It was a big difference going from a light romantic comedy to a heavy drama, but Gable liked the idea of exhibiting his versatility as an actor by playing a much different role in a much different film.

Sidney Kingsley's *Men in White* was a very popular Broadway play. The original Broadway production opened at the Broadhurst Theatre on September 26, 1933, ran for 351 performances and went on to win the Pulitzer Prize in Drama. MGM was interested in securing the film rights and wanted to get the film produced and released before the play had run its course. Thus, despite it being a serious A-movie production, *Men in White* was shot in only 15 days. In fact, when it was completed, the movie had to be withheld from release where the play was still running.

Gable and Myrna Loy were presumably cast in January 1934, based on this article that was syndicated in newspapers[62]: "Clark Gable and Myrna Loy have been selected for leading roles in Metro-Goldwyn-Mayer's forthcoming picturization of the current Broadway stage success, *Men in White*.... Production is scheduled to start in the near future."

Despite the play's massive popularity and critical acclaim, at least one syndicated columnist was underwhelmed and believed it would be better as a movie[63]:

> The most important thing to me about *Men in White* is the fact that the play has been bought for Hollywood for Clark Gable. The most interesting thing about it is the fact that New York critics give it such a high rating as a play. Hospital stories are not new to movies. We have had tales of emergency hospitals—films of ambulance-chasing rustlers—we have had motherhood brought to the screen in closeups that would seem to have done everything to make ether, white linen, pain, distress ... as dramatically interesting as can possibly be made.
> In *Men in White* which all New York has adored, we have the intern's side of the hospital "racket," with a good deal of sympathy engendered for the intern thereby. We have, what is more amusing still, the political and business end of the hospital "racket." The author has, without a doubt, informed himself faithfully on this subject. I still think he could have done a lot more with the material ... and I think the much-despised movies will take his idea and material and work it over into something which will gain in dialog and dramatic values tremendously. I know the reverse is usually the custom but this is going to be the big exception.

Gable agreed completely with this assessment, telling interviewer Wood Soanes,[64]: "I honestly think that the play lost nothing at all by being adapted for the screen. Naturally we had to tone some of it down, but the spirit of Sidney Kingsley's story was maintained and that's all an author can expect when he writes for one medium of expression and is subsequently moved to another."

MGM was noted for being the more polished studio, avoiding the edgier content that was a mainstay at Warner Brothers and Paramount, especially during the pre–Code era. Thus, *Men in White*, a hospital drama featuring Gable as an idealistic doctor and Myrna Loy as his spoiled socialite fiancée, was surprisingly against the norm. A film that deals with a back alley abortion as a major plot point within its narrative was quite challenging, especially for the 1930s.

Gable is Dr. Ferguson, who plans to study abroad under the tutelage of Dr. Hochberg (Jean Hersholt) for only $20 per week. His entitled rich fiancée Laura (Loy) instead wants him to set up a practice and settle down. Her wealthy father agrees. The hospital administration also supports this, because they would like the father to underwrite their losses and believe a position for Dr. Ferguson would be a good bargaining tool.

In a powerful scene, a little girl with diabetic hypoglycemia is diagnosed by a senior doctor who believes the child is in a diabetic coma and needs insulin. Dr. Ferguson overrules his superior, insisting that she is suffering from insulin shock and needs glucose. He is correct and the child lives. The scene is very moving, with Gable purring his lines to the child, who is comforted by his strong, confident and soothing presence.

One night, Ferguson is asked once again to work late, forcing him to cancel his plans with Laura. When the patient dies, he sadly lets her know he will be able to make their appointment, but she haughtily explains she has made other plans. Disgruntled and exhausted, he responds to the advances of a pretty nurse, an inevitable joining of two people who share the same beliefs regarding their profession and are so overworked and frustrated that they don't really have anyone else. This nurse is later admitted to the hospital as an emergency case because she became pregnant and arranged for a back-alley abortion, causing serious injuries that eventually prove fatal. Director Richard Boleslavsky offers a closeup of Gable lowering her head onto the bed, it slowly disappearing into the frame.

This scene is followed by one in which the child who had been in insulin shock runs up the corridor to Ferguson and proudly announces she is cured and going home. So a life the doctor was unable to save is offset by presenting a child whose life he has saved. It is one of the most impressively shot sequences in the film.

Gable offers strength, determination, intelligence and power. He is light-heartedly cavorting with intern friends at one point, romancing his fiancée at other times, and then responding to the hard drama of emergency surgery. Loy maintains a level of superficiality that is forced into seriousness and caring. Jean Hersholt's measured performance is a harbinger to the Dr. Christian series where he did some of his most notable screen work. The edginess of the content, and the melodrama that is notable for 1930s features, are bolstered by fine performances and brilliant direction by Boleslavsky.

The dynamic between Gable's character and Loy's has an interesting connection to the one between Gable and Claudette Colbert in *It Happened One Night*. Both women are entitled rich snobs. Gable is, in each film, a rugged idealist. But where one is played for comedy and creates the screwball comedy dynamic, this one is played for dramatic conflict. Loy's snooty dismissal of the doctor with no regard for his

Gable relaxes between scenes with Elizabeth Allan on the set of *Men in White* (1934).

position or his patients soon evolves into one of greater understanding. Similarly, Colbert's character, in a comic vein, goes from snobbishness to infatuation, revealing that her entitled life isn't all that attractive.

There isn't a great deal of narrative structure in *Men in White*, the film resting mostly on a series of different scenes, not all of which organically connect to one another. The hospital's financial situation is introduced but not fully explored. The comic relief showing the interns fighting over girls is pleasant and could very well have distracted from the central narrative. However, the drama between the central characters is compelling enough that the tangential scenes don't really distract from it. If they serve no other purpose, they at least give the viewer a sense of what the atmosphere is like at a busy hospital. The strongest scenes, the courage of challenging the parameters of the newly enforced Production Code, the performances, and the artful direction are what make *Men in White* a solid 1930s melodrama. The film carefully allows its audience to breathe after the more emotional scenes.

When it was released, the Legion of Decency found *Men in White* unfit for the public. It was banned in some cities and heavily edited when shown in others. Although there were no overt references to abortion in the original script, the Hays Office found the story to be in violation of the Production Code because they believed that there were clear indications that nurse Barbara Denham's illness was brought about by an attempted abortion. MGM cut some lines to allay their concerns. Despite these changes, there were protests against the film by moral reformers and religious groups.

Men in White was one of the first films condemned by the Legion of Decency, which had just been founded in 1933. It was an organization dedicated to identifying content in motion pictures that was considered offensive from the perspective of the American Catholic Church. After being approved by Hollywood's Production Code, films were then submitted to the Legion of Decency before being released to theaters. When a film was condemned by the Legion of Decency, it would hamper the film's box office success. There were around 20,000,000 Catholics in America who would be forbidden from attending the movie, as doing so would be considered a mortal sin.

It is fascinating, and commendable, that a play and its subsequent film adaptation in the early '30s recognized that botched abortions were a big issue and sought to address it. It is unfortunate that the film version never got the opportunity to discuss it more bluntly.

Despite any limitations in exhibition on the part of the Catholic church, *Men in White* was enormously successful, grossing nearly seven times its $213,000 production cost. The reviews were positive, with *Photoplay* stating[65]:

> By no means are you to consider [*Men in White*] just another of those medical things. It is a hospital picture to end all hospital pictures! …It is a film long to be remembered—fine and honest. In the scene with the little sick girl, Gable does a remarkable acting job. And he has your sympathy all through the episode with the nurse who dies as a result of an operation that should not have been performed.

The movie was such a hit, it was parodied by the Three Stooges in their comedy short *Men in Black*, which was nominated for an Academy Award. The Stooges film was shot in five days, from August 28 until September 1, 1934, and released on September 28. While it wasn't a direct parody of the MGM movie, the title was a play on its title, and it was set in a hospital with the Stooges as doctors.

Loy and Gable found themselves in several films together. She had appeared in *Night Flight*, but this is the first movie in which the two of them are co-stars. Loy recalled that because she had rebuffed Gable's advances at a party prior to the filming of this movie, he ignored her on the set, only speaking to her when filming a scene. However, Gable settled down considerably as filming continued, and by the end of the shoot, the two were good friends and remained so. Loy appeared in Gable's next film, *Manhattan Melodrama*.

Manhattan Melodrama

Directed by W.S. Van Dyke
Screenplay: Oliver H.P. Garrett, Joseph L. Mankiewicz

Manhattan Melodrama (1934)

Story: Arthur Caesar
Produced by David O. Selznick
Cinematographer: James Wong Howe
Editor: Ben Lewis
Cast: Clark Gable, Myrna Loy, William Powell, Nat Pendleton, Leo Carrillo, George
    Sidney, Isabel Jewell, Muriel Evans, Thomas E. Jackson, Isabelle Keith, Frank Con-
    roy, Noel Madison, Jimmy Butler, Mickey Rooney, William Bailey, Jack "Tiny"
    Lipson, John Marston, Larry McGrath, Shirley Ross, Oscar Apfel, Vernon Dent,
    G. Pat Collins, Stanley Blystone, William Arnold, John Bleifer, Curtis Benton,
    Wade Boteler, Cullen Johnson, Lew Harvey, Donald Haines, Mary Gordon, Jay
    Eaton, Charles Dunbar, James Eagles, William Irving, Lew Harvey, Eddie Hart,
    Harrison Greene, Jimmy James, George Irving, Leonid Kinskey, Payne John-
    son, Sam McDaniel, Larry McGrath, Leo Lance, Dixie Lotten, Pat Moriarty, Pete
    Smith, Lee Shumway, Charles R. Moore, Tom McGuire, Bert Russell, Harry Sey-
    mour, Landers Stevens, Edward Van Sloan, Emmett Vogan, William Stack, Al
    Thompson, W.R. Walsh, Pepi Sinoff
Released May 4, 1934
MGM
93 minutes

It Happened One Night was in release for about a week when MGM announced that Gable would next star in David O. Selznick's production *Manhattan Melodrama*[66]

What with adoring femmes trying to steal his handkerchief and the whole town of New York reported to have gone Gable, Metro-Goldwyn-Mayer studio will greet their star three weeks hence with a new scenario laid in the very town he conquered. Since Clark went out and made himself a matinee idol he will be more carefully studied. MGM will put him into more dramatic roles. His next [will be] *Manhattan Melodrama*....

The article also featured Myrna Loy, who had clicked with Gable in *Men in White*, and William Powell. Powell had been active since the silent era at Paramount and Warner Brothers but was now freelancing.

The story of two childhood friends who end up on opposite sides of the law as adults is now a cliché, but in 1934 it was popular drama. Its best example might be the 1938 Warner Brothers feature *Angels with Dirty Faces* starring James Cagney and Pat O'Brien as the pals who become a gangster and a priest, respectively. In *Manhattan Melodrama*, Gable grows up to be the gangster, Blackie, while Powell is Jim, a district attorney. Loy is Eleanor, the woman who comes between them, first with Blackie and later with Jim, whom she marries. When Blackie is implicated in a gangland murder, Jim must testify against him and ultimately send him to the electric chair.

The narrative sets up the characters of Jim and Blackie as childhood friends who lose their parents in the General Slocum steamer disaster in June 1904. The steamer caught fire in the East River while transporting passengers to a church picnic. Over 1000 fatalities were the result, many of them women and children. This was believed to be New York City's greatest tragedy before 9/11.

Orphans Jim and Blackie are taken in by the kindly Mr. Rosen, who lost *his* son

Gable (left) and William Powell play grown-up childhood buddies in *Manhattan Melodrama* (1934). Gable is a criminal. Powell is a district attorney.

in the fire. When Mr. Rosen is killed after violence breaks out during a demonstration featuring Leon Trotsky, young Blackie vows revenge. Mickey Rooney, who plays Blackie as a child, recalled for the author during a 2001 interview[67]:

> I remember this picture for being the first time working with Woody Van Dyke as a director, and I think it is when I met both Jim Butler [who plays young Jim] and Don Haines [who plays Blackie's henchman Spud as a child]. Both those boys were killed in the war, and Woody killed himself right around the same time.[68] He had cancer and wanted to die on his own terms. Good memories and sad memories with this picture.

After these establishing scenes, the film quickly jumps to current times, with Gable as Blackie running an underground gambling record that stays a jump ahead of raids, and Loy as his devoted girl who wishes he'd quit the rackets. On the street, Blackie runs into Jim (now played by Powell), who is rising as a prosecutor.

The film then presents both characters and their parallel lives. Gable and Powell offer striking, charismatic portrayals that are immediately attractive to the viewer from different perspectives. When Blackie cannot meet Jim as planned, he sends Eleanor in his place. It is fascinating how the narrative has them connect due to their mutual attraction to Blackie. The attraction that develops organically results from

Eleanor's continued longing to get away from the rackets. This results in Eleanor asking if Blackie will marry her. Blackie responds:

> You're talking a lot of hooey, right out of nice, clean storybooks. You got a good load of Jim tonight, probably did you a lot of good outside of these silly notions. But get this: Jim's as much out of your class as he is out of mine. I used to get ideas too, listening to Jim. Ideas that could be something. But I forgot them because they're not my stuff.

Eleanor responds by telling Blackie she is leaving him. He doesn't accept it at first, even tries to laugh it off. When that doesn't work, he tries to make love to her. She resists, stating:

> Up to a minute ago, I loved you very dearly. You were all that mattered to me. But right now, I can't even remember having been in love with you. I got some ideas of my own now. They may be old and discarded, like oil lamps or horse carts. But they're mine. And I'm stuck with 'em.

Eleanor walks to the door to leave, then turns and tearfully says, "Goodbye, Blackie." Van Dyke shoots this in closeup and Loy wisely pauses for a beat before delivering the line. It is one of the most emotionally stirring scenes in the film.

It is months before Eleanor runs into Jim again, and they connect as comfortably as they had when they first met. The scene that follows is significant in how it presents Gable's interpretation of the Blackie character. In Gable's hands, the character is very layered, able to be a secure leader with his gangster connections, a romantic partner for Eleanor, and a light-hearted buddy to Jim. But when he is alone with gangster Manny Arnold (Noel Francis), who is long past paying a debt he owes Blackie, Gable draws from his experience in playing evil gangsters. Speaking in a quiet, measured tone that is almost a monotone, Blackie states:

> A couple of months ago, I might have felt sorry for you and let you crawl out. But a lot of things have happened to me since then and I don't feel the same about you anymore. You better cross yourself, Manny, and make it double. This is once you double-crossed yourself.

Gable plays the scene with no movement. He is still, stern, his eyes fixed on Manny. The character is drawing on the bitterness he's felt since Eleanor left him. He kills Manny while remaining still, unmoved emotionally or physically. Van Dyke cross-cuts between Blackie's cold stare to Manny's wide-eyed fear. It is one of the film's strongest scenes.

The narrative offers a complication when it is discovered that henchman Spud, whom Blackie ordered out of the room before the murder, left an overcoat behind. The problem is the overcoat was Jim's; he lent it to Eleanor the night they met. Spud had been instructed to return it to Jim, but began wearing it himself.

Jim summons Blackie to his office and tells him that he and Eleanor plan to be married. Blackie, who is surprised at first, tells Jim he supports their union, stating, "She couldn't have picked a better man." Jim then informs Blackie that he is a

Myrna Loy (left) dumps Gable (right) for William Powell in *Manhattan Melodrama* (1934). Later that year, she and Powell would make movie history with *The Thin Man*.

suspect in the Manny Arnold murder, and the fact that his coat was in the room is what makes him realize this. There isn't enough evidence to convict, so it is considered a warning. Jim tells Blackie, "I'm going to clean out every rotten spot I can find in this city and, Blackie, I don't want to find you in any of them!" Blackie states that if Jim finds him, "You're gonna give me everything I've got coming to me! You're gonna nail me every time I step out of line and sock me to the limit. And as cockeyed as it all sounds, I'll be proud of ya!"

This allows us to further explore the depth of the Blackie-Jim relationship. It is stronger than their being on opposite sides of the law. Each must do what is necessary and both respect that. It can be considered ominous foreshadowing in the context of the narrative. Then, when Jim and Eleanor marry and Blackie is best man, he sends a congratulatory telegram rather than attend. He doesn't want to give Jim negative publicity. Jim's secretary feels the same way, stating, "Some people think you let Blackie go free for the Manny Arnold killing because of your friendship." Jim is not bothered by what people say.

Blackie learns from Eleanor that Jim's former assistant, Mr. Snow, holds a grudge against him, so he murders the man. This scene is also well done. It takes place at a Madison Square Garden hockey game. Blackie summons Snow into the men's room. As Snow enters, Blackie is facing away from him, washing his hands. When Snow asks what he wants, Blackie turns around and says, "I want to do a favor for a friend" and empties his gun at Snow. A phony blind beggar is a witness, and he turns Blackie in.

When Jim is forced to send Blackie to the electric chair, he is riddled with remorse. Blackie takes it completely in stride. Even during the court proceedings, Blackie nudges his defense attorney and points out how Jim, the prosecutor, has "class," and states, "You've been licked by the best." Meanwhile, Jim states in court, "I once made a boyish effort to save Blackie's life. Now I ask for his death." As the judge addresses the jury, Jim sends Blackie a note that states, "Sorry kid, I had to do it." Blackie returns a note which states, "It's ok, I can take it. And can you dish it out!" Even though his lifetime friend is sending him to the chair, Blackie accepts his fate, telling Jim: "Don't commute me—I don't want it. Hey, look, Jim, if I can't live the way I want, then at least let me die the way I want." As he is moved to Death Row, Blackie stops and tells a young inmate, "Die the way you lived, all of a sudden, that's the way to go. Don't drag it out."

This is a very different kind of gangster than what we've seen Gable play before, in that he consistently shows so much respect for Jim and what Jim stands for, even if doing so puts his own life at risk. Gable's performance in his final scene with Powell, just before the execution, is strong because even though he tries to play off the situation in a very casual manner to alleviate Jim's remorse, the pain at their parting is apparent in his face. The shot of Jim walking away and the lights dimming, then coming back on, is very powerful.

While *Manhattan Melodrama* has a plot that has since become clichéd, it functions well here as a study in characters who love each other but must remain true to themselves. Gable plays Blackie with strength and stoicism, a character who is attractive and charismatic in spite of his exploits. Powell has the same level of charisma, and functions solidly in his role, especially toward the end when his remorse is so overwhelming despite his realizing it was the best thing to do.

Loy must balance between these two extremes and does so expertly. Leo Carrillo, probably best known for playing Pancho on the *Cisco Kid* TV series of the early 1950s, plays a priest who was with the boys on the ship at the beginning of the film, and is back with them when Blackie is about to go to the chair. He is a random yet consistent presence that helps bolster the emotional impact of the film. Carrillo, an actor who can play light-hearted or heavy emotion, is well-cast. Four years later he worked with Gable again, in a more comical role, in *Too Hot to Handle*.

MGM didn't expect a great deal out of *Manhattan Melodrama*, but it became an enormous hit, further solidifying Gable's stardom. It also made bigger stars out of Powell and Loy. *Manhattan Melodrama* allows us our first chance to see the chemistry between Powell and Loy, who would later score with *The Thin Man*, released a few months after this movie. They co-starred a total of 14 times, three of those during this same year. In fact, when retakes were shot for *Manhattan Melodrama*, W.S. Van Dyke was busy directing *The Thin Man* so George Cukor stepped in.

Columnist Sidney Skolsky was on the *Manhattan Melodrama* set when the courtroom scene was filmed. He reported[69]:

Tense William Powell is standing at the railing ready to address the jury. Director Woody Van Dyke then turns to Cameraman James Wong Howe, the only Chinese cameraman in the flicker industry. He came here from China when he was 3. He is one of the few cameramen who favors natural light for his scenes and uses fewer studio lamps than any other cameraman. Van Dyke gets the okay from Howe and passes it along to Powell. "Let 'em roll," yells the assistant director. Powell twitches his face and then lets his tongue glide over his lips to moisten them. The film in the camera is rolling and Powell is addressing the jury. It is a long take, for Powell has a lengthy speech. It consumes about two minutes: Powell is asking the jury to send Clark Gable, the gangster, to the electric chair. It is a dramatic point in this dramatic yarn for this, in brief, is the story of *Manhattan Melodrama*.

In another widely syndicated column, Powell himelf recalled his reaction to Gable's approach when performing the scene where he kills Manny[70]:

When an actor of the olden days announced his decision to kill another, the announcement was delivered with a clenching of fists, a contortion of the face muscles, the glare of fire-darting eyes, and a voice that was a cross between a snarl and a yelp of pain. In a similar sequence which Clark Gable plays in this present picture …, the important line is delivered calmly, evenly … in a low tone of voice. The modern delivery is by far the most effective, because in a talkie we can have true realism. On the old-time stage, in the old-time theater, with all its acoustic and lighting defects, there had to be great variations from that norm, or your line wouldn't get over. And, for many years, these variations from realism came to be accepted as an established technique.

Another visitor to the set, Wood Soanes, asked Gable if he missed his days as a stage actor. Gable stated[71]:

I served my time in the theater, and got little or nothing out of it except experience. I don't owe the stage, as an institution, anything at all. I'm not beholden to any managers or producers either. But I do owe a definite debt to the screen. When I got into pictures, I was a nobody. I'd done a few parts that won attention, but I certainly was no great shakes of a personality. Hollywood built me up into the star class, paid me well while it was building me, and gave me an opportunity to enjoy a taste of home life I hadn't had since I was a boy. Why should I want to chuck this in favor of the stage? I had a taste of the theater not so long ago. I went to New York on a pleasure jaunt and let myself get talked into some personal appearances. I did it because the studio wanted me to, not because of personal choice. And I was glad when it was all over. It's great to meet your friends face to face, but a little of it goes a long way. And I found out, incidentally, that all this talk of the stage being in the ascendancy again is largely talk. One of the first things an actor has to do is find a play, and plays are still few and far between. Broadway is in pretty good shape, but a lot of bad plays are being given runs. There weren't many good ones on display when I was there. If I went back to the theater right now, all the producers would do is flip back the pages of their minds and immediately classify me as a gangster. Talk about Hollywood typecasting, Broadway taught Hollywood that game.

The reviews for *Manhattan Melodrama* were strong, with *The Hollywood Reporter* stating[72]:

> Even if *Manhattan Melodrama* were only half as good as it is, you would have a hit picture in the combination of Gable, Powell and Myrna Loy. But with the sure-fire audience plot contained in the story…, plus the powerful direction by W.S. Van Dyke, it has all the elements of a sensational smash hit. Chalk up another for David O. Selznick and MGM.

Manhattan Melodrama is also noteworthy for some trivia connected with the film. During a nightclub scene, Shirley Ross sings the Rodgers and Hart song "The Bad in Every Man," which was later given more positive lyrics and became the classic "Blue Moon." This is a rare presentation of the song as it was originally written. *Manhattan Melodrama* is also the only film pairing Gable and Powell. Both were married to Carole Lombard. Powell was married to her from 1931 to 1933, during the time she appeared opposite Gable in *No Man of Her Own*. Gable was married to her from 1939 until she was killed in a plane crash in 1942. Finally, and even more famously, *Manhattan Melodrama* was the movie playing at Chicago's Biograph Theater on July 22, 1934, when gangster John Dillinger, just outside the building, was shot to death by federal agents. Dillinger had plans to see the movie, as he was a fan of both Loy and Gable, but he was set up by the notorious Lady in Red.

On September 9, 1940, *Manhattan Melodrama* was presented in a *Lux Theater* radio broadcast, with Powell and Loy repeating their screen roles. Blackie was played by Don Ameche.

While *Manhattan Melodrama* was being filmed, MGM announced that Gable would next co-star with Wallace Beery in a story based on the life of John J. McGraw, famous manager of the New York Giants. It had the working title *The Coach*, and Larry Weingarten was to produce. For whatever reason, this movie was never made. Gable was next put into the romantic melodrama *Chained*, which reunited him with Joan Crawford.

Chained

Produced and Directed by Clarence Brown
Screenplay: John Lee Mahin
Story: Edgar Selwyn
Cinematographer: George Folsey
Editor: Robert Kern

Clark Gable in the 1930s

Cast: Clark Gable, Joan Crawford, Otto Kruger, Stuart Erwin, Una O'Connor, Marjorie Gateson, Akim Tamiroff, Ward Bond, Francis X. Bushman Jr., Tommy Bupp, Mickey Rooney, Nora Cecil, Grace Hale, Paul Porcasi, Wade Boteler, Theresa Maxwell O'Connor, Nick Copeland, George Humbert, Chris-Pin Martin, Franklin Parker, Adrian Rosley, William Stack, Ernie Alexander, Colin Chase, Gino Corrado, Gordon DeMain, Sam Flint, Gladden James, Tom Mahoney, Edward LeSaint, Phillips Smalley, Adrian Rosley, Louis Natheaux, Edward Mortimer, Kendall McComas, Delmar Watson, Frank Puglia, Lloyd Whitlock, August Tollaire
Released August 31, 1934
MGM
76 minutes

By the time Clark Gable made *Chained*, once again co-starring with Joan Crawford, he extended beyond movie stardom into the fashion world. According to *New York Daily News* fashion reporter Al Taylor[73]:

> Hope is evidently springing eternal in the breasts of the younger male citizens who would like to move the heart-strings of the girls, even as does Clark Gable. When I went to look at the Fall line of a well-known clothing house, they brought out a coat which they called the Clark Gable coat, a copy of one he wore in the picture *It Happened One Night*. It seems the boys are going to believe that clothes make the man. That particular coat was a sport model, and had all kinds of belts, patch pockets, plaits and whatnot. The Metro Studio has just sent me pictures of the popular Clark in a suit he is wearing in his latest picture, *Chained*.... The suit, you will observe, is single-breasted, with peaked lapels. Shoulders are broad, waist high and snug, trousers full and plaited. A white shirt, striped tie, white handkerchief and gray spats complete the picture. So there you are, boys. If you want to dress like Gable, get yourself made a suit *comme ca* ("like that, to you"), and all you need is the personality that goes with it.

It appears Clark Gable had an impact on men's fashion somewhat beyond merely causing undershirt sales to plummet.

The real-life affair between Crawford and Gable was troublesome for the studio when the two were filming *Possessed*, but MGM now chose to look the other way rather than keep them apart. They realized with the more recent *Dancing Lady* that the two of them together guaranteed a strong box office result.

Crawford had just completed *Sadie McKee*, and while she had a troubled relationship with director Clarence Brown during that production, she still considered him her best director, and asked for him for *Chained*. Gable, who was also fond of Brown, had no objection.

Shipping magnate Richard Field (Otto Kruger) is in love with his secretary Diane Lovering (Crawford), but cannot marry her until he secures a divorce from his wife Louise (Marjorie Gateson). When Field sends Diane on a cruise, she meets Mike Bradley (Gable) and there is an attraction. Diane remains true to Richard, despite Mike's best efforts, and the flirtations of his friend Johnny (Stuart Erwin). Diane finally falls in love with Mike, tells him about Field, and agrees to break it off with Field when she returns home. Upon her return, she learns that Louise is now open to divorcing Richard so, due to her loyalty, she agrees to marry him. Mike confronts Richard but is moved by how kind he is and decides to back off. Richard realizes that Diane truly loves Mike and decides to be noble and allow her to be with him. In the end, Diane marries Mike and settles on his ranch in Argentina.

The last time Gable and Crawford appeared together, it was the pre–Code era. The *Chained* narrative is careful to emphasize that Diane and Richard's relationship is chaste, because he is a married man. And despite its melodrama, the cast plays it naturally, especially Gable, whose natural ability impressed a reporter visiting the set[74]:

> The scene called for him to speak a few light-hearted lines to Joan Crawford, who sat at a table all tied up in emotional knots. As a prelude, a phonograph offstage was playing "Butterfly" to aid Miss Crawford, while Gable, paying no attention to her at all, was chatting off the set with an important lady producer from Sweden who was on her annual tour of the studios. When it came time for Gable to speak his piece, the phonograph was turned off, the cry of "Camera!" sounded, the assistant director cried, "Quiet—quiet please!"—the outside doors were shut, the director went to his post, several cameramen went to theirs, those monster lights flashed on those blinding streams of light. Miss Crawford clutched her hands and suddenly there was Gable tossing out his light, amusing lines—and then suddenly going into the kind of a love siege that only the films reveal. It all seemed very easy—very natural.

It is this type of natural performance that helps even Gable's more melodramatic romance films hold up well today.

The film is manipulative in making us like and admire the wealthy man who wants to leave his marriage to hitch up with his younger, attractive secretary. We see him as trapped in a loveless marriage because his wife clings to her social status. She wife even suggests that he engage in a sexual affair with Diane while they remains married. However, in a Production Code–era film, the man balks at such an idea. Of course, they don't come right out and say such a thing but the inference is clear. What is most impressive is that all of this set-up and backstory is established within the film's first ten minutes.

In one of Gable's first big scenes with Crawford, he cavorts in the cruise ship pool while she is trying to swim and trying harder to ignore him. He wins her over with his playful manner. Two young boys appear in this scene, one of whom is Mickey Rooney. He recalled for the author[75]:

> We were splashing around in the cold water for a couple of days. Joan Crawford was very nice to us, but Clark Gable was like one of us kids. We did a scene where we are all throwing a ball around in the pool and having a lot of laughs. So we forgot how cold and uncomfortable it was.

Both Gable and Crawford are amusing and carefree in this scene, which is the portent to their breezy relationship that develops into romance.

The film drags, even within its rather brief 76-minute running time, and the development of the Mike-Diane friendship into romance is not terribly compelling. The stars bank on their natural charisma, and their presence overcomes what is essentially a weak story. *Possessed* had been filmed as a silent in 1921 with Elsie Ferguson and Conrad Nagel in the leads; the update didn't offer enough of a story or enough good dialogue to sustain it as well as Gable and Crawford's other movies together. It was especially a letdown after Gable hit bullseyes with *It Happened One Night*, *Men in White*, and *Manhattan Melodrama*. Empty scenes like Mike and Diana running after a baby horse who has galloped off Mike's ranch, eventually stumbling into the weeds and kissing, seem more perfunctory than emotionally gripping.

Gable and Crawford's cruise ship scenes are perhaps the most fun. But their chemistry is the only thing that makes them interesting, and everything that comes later is trite and predictable. This sort of story has been done so many times before and since. Gable really has nothing to do here except react to Crawford.

Crawford was having a difficult time in her personal life while filming this movie. Her marriage to Franchot Tone was shaky, mostly due to his insistence that she leave movies and concentrate on the legitimate theater. In a Louella Parsons column promoting the production of this film, the columnist writes: "Miss Crawford is going 'arty' these days with her little theater movements and other Franchot Tone ideas."[76] Another situation arose when Joan's estranged father visited the set. It was the first time she ever saw him. And the last. According to Margarita Landazuri at the Turner Classic Movies website[77]:

> Her father, Thomas LeSeur, had abandoned his family before Joan was born, and she had never met him. After she became famous, he began writing to her, and they corresponded for several years. Finally, he came to Hollywood and they met on the set of *Chained*. The meeting was strained, and they never saw each other again.

Landazuri continued:

> *Chained* was the first of eight films Crawford would make with cinematographer George Folsey. Quite by accident, Folsey discovered a lighting scheme which dramatically emphasized her best features. As the crew prepared for a shipboard-in-the-moonlight scene, a single small spotlight shone down on Crawford from high above the stage. Folsey noticed how the soft light highlighted her eyes and cheekbones, and designed her key lighting around that. Crawford was thrilled with how she looked, and demanded the same kind of lighting for the rest of her career.

Gable and Crawford worked so well together, and understood their characters so thoroughly, they found themselves often straying from the script and improvising dialogue. Under most circumstances, this would not be allowed; it would even be considered a disruption. But director Brown saw that it flowed more naturally and effectively so he left it in.

Otto Kruger specialized in the urbane type of role he played in *Possessed*, and comes off effectively. He is called upon to exhibit the sort of character that remains appealing despite his actions. His pleasant demeanor makes it work. The scene where Mike confronts Field and he responds by welcoming him and setting a place at the dinner table, is effective. Kruger's role is an interesting counterpart to Gable's more dazzling character, and Crawford has the ability to play off of either, with consistent aplomb. Stuart Erwin, providing much-needed moments of humor, stands out as well.

Despite some positive elements, *Chained* isn't a good movie for Gable or for Crawford. The October 1934 issue of *Movie Classic* stated[78]:

> *Chained* is a better picture than it deserves to be, considering its well-worn and hokumish theme. There is no villain so the hero pursues her. What should she do? That's what the scenarists wondered. Their solution to the predicament looks decidedly makeshift, solves nothing, proves nothing. If it weren't for the acting, and the settings, it would be time wasted.

Other reviewers were no more impressed, essentially dismissing the film as "ho-hum" despite the stars' appeal.

The critical reaction didn't hurt the box office. *Chained* was a big hit, and most moviegoers were happy and satisfied. Exhibitors reported in *Motion Picture Herald*:

> "These two make a wonderful pair of lovers. The picture went over fine."
> "By far the best that this team has ever made. Patrons surely praised this one."
> "Did the best business of the week in a steady downpour of rain both days of its run."

The film more than tripled its production costs, and certainly pleased the studio.

Next on the assembly line, Metro's *Forsaking All Others* was originally intended for Loretta Young, George Brent and Joel McCrea. But the company wanted to further capitalize on the Gable-Crawford combo, so the film was recast.

Forsaking All Others

Directed by W.S. Van Dyke
Screenplay: Joseph L. Mankiewicz
Based on the play by Frank Morgan Cavett, Edward Barry Roberts
Produced by Bernard H. Hyman
Cinematographers: George Folsey, Gregg Toland
Editor: Tom Held
Cast: Clark Gable, Joan Crawford, Robert Montgomery, Charles Butterworth, Billie Burke, Frances Drake, Rosalind Russell, Jan Duggan, Eily Malyon, Greta Meyer, Tom Ricketts, Arthur Treacher, Sidney Bracey, Harold Huber, Pat Flaherty, Jay Eaton, Clarence Wilson, Ernie Alexander, Eddie Phillips, Louise Henry, Kane Richmond, Perry Ivins. The following actors appeared in the film, but their scenes were deleted: Ted Healy, Edward Brophy, Lillian Harmer, Hooper Atchley, Forrester Harvey.
Released December 23, 1934
MGM
83 minutes

Gable and Crawford next co-starred in an upbeat romantic comedy. He turned in a winning performance in this breezy item, but it did little for his career, other than placing him in yet another hit. It ended up being the most profitable Joan Crawford movie to date.

Forsaking All Others had been a play featuring Tallulah Bankhead, Ilka Chase, Barbara O'Neil, Cora Witherspoon, Fred Keating, Anderson Lawler, Harlan Briggs and George Lessey. It opened in New York on March 1, 1933, and ran 110 performances. When MGM bought the movie rights, they planned to cast Claudette Colbert in the female lead. A syndicated article stated[79]:

> The screen star who can chalk up the greatest advance from both a popular and a financial standpoint is Claudette Colbert. A year ago she was discouraged and unwilling to continue unless she had better stories. Then came *Torch Singer* and *It Happened One Night*. The latter picture put her in the money class. Now Metro-Goldwyn-Mayer is trying to borrow her for *Forsaking All Others* (Tallulah Bankhead's stage play) and another producer is also angling to get her.

However, only a month later, newspapers were announcing that MGM had signed Loretta Young for the role[80]: "[Young] will be the leading light in *Forsaking All Others*…. Frank Davis, who started in his film life as a cutter and who has been gradually promoted, will co-direct with Irving Rapper and stage director Joseph Mankiewicz."

Shortly after this announcement, Young underwent surgery and her illness was holding up production. It was then that Crawford was given the role, and the leading cast was rounded out with Gable and Robert Montgomery.

Forsaking All Others was hailed by MGM as their first all-star production since *Dinner at Eight* (1933), which had featured Marie Dressler, Jean Harlow, Lionel Barrymore and Wallace Beery. This film not only had the three leads, but a supporting cast that included comedians Charles Butterworth and Ted Healy, as well as newcomers Frances Drake and Rosalind Russell, plus reliable character actors Ed Brophy, Billie Burke and Arthur Treacher. Unfortunately, neither Healy nor Brophy made it into the final edit.

Jeff (Gable), Mary (Crawford) and Dill (Montgomery) have been friends since childhood. Jeff always loved Mary and plans to propose upon returning from Spain, but discovers she is about to marry Dill. He keeps his feelings to himself and agrees to be best man. Dill jilts Mary and runs off to marry Connie (Drake), an old girlfriend. Mary is furious but can't shake her underlying love for Dill. The unfaithful Dill continues to connect with Mary. Distraught Jeff plans to return to Spain. When Mary learns of Jeff's feelings, she changes her mind about everything and finally realizes what should have been obvious all along.

Gable plays a glorified supporting role here, which is a bit curious in that he was now a bigger star than Montgomery, who essentially has the lead. But Gable also plays the more appealing, genuine character, which is some consolation. Crawford is at her most attractive and appealing.

Forsaking All Others (1934)

Robert Montgomery, Joan Crawford and Gable make a comical love triangle in *Forsaking All Others* (1934).

Even though the beginning of this film seems to set up a trio dynamic, it feels like Gable has significantly less screen time than Crawford and Montgomery. Gable really sells his feelings for Crawford's character, but her realization that she actually loves him in the end is almost too sudden.

The film's rhythm is consistently quick, exploding immediately with an opening scene showing Mary getting a massage and a facial before the wedding. Dill bursts in and is angrily removed by Mary's aunt Paula (Billie Burke). This noisy raucousness cuts to Jeff calling to announce that he has returned from a long stint in Spain. Gable exhibits his usual charisma at top volume in a beautifully done tracking shot as Jeff and buddy Shep walk to a cab. Jeff maintains an enthusiastic conversation with Shep, announcing that he is headed to propose to Mary, all the while buying items in bulk from street vendors (flowers, balloons, bags of peanuts) and dropping them into Shep's arms. It is expertly performed and beautifully shot in one long take.

Acting-wise, Gable's at his best: When he finally sees Mary, he exhibits the same level of charisma, but allows his face to subtly darken as he is told that she and Dill are about to marry. Jeff is hurt but wants to hide it from Mary. Gable displays the character's disappointment subtly enough to convey it to the audience, but without his character revealing it to Mary. It's only seconds long, but reveals just how brilliant a screen actor Gable had become. When he has to go to a more serious level upon delivering the news to Mary that Dill has jilted her, the rhythm of the film stops long enough to convey the impact of the situation. Within the first 20 minutes, *Forsaking All Others* introduces itself as a comedy, but is able to convey its serious moments without seeming uneven.

A transitional scene where Jeff, Mary, Aunt Paula and Shep all get away to a cabin in the woods is a further delight, and continues to maintain the film's pace. Charles Butterworth, a droll comedian who fits in well here, is very much a part of the film's humor. Upon his arrival, Shep asks, "What is that smell? Fresh air?" Jeff explains the virtues of "early to bed, early to rise" and Shep responds, "Have you ever seen a milkman?"

The scene where Jeff and Mary attend a party given by Dill and Connie isn't as amusing in its awkwardness as the other scenes. It does present a conflict between Dill and Connie that causes him to realize he should never have jilted Mary: He says, "Mary, I did something so horrible to you, that it doesn't even seem real. I'm not going to say I'm sorry because that's such a weak word. But you don't know how miserable it's made me." He proclaims his love for her, she denies she still loves him, he insists she must, and embraces her. Connie walks in on them. Jeff jumps in, stating that he can explain. He, Dill and Mary then jump into the sort of routine that only very old friends could possibly improvise:

> JEFF: You know, I started life in the service of Mary's grandfather, one Colonel Lionel Q. Clay, of the Confederate army.
> DILL: Union army.
> JEFF: Confederate.
> DILL: Union army.
> JEFF: Confederate.
> DILL: I beg your pardon, Union army.
> JEFF: I was, at that time, a slave and very anxious for the South to win, so I could collect my back pay. I'm still trying to collect.
> MARY: How dare you say that! We once paid you a dollar eighty on account.

Connie is unimpressed with the attempt at a dodge, and not the least bit amused. But this leads to the point that Dill and Mary still love each other. Jeff realizes it and continues to hide his feelings for Mary.

Gable's best moments are when he is being amusing, saying absurd things like, "We're going to Coney Island to throw baseballs at cops. Wanna come with?" But he is also very effective at balancing his comic moments with the more serious, dramatic ones. When Mary goes back to Dill, and Jeff scolds her, he is told that it doesn't really involve him. He responds, "If I walk by and see a man beating a dog I'll stop it every time."

Montgomery comes off well as a man who is handsome and appealing, but whose actions are pretty despicable. As with most films from this period, it all ends well, but Mary's attraction to a man we know she cannot trust, makes the viewer more sympathetic to Gable's character. But it was still not a big enough role for a star of his stature.

Columnist Louella Parsons noticed that Gable, while perhaps the movie's most appealing character, was still in a supporting role[81]:

> I don't know why MGM put Clark Gable into this picture. He gives, it's true, a beautiful performance, and the picture is entertaining; but the part is hardly big enough for Clark, who today is at the very top. He's the best friend of Joan, and after much watchful waiting he finally succeeds in winning her away from Bob—I mean after she has forgotten Bob's desertion and he has divorced the vamp who carried him away. Frances Drake, as that siren, reveals unexpected ability. She is a worthy screen companion for those three accomplished players, Joan, Bob and Clark. In fact, in several instances she is a bold scene stealer. Billie Burke, as the fluttery mother of Joan, again looks absurdly young, and, as usual, is splendid in her light comedy moments. As for Charles Butterworth, as Gable's close friend—well, he is himself.... [Director Van Dyke] manages to get in all the little touches that mean so much to a picture of this kind.... [W]hile it's not a great picture, it's the kind that is entertaining and amusing enough to offset its shortcomings.

Forsaking All Others was a significant production for Crawford: It not only generated the strongest box office of all her films thus far, but it was her first collaboration with screenwriter Joseph L. Mankiewicz, with whom she would connect strongly, as he understood her approach and her appeal. It also highlighted some of her comedic talents more effectively than her previous films. Crawford got a byline for a syndicated article discussing her experience while making the movie[82]:

> My director is W.S. Van Dyke. How tall and strong he looks as he walks, or rather swings, along. The most athletic figure on the lot, and the most versatile director, imagine doing both *Eskimo* and *The Thin Man*! Strange about Van Dyke, the exterior of a cowpuncher with the sensitivity of a violinist. If you look closely you'll see he has the long fingers of a musician. Met his mother on the set the other day, a charming woman, she looks like Mrs. Franklin D. Roosevelt. It's a pleasure having Van Dyke for a director. He races with exhaustion and always wins. If *Forsaking All Others* is as good as it was fun to make, we'll all be happy, There goes Clark Gable tearing by in his classy roadster. There would be a fishing pole hanging on the side. This is our sixth picture together. Clark hasn't changed a whit. As kind and considerate as the first day we met. Only more fun, now that he's lost his shyness. He's that rare combination, a good actor and a good fellow, and my friend. Back on the set. Billie Burke, sitting smiling at Charlie Butterworth's anecdotes. Two good people, two of the best. Took me days to control bursts of laughter in the middle of scenes with Charlie. Such droll, excruciating humor. With hardly a change of expression, maybe just an awkward gesture, he sends you into stitches.

Another reaction to filming came from columnist Sidney Skolsky, who visited the set[83]:

> Clark Gable, Joan Crawford, Charles Butterworth and Billie Burke are gathered about a bridge table in a mountain cabin eating mulligan.... Director W.S. Van Dyke sits in his chair,

which is so close to the bridge table it is almost in the picture. Speaking quietly, but with force, Director Van Dyke tells Gable, Crawford, Butterworth and Burke every piece of business they are to do at that table. The scene is completely his and they play it for him. At the same time that he is issuing orders to his players he is also directing the cameraman how he wants the camera to move so this scene will lap right into the next one. Later, while waiting for a set-up, Clark Gable calls over the script girl and reads his lines to her. She is doing what plenty of girls would like to do: play a scene with Clark Gable.

News stories indicated that Gable bought the first topcoat of his career for this movie, stating that he planned to give it away as soon as production ended. Another told about his going on a hunting trip to Wyoming during a break in filming. These little publicity tidbits attracted movie fans, making them feel connected to the production.

Forsaking All Others was another big hit for MGM, taking in around five times its production costs and making a very substantial profit for the studio. Exhibitors reported very happy patrons; one stated in *Motion Picture Herald*[84]:

Swell entertainment if your patrons enjoy the light breezy comedy of picture. The cast is perfect in this and they romp through the whole thing as though they were having the time of their lives. A wow of a picture.

The studio felt that since comedies like this and *It Happened One Night* were such big successes for Gable, it stood to reason that they should cast him in another comedy. Depression-era America was also responding better to comedy, desiring something light and entertaining to take their minds off of their economic situation. Movies were inexpensive entertainment and even those with a low income could enjoy this escapist activity.

After Office Hours

Directed by Robert Z. Leonard
Screenplay: Herman J. Mankiewicz
Story: Laurence Stallings and Dale Van Every
Produced by Bernard H. Hyman, Robert Z. Leonard
Cinematographer: Charles Rosher
Editor: Tom Held
Cast: Clark Gable, Constance Bennett, Stuart Erwin, Billie Burke, Harvey Stephens, Katherine Alexander, Hale Hamilton, Henry Travers, Henry Armetta, Charles Richman, Herbert Bunston, Margaret Dumont, William Demarest, Sayre Dearing, Bud Jamison, Wilbur Mack, Bess Flowers, James Ellison, Pat Flaherty, James Ellison, Tom Dugan, Rita LaRoy, Olaf Hytten, George Guhl, Dale Van Sickel, Alexander Pollard, Tom Mahoney, Mary MacLaren, Monte Vandergrift, David Thursby, Pat O'Malley
Released February 22, 1935
MGM
72 minutes

One of the more inconsequential films of Gable's career, *After Office Hours* has almost nothing to offer. Some films just lie there. They may have the great potential of a good screenwriter, a strong cast and a top director. They may be of a certain genre or subgenre and come from an era where the style and methods are not only attractive, but also effectively lasting. But they don't add up to anything more than a few dollops of casual entertainment, at best.

After Office Hours has none of the interesting backstory or cinematic significance of other Gable films from that time. Even when taken on its own terms as entertainment, and accepting its energy and the appeal of the performances, *After Office Hours* really doesn't amount to much.

Gable is well-cast as fast-talking newspaper editor Jim Branch, who runs sordid gossipy stories if they'll attract readers. In his opening scene, he states, "A newspaper should print any news that can be found, stolen or bought to print!" This cynical approach is often featured in journalism films of the 1930s (most effectively in the 1931 Warner Brothers drama *Five Star Final*), mostly because of the many tabloids available at the time.

Branch falls for wealthy Sharon Norwood (Constance Bennett), who writes music reviews for the paper. Her employment is a hobby, as she doesn't need the money. She is snobby and detached, and when Gable fires her as excess baggage, she responds as if entitled, and above the decision of the commoner who is still her superior.

Branch develops an interest in Sharon because he wants to write an exposé on a millionaire with whom she is acquainted. When a married woman with whom the millionaire is connected turns up dead, Sharon and Branch team to solve the mystery. The evidence points to the woman's alcoholic husband, but it isn't conclusive so the two of them, arguing over who is the more likely suspect, explore it further. Because MGM was noted as the studio who gave the world the Thin Man movie series (the first of which had been released the previous year and was still circulating in second run theaters), the comparisons are natural. *After Office Hours* isn't nearly as good.

The romantic connection between Branch and Sharon is probably in an attempt to replicate the *It Happened One Night* dynamic. While in the Capra film there is solid development between Gable and Claudette Colbert, in *After Office Hours* he is proposing only a few scenes after he angrily fires her (which occurs in the same scene as when he first meets her). It is worth noting that Bennett was among the actresses who turned down the female lead in *It Happened One Night* before it went to Colbert.

After Office Hours features some amusing moments. Stuart Erwin is a photographer on the paper who sneaks into the crime scene pretending to be the coroner's assistant. William Demarest is typically great as a fast-talking detective. At one point when the maid explains that the husband slapped the murder victim, the detective asks "How hard?" and the maid slaps him. Billie Burke, as Sharon's mother, is delightfully fluttery. Seeing veterans like Henry Armetta, Margaret Dumont, Bess Flowers

Constance Bennett and Gable in *After Office Hours* (1935), one of his less interesting '30s movies.

and Bud Jamison pop up, even if only briefly, raises the movie's entertainment value to some extent.

After Office Hours maintains its comic energy throughout, and the Herman Mankiewicz screenplay is occasionally crisp and witty. Mankiewicz is today known for penning the Orson Welles masterpiece *Citizen Kane*, but at this time he was writing amusing plays and screenplays, including *Dinner at Eight*, and doing quite well at it.

The film's director Robert Z. Leonard, a veteran from the silent days, had directed Gable in *Dancing Lady* and would later helm the Oscar winner *The Great Ziegfeld*. There doesn't appear to be much that he can do with this film, other than allow the narrative to play.

Despite all the positive elements, *After Office Hours* is really quite uninvolving. Perhaps its chief interest is in the fact that it fails at what it attempts. It is an example of top people trying to make a good movie, but not succeeding.

One of its biggest problems is that the connection between Gable and Bennett doesn't have quite the magic as his pairings with Colbert, Joan Crawford, Jean

Harlow or Myrna Loy. In fact, Gable's scenes with Stu Erwin are more amusing and appealing than those he shares with Bennett. The scene in which they investigate the murder scene is quite amusing, Erwin telling Gable, "You have the mind of Einstein. *Mike* Einstein, who runs the lunchroom down on Beesy Street."

The tone of the movie also feels off at times. It is primarily a comedy, but the characters seem a bit too gleeful to hear about the murder of someone they knew. You can also definitely tell that the Production Code was in full force at the time of this film. The ending shows Gable and Bennett in bed together and Bennett's mother shocked, but the statement that they were married the night before makes it okay.

Reportedly, Constance Bennett treated Gable condescendingly on his early film *The Easiest Way* where she was a lead, and he was a supporting player. Now that he was an established star, Bennett was flirtatious on the *After Office Hours* set and he rebuffed her. They never worked together again.

All of these shortcomings did not hurt its box office when it was released. *After Office Hours* effectively represented its era's entertainment at the time it came out—its box office nearly quadrupled its production costs, and it was a big hit to open the year 1935 for Gable. He made some of his best movies that year.

After Office Hours should come off as a typical fast-talking romantic comedy of the 1930s that boasts a great cast and a strong writer. But the final result in the realm of the Clark Gable filmography is that it is a very basic, only mildly amusing movie that pales in comparison to even something like *Forsaking All Others* let alone a triumph at the level of *It Happened One Night*.

China Seas

Director: Tay Garnett
Screenplay: Jules Furthman, James Kevin McGuinness
Based on the novel by Crosbie Garstin
Producer: Irving Thalberg
Cinematographer: Ray June
Editor: William LeVanway
Cast: Clark Gable, Jean Harlow, Wallace Beery, Lewis Stone, Rosalind Russell, Dudley Digges, C. Aubrey Smith, Robert Benchley, William Henry, Lilian Bond, Edward Brophy, Soo Yong, Akim Tamiroff, Malcolm McGregor, Hattie McDaniel, Emily Fitzroy, Daisy Belmore, Pat Flaherty, Willie Fung, Forrester Harvey, Charles Irwin, John Ince, Bobby Watson, Chester Gan, Tom Buggins, Sherry Hall, Eddie Lee, Richard Loo, Carol Ann Beery, Donald Meek, Sam Harris, Harry Bradley
Released August 9, 1935
MGM
87 minutes

A good adventure drama, *China Seas* was filmed after Gable went over to 20th Century and starred in *Call of the Wild*, but that film was held back by the studio, and released on the day that this movie premiered. So Gable had two popular adventure dramas playing the major theaters at the same time.

The pre-production of *China Seas* was fraught with complications. The film rights to the novel were purchased by Irving Thalberg for MGM in 1931. The author, Crosbie Garstin, had died a few months earlier, and the rights were secured from his widow. The original story dealt with a romance between a Chinese girl and a ship's captain, with a subplot involving pirates in violent conflict.

The project was shelved until late 1932 when Myrna Loy and Gable were considered for the leads, and Tod Browning was set to direct. Loy had already played Asian characters before, most significantly opposite Boris Karloff in *The Mask of Fu Manchu* (1932); MGM went so far as to release promotional stories that claimed the name Loy was of Asian origin. (Loy's real last name was Williams. The actress changed it to Loy when she signed a contract with Warner Brothers in 1925.)

While plans were being made to film *China Seas*, the script endured many rewrites by several writers. While it was being revised, Gable got busy with other projects and was replaced by John Gilbert as the leading man, while Browning was replaced by Richard Boleslavsky as director. Thalberg eventually lost interest, as the project was causing too many distractions and challenges, so in 1933 he decided to drop his plans to produce it. When he decided to revive the project, he hiring Jules Fuhrman to rewrite the screenplay. Furhman revamped the original story and created the character of China Doll, which went to Jean Harlow. Wallace Beery was hired to play Jamesy McArdle. It was then that Tay Garnett signed to direct. Garnett recalled for John Gallagher in a 1977 interview[85]:

There never was an actor who was more of a director's actor than Clark Gable. He was a director's dream. You told Clark and that was what he did and he did it well most of the time. Harlow was not the natural actor that Gable was nor had she had his training, but she was trying. She was a worker. She came in prepared, she knew her dialogue, and she would say, "Look, you know, this is a tough scene, this is an emotional scene, and I'm not much of an actress so try and be patient with me." But it was easy to be patient with her because you knew that every time she was coming to bat, she was giving everything she had. Now sometimes she gave you too much, more than you could use, or more than she could handle. But in any case she was easy to direct because she would listen to you and try and do exactly what you asked her to do. Wallace Beery was a difficult man. He was a bully. He felt his position as a star very heavily on his shoulders, and he never read a line of dialogue in his life the way it was written. He *always* rewrote it but one didn't mind that too much because the way he rewrote it, it fit Wallace Beery and the character he was playing perhaps better than the written word would have done. So all in all he was not too difficult once it had been established who was the boss. One had to establish that early because he had shoved several of the younger and less experienced directors around pretty badly at MGM before I got him on *China Seas*. I had a very frank understanding with him before we started the picture that if there was to be any doubt as to who was the boss on the picture, he'd better read his contract again and it would tell him that the director was to tell him what to do. Now, my contract said I was that director and I was to tell him what to do and how to do it. After that first

Gable, Jean Harlow and Wallace Beery, the stars of *China Seas* **(1935).**

understanding, he tried a couple of times to push me around as he had the younger guys, and failing that, he stopped trying and we got along very well.

Gable clashed with the director by insisting on doing his own stunts. But because he was now an Oscar winner and top box office attraction, MGM let Gable do as he wished.

Gable plays Alan Gaskell, the captain of a steamer sailing from Hong Kong. A tough, no-nonsense sort, he is fully in charge of his crew. Gaskell also takes charge upon discovering pirates trying to sneak aboard his ship by disguising themselves as women. Next he finds that ex-girlfriends Dolly Portland (Harlow) and Sybil Barclay (Rosalind Russell) are also aboard. Sybil plans to marry Gaskell once they dock in Singapore; Dolly tries to win him back.

While this is the set-up for Gable's character, much of the plot revolves around passenger James McArdle (Wallace Beery), who has joined the pirates planning to steal a gold shipment aboard the ship. James is also interested in Dolly. She finds a torn bank note that connects McArdle to the pirates, but he keeps her from telling Gaskell. When a typhoon strikes, the ship is boarded by McArdle's pirates. They go to retrieve the gold, and find the boxes' contents have been replaced by sand. They torture Gaskell, but he's too tough and won't reveal where the gold has been hidden.

The pirates eventually leave the ship, but a wounded officer sacrifices himself by falling among them with explosives, killing them all and sinking their ship. A defeated McArdle commits suicide. The ship docks in Singapore, and Gaskell realizes his love is for Dolly.

A few ideas were added to the final treatment. This included Lewis Stone as the officer who sacrifices himself to destroy the pirates, and popular humorist Robert Benchley as a drunken passenger who lightens the dark story with bright comedy relief. Benchley's inclusion is sometimes distracting but serves its purpose. Stone's performance is significant as being a separate arc. He plays a veteran shipman who can no longer handle tasks, so he is disciplined. He heroically saves the day by sacrificing himself to destroy the pirates in one of the film's most effective scenes. The injured man painfully drags himself to his destination, carrying a box of bombs. Because it was established early in the film that he is cynically considered a has-been and a coward, his bravery is emotionally stirring.

The torture scene is especially brutal and unsettling, with the pirates capturing the captain and putting his foot in a Malay boot which slowly crushes his bones. Gaskell struggles through the intense pain with a toughness that Gable is exceptional at conveying. Meanwhile, McArdle feigns concern in brilliant Wallace Beery manner by stating, "I hate to see you suffer like this."

In a male-dominated movie, Harlow turns in one of her best performances. The important link between Beery's character and Gable's, she exhibits toughness, humor and a sense of pathos, while the conflict with Russell's character bolsters the narrative. Despite playing rivals, Jean and Rosalind became good friends and Russell remembered Harlow fondly in her autobiography *Life Is a Banquet*. She did not, however, recall *China Seas* with any real affection: "It was ludicrous. There would be Jean, all alabaster skin and cleft chin, savory as a ripe peach, and I'd be saying disdainfully … 'How can you spend time with her? She's rather vulgar, isn't she?'"[86]

Producer Thalberg wanted to create another movie like *Red Dust*, but his intrusions on the set were a problem for director Garnett. Thalberg offered ideas to the actors, who were confused as to whose direction they should follow. Garnett eventually confronted the producer and asserted his authority. Both were pleased with the final product.

The similarities to *Red Dust* are obvious, but this movie is much heavier on action than romance. Gable handles both very well, exhibiting the macho persona that he was becoming known for.

The trades offered positive reviews overall. *Variety* was suitably impressed[87]:

This is a story of love—sordid and otherwise—of piracy and violence and heroism on a passenger boat run from Shanghai to Singapore…. Clark Gable is a valiant sea captain, Wallace Beery a villainous pirate boss, and Jean Harlow a blond trollop who motivates the romance and most of the action. All do their jobs expertly. The pirate raid and its unsuccessful termination (for the pirates) is full of shooting, suspense and action. Add a running atmosphere of suspense through the picture, and there's plenty of excitement.

Moviegoers agreed. *China Seas'* box office receipts almost doubled its formidable budget.

Harlow became sick after being drenched with water in several scenes, getting an acute ear infection that resulted in pain and a fever. Still, the dedicated actress completed the scenes, so as not to cause a production delay. Gable contracted the flu during filming, telling syndicated journalist Florence Fisher Parry for her "On with the Show" column: "I felt rotten all through *China Seas* and yet it didn't seem to matter much. We had a good time making it anyway. It got to be a joke when we'd meet in the morning on the set and all begin comparing notes on our new symptoms of the day." Harlow was pleased to once again be working with her friend Gable, telling Parry:

> It's funny about Clark Gable. Here I am playing with him in a picture, I'm supposed to be his sweetheart, we're wild about each other. I'm supposed to be completely nuts about him. Well, I go to the rushes and the minute I get in that little projection room and being able to watch Clark, I become a regular movie fan. I get thrilled just the same as any girl might at a movie he is in. I even forget that I am in the scene.

There was a lot of studio publicity claiming that Harlow and Gable got along with Wallace Beery, even claiming that Gable called him Teacher and Jean addressed him as Grandpop. In fact, Beery continued to be difficult, even with his four-year-old daughter Carol Ann on the set essaying a small role. MGM publicity claimed that Beery wanted her to become an actress. She appeared in one other movie, her father's 1944 MGM feature *Rationing*.

China Seas' publicists had a lot of interesting promotion and marketing ideas. The May company offered prizes to the best essay entitled "Why I Want to Visit the Romantic China Seas." And the showing of *China Seas* at the Wisconsin Theater in Milwaukee resulted in 30 days' worth of 24-sheet boards, a serialized version of the story in a local newspaper, trailers, a teaser ad, daily announcements over WTMJ radio, even posters of Wallace Beery and his daughter placed in the Children's Department of Boston Store and Gimbels.

Call of the Wild

Director: William Wellman
Producer: Darryl F. Zanuck
Screenplay: Gene Fowler, Leonard Praskins
Based on the novel by Jack London
Cinematographer: Charles Rosher
Editor: Hanson T. Fritch
Cast: Clark Gable, Loretta Young, Jack Oakie, Reginald Owen, Frank Conroy, Katherine DeMille, Sidney Toler, James Burke, Charles Stevens, Lalo Encinas, Thomas E. Jackson, Russ Powell, Herman Bing, George MacQuarrie, Marie Wells, Arthur Housman,

Harry Woods, Sid Grauman, Philip G. Sleeman, Samuel T. Godfrey, William R. Arnold, Perry Ivins, Walter McGrail, Wong Chung, Loo Loy, LeRoy Mason, Frank Moran, Wade Boteler, Arthur Aylesworth, John Ince, Hank Bell, Jesse DeVorska, Joan Woodbury, Frank Campeau, Pat Flaherty, Syd Saylor, Larry McGrath, Jack Stoney, Leon Beaumont, Tyler Brooke, Gay Seabrook, Celia Marcel, Carol Mercer, Harriet King, Kay Johnson, Gladys Johnson, Kay Deslys, Pearl Varvelle, Helen Chadwick, Mary MacLaren, Frank Mills, Bud Osborne, Jack Grey, Loretta Rush, Ted Lorch, Edwin Argus, Hazel Mills, Kay Howard, Harvey Parry, Duke Green
Released August 14, 1935
20th Century Pictures
80 minutes

Twentieth Century Pictures picked the right time to make a movie version of Jack London's 1903 story *The Call of the Wild*. London's daughter Joan had been appearing at literature clubs throughout the California area, discussing her father's enduring books. Joan told of how her father knew the worst of poverty as he went through many jobs with little or no success. He joined the gold rush, found no gold, but decided to write about the experience.

Darryl Zanuck at Twentieth Century Pictures secured the *Call of the Wild* movie rights in July 1934 and announced plans to star Fredric March. The studio had already borrowed Gable from MGM, but it was to star opposite Constance Bennett in the film *It Had to Happen*. When that project was cancelled, it was decided to put Gable in *The Call of the Wild* and March in *Les Miserables*. Columnist Louella Parsons believed this worked out well for both actors[88]:

> Clark Gable will be moving to Twentieth Century on a loan, of course, from MGM. He plays the lead in Jack London's *Call of the Wild* on account of Fredric March cannot possibly be in two pictures at once. Darryl Zanuck was particularly eager to get going with *Les Miserables* when Freddie returned from the South Seas. They talked over the situation with the result Gable was borrowed for *Call of the Wild* and March was kept in the Victor Hugo classic. Seems to me the decision is a wise one. The London role is more to the Gable type and no one could be a better Jean Valjean than Freddie who can out–Barrymore Barrymore when it comes to these unusual characterizations. Both productions are scheduled for December production.

Subsequent newspaper accounts claimed that Wallace Beery would be co-starring with Gable. The first leading lady announced was Claudette Colbert, then Madeleine Carroll. Edward Arnold was to be cast as the villain. William Wellman was slated to direct.

Wellman began scouting locations for filming, and first settled on Plumas County in Colorado, but this was later changed to Washington state. Only a few days were spent shooting at the studio; the remainder of the footage was filmed in snowy Washington. While the film was being shot at the studio, Joan London was invited to watch from the sidelines.

The story is set in 1900 Skagway where Jack Thornton (Gable) has struck it rich

Jack Oakie, Gable and Buck the Dog in Jack London's *Call of the Wild* (1935).

mining for gold, and plans to go home. After gambling away a large sum, Jack runs into an old friend, Shorty (Jack Oakie), who just got out of jail for reading others' mail. Shorty reveals to Jack that he read a letter that contained the map to a gold mine. The prospector died before staking a claim, so he sent the map to his son John Blake. Planning to find the mine based on Shorty's memory of the map, Jack and Shorty buy a team of dogs and other equipment to get through the snowy Yukon. While purchasing dogs, they see a haughty Englishman named Smith (Reginald Owen) who is interested in purchasing a vicious St. Bernard. When the large dog attacks Smith, he plans to shoot it, but Jack stops him and purchases the dog himself as part of his team, naming it Buck.

En route to the mine, Jack and Shorty find a woman alone, about to be attacked by wolves. They rescue her and discover it is John Blake's wife Claire (Loretta Young). She tells them John went to look for food two days ago. The men presume he has died, but Claire refuses to leave the spot and insists on waiting for them. Jack picks her up and carries her to their sled and ties her in, to save her life, but she is very angry. Eventually she settles down, realizes the men have saved her, and appreciates what they've done. She agrees to help them find the gold, as she knows which portions of Shorty's memory of the map are inaccurate.

The trio stops in Dawson and run into Smith again. Buck spots him and attacks him in a saloon. Smith announces he will give Jack $1000 for the dog. Jack refuses when Smith admits he plans to kill the animal. Jack later makes a flippant remark that his dog could pull 1000 pounds, and Smith bets Jack the $1000 that the dog can't do it. If Jack loses the bet, he must give up the dog for Smith to destroy. The dog does it, and the money Jack wins finances the rest of the trip to the mine. When they reach their destination, the mine is all that had been described, so Shorty goes to town to stake the claim.

John Blake is found, barely alive, and brought to a nearby town. He connects with Smith, who uses his knowledge to find the gold. Blake doesn't trust the Englishmen and his two henchmen, and his fears are borne out when they reach the destination and Blake is attacked and left for dead. Smith finds Jack and Claire in the cabin and, at gunpoint, takes their gold, kills their means of transportation and escapes in their boat. The boat hits a violent current and capsizes, killing Smith and his henchmen.

Buck the dog discovers John Blake and Jack carries him into the cabin. Claire reacts to seeing her husband who was believed dead. Jack and Claire had started to fall in love, but now that her husband turns out to be alive, she goes with him. Jack is left alone, until Shorty returns, having filed their claim, and he brings a heavyset Native American woman with him as "their new cook," indicating, "I won her in a crap game!"

The Call of the Wild showed Gable to his best advantage; the way audiences wanted to see him: ruggedly attractive, able to handle himself in any situations. Loretta Young is soft and doe-eyed, but determined to keep up with the men and not be any kind of hindrance to them. Jack Oakie is typically amusing and appealing. Reginald Owen is magnificently creepy as the evil Smith, who is so effete he brings along a collapse-able bathtub on the quest and has his two goons bathe him.

The connection between Jack and Buck the dog is a more central part of London's original story, but here is best represented by the scene in which the dog pulls the 1000 pounds of equipment. Wellman shoots it in a tracking shot from Jack's perspective, cutting back to a close shot of Gable cheering the dog on. The negative space on either side is filled with onlookers cheering; this sound, along with Gable, fills the soundtrack. It is very exciting and emotionally stirring, one of the best scenes in the film.

The St. Bernard playing Buck was really named King, and was making his first movie. He was owned and trained by Carl Spitz, who was always on the set, out of camera range, when one of his dogs was in a scene. He gave the dogs their instructions and cues. Spitz received $450 a week for his services. In the scene where Buck pulls the freight, Spitz was one of the extras, shouting at the dog to run faster, and then to roll over. Spitz shouted his instructions in German, which was the language the dog best understood. This scene was shot at the RKO Ranch in California, on a set built for *The Silver Horde* (1930).

Gable held up production for a couple weeks while doing retakes on his previous film, *After Office Hours*. There was a blizzard with temperatures at 14 degrees below zero. The newspapers reported[89]:

Call of the Wild (1935)

Hollywood's snow-seeking film colony, here to film *The Call of the Wild*, was getting what it wanted today in large quantities as fast-falling snow split the company in three sections and held them snowbound. Director William Wellman was reported at Mount Baker lodge; equipment aboard trucks was stalled by the storm in the small mountain community of Shuksan; Clark Gable and Jack Oakie waited developments at Bellingham while Loretta Young, Reginald Owen, Lalo Encinas and Charles Stevens were forced by the storm to halt at Glacier.

Gable contracted laryngitis, and William Wellman became ill. Loretta Young recalled for John Gallagher[90]:

The Call of the Wild was really a tough location…. We were up at the top of a mountain and they had about 60 men in the cast and crew. It was ten degrees below zero. We were in the summer cottages freezing to death because the main hotel burned down the year before. We were there for nine weeks and all I did was crab. I never heard Clark Gable open his mouth. He was very easy to work with, a marvelous disposition. I don't know anybody who worked with Gable, whether it was man, woman or child, who wasn't crazy about him.

Jack Oakie recalled in the book *Jack Oakie's Double Takes*[91]:

It took longer than scheduled to make *Call of the Wild*; not only were we continually fighting the unusual weather conditions, but we also lost time over what I called "the snowshoe rabbit escapade." Wellman ordered about 50 snowshoe rabbits. He wanted them to run through the background of a scene. The rare, sensitive little animals, named snowshoes, were very hard to catch. It cost a fortune to send out a special crew to set nets for them. The men kept complaining that it was almost impossible to gather them, and that 50 was out of the question. Wellman finally agreed that the few they had collected would have to do for the scene. "Action!" Bill called. "Let 'em go!" The rabbits were let loose. The dogs, with their mouths wired to protect the rabbits, were sent to chase them, but the scared little things wouldn't move. "Scoot!" Wellman shouted, trying to get them to act for the cameras, but they wouldn't budge. The property men fired guns at them, but they wouldn't take Wellman's direction. They gave the little things some Spanish fly, but even that wouldn't rouse them. They just wouldn't run through the background of the scene. Wellman tried every trick he knew and finally gave up. "Those aren't snowshoe rabbits!" he screamed. "They're fireside rabbits!" The following day the crew went into town and rounded up all the stray cats they could find. They glued rabbit ears on the alley cats and when the dogs were let loose to chase them, they did just as Bill directed, they scooted!

This extended the production of the film, keeping Gable from beginning work on *China Seas* and forcing Cecil B. DeMille to shoot around Loretta Young on the Paramount movie *The Crusades*.

While scenes were being shot in Hollywood, columnists visited the set and reported the more interesting and amusing incidents to movie fans. According to columnist Sidney Skolsky[92]:

Director Bill Wellman is filming a big Alaskan saloon scene … and eager to help needy actors; he has an old trouper playing a bit. It means $15 for the day to this actor who doesn't work often because of his great love of whiskey. Now the actor is seated at a table with a bottle of whiskey in front of him. He sees his wife enter the saloon with a drunkard and he is to stand and shout: "You dirty drunkard, leave my wife alone." He stands to play his role but topples

Jack Oakie looks on as Gable comforts Loretta Young in *The Call of the Wild* (1935).

over. The actor playing the drunkard is sober but the prop whiskey is too genuine for the actor who is to denounce the drunkard. Another extra has to be given the part. This sequence is completed and Clark Gable enters the saloon, stands near the bar and rehearses his big speech which he delivers to the crowd. After several rehearsals, Director Wellman is ready to take the scene. Meanwhile, some official delegation, numbering about 75 people, have come on the set with a studio executive. They want to see a picture being made. The camera is turning. Clark Gable makes his entrance into the saloon. He starts to deliver his long speech. He notices the large audience of tourists. He continues, but becomes a little nervous. Gable comes to the line: "And you'll never see me again. You'll never hear from me again…." He hesitates and fumbles. "You'll never hear from me again," he repeats, and then adds, "because I can't remember the damn words."

Call of the Wild (1935)

Once the film was on location, there continued to be movie fans excited by the appearance of the actors. One article indicated[93]:

The announcement "Clark Gable is coming here to lunch" at the fashionable Monday luncheon at the Olympic hotel in Seattle set the entire dining room a flutter. Loretta Young, winsome star, was with Gable and the two had cordial smiles for everyone in the room. They are filming *Call of the Wild* at Mount Baker. Incidentally, Mr. Gable had a fine growth of whiskers, cultivated as essential to his part. Mrs. Wilbur Coman and Mrs. Walter Wyckoff (Jane Brown), both formerly of Spokane, were present at the exciting event.

Despite these events, the grueling conditions that made much of the shooting difficult caused some tension between Gable and Wellman, despite each man's respect for the other's work and Gable's otherwise easygoing disposition. Gable was awarded his Academy Award for *It Happened One Night* at the Oscar ceremonies during the filming of *The Call of the Wild*.

Director Wellman was also upset by the liberties taken with the original Jack London source material. According to Frank Thompson and John Gallagher in their book *Nothing Sacred: The Cinema of William Wellman*[94]:

Wellman gave the material rugged treatment, and [*Call of the Wild*] was one of his favorite films, though very little of Jack London made it onto the screen. Zanuck and Wellman argued over the screenplay, since the producer took drastic liberties with the source material, interpolating such dialogue between Gable and Young as "I'll be seeing you every day, every hour, every minute."

The emphasis was shifted from Buck, the St. Bernard who, in London's novel, progresses from pampered pet in California to abused sled dog in the Yukon and finally to noble beast living among the wolves. In the final script, the story of *The Call of the Wild* focused mainly on the gold-hunting adventures of Gable, Oakie and Young, and the romance between Gable and Young. Buck was relegated to subplot status, though Gable's scenes with the dog are natural and affectionate, the emotional center of the film.

Despite not being particularly faithful to the original story, *The Call of the Wild* was a big hit and continues to be among Gable's best and most enjoyable films of the 1930s. Edwin Schallert of *The Los Angeles Times* stated: "Wellman has imbued with poetry the love story between Gable and Miss Young. He also returns to the screen the old-time sweep of Frozen North scenic films." *Photoplay* stated: "The familiar story has been changed in spots, but the revisions make for stronger screen fare. And all the humanness, the drama of the novel has been retained.... The direction of William Wellman deserves high praise." And Buck Herzog of *The Milwaukee Journal* raved:

Completely as refreshing and welcome as the first sign of spring ... endowed far beyond the ordinary limits for this type of film. It has colorful portrayals, comedy, scenic backgrounds and romance. By diligently blending human interest with melodramatics, preserving of course the Jack London flavor, the filmmakers have provided a great outdoor picture.... *Call of the Wild* is a cinch for gaining the complete favor of each member of the household.... I'm sure most of the paid contingent will agree, (the movie) is a real cinema treat.

One scene disappointed preview audiences. Originally, Oakie's endearing Shorty character was shot to death. There is a running gag in the film where Shorty manages to roll a seven with a pair of lucky dice he always carries with him. When he leaves to file the claim, Jack throws him the dice and they land on unlucky snake eyes, a bad omen. In the original film, Shorty is shot by the evil Smith over a gambling debt. There is a shot of him after being shot, stating: "I knew those dice weren't lying." He then smiles faintly and says, "The homestretch..." before dying. This footage so upset preview audiences, Wellman was asked by Zanuck to remove the scene and shoot the happy ending where Shorty returns triumphantly at the end.

During the scene when Smith holds Jack and Claire at gunpoint, Jack smirks, knowing that Shorty has filed the claim. Smith states that he looks like he has something up his sleeve, and says, "Check your sleeves, there's nothing there." The scene then cuts as Jack starts for Smith. Originally, it is here where Smith reveals to Jack that Shorty is dead. With that part cut out, the scene plays differently. But Smith and his henchmen's fate is no less gratifying, while the tacked on happy ending is more appealing. The original footage featuring Shorty's death exists in the holdings of the UCLA film archive.

The Call of the Wild originally ran 92 minutes but was cut for reissue and not restored until its 2013 Blu-ray release. This contains a scene with Katherine DeMille and LeRoy Mason that does not exist in the shorter version, as well as other moments that were edited out of the 81-minute version that was used for theatrical re-release in 1945, and again in 1954, and subsequently for television and home video until the restored Blu-ray.

One notoriously significant event occurred during the filming of *The Call of the Wild*. A romance developed between Gable and Loretta Young, and the actress became pregnant. Because Gable was married, the situation was covered up and never reached the press. Young, a strict Catholic, refused to abort the child, so she went away and gave birth on November 6, 1935. She later showed up in Hollywood with a baby that she claimed was adopted. In 1940, Loretta married Tom Lewis, who adopted the child. Judy Lewis was not told who her real father was until she was an adult. She wrote about this situation in her 1994 book *Uncommon Knowledge*, which stated that she met Gable only once, when she was 15. Loretta Young was angered that Judy revealed this information.

The Call of the Wild was the last film made for Twentieth Century Pictures before it merged with Fox to become 20th Century–Fox. The studio was renamed 20th Century Studios in 2020, and, interestingly, the first film made under that new banner was another version of the Jack London story, this one featuring actor Harrison Ford.

Mutiny on the Bounty

Produced and Directed by Frank Lloyd
Screenplay: Talbot Jennings, Jules Furthman, Carey Wilson
Based on the book by Charles Nordhoff, James Norman Hall
Cinematographer: Arthur Edeson
Editor: Margaret Booth
Cast: Clark Gable, Charles Laughton, Franchot Tone, Herbert Mundin, Eddie Quil-
lan, Dudley Digges, Donald Crisp, Henry Stephenson, Francis Lister, Spring
Byington, Movita, Mamo Clark, Byron Russell, Percy Waram, David Torrence,
John Harrington, Douglas Walton, Ian Wolfe, Robert Livingston, DeWitt Jen-
nings, Ivan F. Simpson, Vernon Downing, William Bambridge, Marion Clayton
Anderson, Stanley Fields, Wallis Clark, Crauford Kent, John Power, Pat Flaherty,
Alec Craig, King Mojave, Charles Irwin, Dick Winslow, Derek Blomfield, Lucy
Chavarria, Harold Entwhisle, Sam Wallace Driscoll, Hal Le Suer, Will Stanton,
David Thursby, Robert Adair, Harry Allen, Lionel Belmore, Nadine Beresford,
Harry Cording, Sig Frohlich, Mary Gordon, Jon Hall, Lilyan Irene, Doris Lloyd,
Lotus Thompson, Eric Wilton, William Stack, Julie Bescos, Ray Corrigan, Charles
Dunbar, Edgar Edwards, Fred Graham, Dick Haymes, Clarke Jennings, Stubby
Kruger, David Niven, Jack Sterling, Harry Warren, James Cagney
Released November 8, 1935
MGM
132 minutes

Mutiny on the Bounty was a three-part story by writers Charles Nordhoff and
James Norman Hall, but only the first two were adapted into a screenplay. Wallace
Beery was originally set for the role of Captain Bligh, and MGM wanted to borrow
Cary Grant from Paramount to play either Fletcher Christian or Roger Byam. Para-
mount didn't want to loan Grant, so MGM then chose Gable for the role of Christian.
Gable got the assignment while he was filming *The Call of the Wild*; he then made
China Seas. Beery bowed out of *Mutiny* because he didn't like Gable and wasn't inter-
ested in doing a long location shoot with him. It was then that Charles Laughton was
given the role of Bligh.

The conflict between the actors was covered up by the studio. Louella Parsons
reported[95]:

> Captain Bligh so verra' verra' English in *Mutiny on the Bounty* is not what Wallace Beery con-
> siders a perfect role for him. Wally did not want to say anything but when he found Irving
> Thalberg could get Charlie Laughton he just bowed out. Laughton with his 100 percent Brit-
> ish accent should be okay. *Mutiny on the Bounty*, so long discussed, actually gets underway
> within the next few weeks. Clark Gable and Robert Montgomery continue in their original
> roles.

Gable didn't think he was right for the role of the British Fletcher Christian, and
seriously objected to shaving off his now-trademark mustache for the role. (At the
time this story is set, members of the Royal Navy were not allowed to have any facial

119

hair.) Gable argued that when Ronald Colman shaved his mustache for *Clive of India*, his fan base reacted negatively. But the role had to be played without the mustache.

Robert Montgomery was set to co-star in the role of Roger Byam, but the part eventually went to Franchot Tone. Tone was married to Joan Crawford, who had been romantically connected to Gable prior to their marriage, so there was bad blood between the two men. However, once shooting began, they became friends.

Gable had never worked with Laughton, so to get acquainted on their first day, he took the actor to a brothel, not realizing Laughton was gay. Despite the awkwardness, Laughton later indicated he was flattered by the gesture.

Producer-director Frank Lloyd insisted on as much authenticity as possible, and demanded the film be shot on location. According to the *New York Daily News*,[96] "It is a part of Frank Lloyd's contract that he shall direct *Mutiny on the Bounty* in the South Seas, and not on the synthetic South Seas on nearby Catalina Island." However, much of the film was indeed shot on Catalina, as well as on location.

Set in the 18th century, the story deals with the two-year voyage of the *Bounty*, led by the brutal and sadistic Captain Bligh (Laughton). The ship is to gather breadfruit from a Tahitian island and sail it to the West Indies. Lt. Fletcher Christian (Gable) is tough and experienced, but his inner compassion causes him to be troubled by Bligh's sadism. Midshipman Roger Byam (Tone) is is proud of his family's long naval tradition, but his loyalty to Bligh is shaken by the captain's behavior. Conflict between Bligh and Christian builds throughout the voyage as the lieutenant challenges the captain's methods. When the ship reaches the West Indies, Bligh forbids Christian from going ashore. Byam finds a place with pretty Tahitian girl Tehani (Movita) and her father, island chief Hitihiti (William Bambridge). Hitihiti insists that Bligh allow Christian a day ashore. Bligh agrees and then reneges. Christian ignores this and leaves the ship, engaging in a romance with Maimiti (Mamo Clark), promising to return to her after the voyage.

Once they leave the island, Bligh's sadism results in the death of the ship's beloved doctor, the drunken one-legged Bacchus, and a rationing of water for the men in order to give more to the breadfruit cargo. The crew plans a mutiny, but Christian is against it. However, upon seeing crew members in chains, Christian joins the mutineers who take over the ship and cast out Bligh and his minions. Byam, due to tradition, is against this, and it leads to a conflict between him and Christian. In Tahiti, Byam marries Tehani and Christian marries Maimiti and fathers her child. The two men become friends again, but decide to split up when the British ship *Pandora* approaches the island. Christian mans the *Bounty* and goes to find a new island, while Byam waits for the *Pandora* to take him to England. He is shocked to find Bligh is captain of the *Pandora*. Believing he was part of the mutiny, Bligh imprisons Byam for the voyage to England, and upon their return, has him court martialed. Byam details Bligh's sadism in court and is pardoned by King George III. Christian escapes with his family and crew to the island of Pitcairn and burns the *Bounty*.

While *Mutiny on the Bounty* is an exceptional film, it is not historically accurate. The story worked to make Bligh much more sadistic than he really was. At one

Gable and Charles Laughton in *Mutiny on the Bounty*, 1935's Best Picture Oscar winner.

point early in the film, he even orders the flogging of a dead man; another man is keelhauled[97] for requesting water. These were created for the purposes of the film. *The Bounty* (1984) with Mel Gibson, was much more historically accurate, presenting Bligh as a much more sympathetic person than this film. However, the Gibson film is not as good as this one.

The film version of the stories underwent roughly two years of preparation. The *Bounty* was carefully recreated, down to some of the most minor details. Laughton arranged for his uniforms to be made by the same London company that had done so for the original Captain Bligh. Laughton was quite effective, conveying pure evil with aplomb. (This same year, he played Inspector Javert in Richard Boleslavsky's screen version of the Victor Hugo story *Les Misérables*.) However, playing so despicable a character forced the actor to maintain some balance. To offset the evil character he was playing, Laughton spent his time between scenes telling jokes and making humorous comments, including coining up funny names for foods that were being served. This joviality helped balance Laughton psychologically and he recalled the experience as an enjoyable one as well as being one of his most successful screen performances.

It was a pretty rough shoot, and at least one mishap was quite serious. From an article syndicated in most of the major newspapers of the time:

One man was missing and $50.000 worth of motion picture equipment lost when a ship on which they were working off lonely San Miguel Island suddenly sank.... The missing man was Glenn Strong, assistant cameraman at work filming the story *Mutiny on the Bounty*. Seventy-five persons were rescued from the wreckage, it was said. None of the major stars employed in making the picture were on the vessel, a former barge from Catalina Island, which had been rebuilt to represent a replica of the famed adventure ship *Bounty*.... [T]he mishap occurred after the vessel had been partially filled with water and submerged. For some unexplained reason the barge suddenly lurched, rolled on its side and sank rapidly, hurling its entire crew into the water. There is no direct means of communication with the island where the mishap occurred and complete reports must await a return of a Coast Guard cutter sent to the scene.

Sad to say, crew member Glenn Strong was later found dead.

In a syndicated article detailing the weather conditions, the reporter wrote[98]:

The mutiny would go off as per schedule if the company were not experiencing some of the unusual California weather. H.M.S. *Bounty* has cruised the channel of the late William Wrigley's Santa Catalina island for two weeks now, and has encountered nothing but fog. Well, maybe an hour of sunshine a day. Even if the crew gets ten straight days of sunlight, that will be just about enough to finish up the sequences on the boat. (Messrs. Louis B. Mayer and Irving Thalberg must be tearing their Metro-Goldwyn hair when they contemplate the expenses at the rate of more than $5000 a day.) Also Charles Laughton, who plays Capt. Bligh, was reminded that another company cruised the channel for three weeks looking for sunlight for the picture, *The Captain Hates the Sea*. "You can say for me," said Laughton bitterly, "that Captain Bligh, too, hates the sea." Director Frank Lloyd, who has handled at least six great sea pictures, keeps his fingers crossed and his eye on the heavens.

Another bit of drama that occurred during production. A minister, who wanted to save Gable and convert his soul, made a sincere effort to come on the set of the film. According to the press:

Samuel J. Williams, fiery Ohio evangelist who travelled 2500 miles to snatch Clark Gable from filmland's "primrose path to sin," packed his traveling bags tonight and regretfully prepared to go home. "I am sorry to say," said the Rev. Mr. Williams, "that I did not convert Mr. Gable. I didn't even see him." But the Rev. Mr. Williams was not lost in despair. "Some day he will see the light," he said. "Then he will seek a minister." The Rev. Mr. Williams said he haunted a Catalina island hotel where Gable reportedly was staying when filming *Mutiny on the Bounty*, but did not catch so much as a glimpse of the dark-haired young actor.

Gable found the incident amusing, but had no intention of taking any time to humor the minister.

Despite his misgivings about the role, Gable later referred to *Mutiny on the Bounty* as the best movie of his career. Initially he was put off by the fact that Laughton was classically trained, and his methods were theatrically based more so than cinematically. Gable also didn't like that Laughton never looked him directly in the eye, something Laughton used as part of the character. These elements that angered Gable only helped both actors to draw from it and convey the on-screen conflict of the characters.

Mutiny on the Bounty (1935)

Gable and friend on the set of *Mutiny on the Bounty* (1935).

There was also Gable's initial conflict with Franchot Tone, coupled with the fact that Tone was given a role that was intended for Gable's good friend Robert Montgomery. All of these situations were ironed out rather quickly, and everyone got along fine during the often grueling shoot where they were jostled by wind and doused with water.

123

Many familiar character actors dotted the cast, including Donald Crisp, Henry Stephenson and Dudley Digges. Eddie Quillan's performance as the tragic Ellison resonates throughout the film. It's established that he has a young wife and new baby at the outset of the voyage, and later he is charged with being a mutineer; this is one of the most emotionally stirring portions of the film. Movie critics gave Quillan honorable mention for best motion picture performance of the month (December 1935).

Mutiny on the Bounty was both a critical and commercial success, delighting audiences throughout the nation. A *Hollywood* magazine critic attended a preview in Chicago and reported in the January 1936 issue[99]:

> It's a stark, grim picture that wins nothing but praise from the men and surprised exclamation from a few shocked women. Already there has been a multitude of cries that here is the finest picture ever filmed. Franchot Tone emerges as the big hit of the picture. He drew the only burst of applause at the preview upon completion of his defense in the Admiralty Court on mutiny charges. Clark Gable joins with Tone and Charles Laughton to share top honors.

The *Motion Picture Herald* critic offered similar praise in the November 9, 1935, issue[100]:

> *Mutiny on the Bounty* is melodrama, the ripping tearing power of which leaves one breathless. Always, until the final sequence, it is a melodrama of man's cruelty to man and man's rebellion to cruelty…. It puts right up to the individual showmen the responsibility of selling a valuable piece of screen merchandise, which is almost sure to encounter some adverse reaction on the part of the public, in the same courageous, straight-from-the-shoulder manner in which it was made.

On another page of the *Motion Picture Herald*, exhibitors revealed how their patrons responded to the film. A North Hollywood theater owner stated[101]:

> Every exhibitor who plays *Mutiny on the Bounty* should write MGM and thank them for this great production, thank Charles Laughton, Clark Gable and Franchot Tone for their great performances, and director Frank Lloyd for giving Eddie Quillan the chance to display his wonderful talent alongside these performers. Let's see Eddie more often.

Other exhibitors praised the film and mentioned audiences' reactions to it. One rave came from the recreational director at the state prison in Trenton, New Jersey, who stated: "Made to order for our type of audience. It went over 100 percent!"

Mutiny on the Bounty won the Academy Award for Best Picture. Three of its actors were nominated for Best Actor—Gable, Laughton and Tone—but the award went to Victor McLaglen for *The Informer*. Because so many actors were nominated for the same film, at the next Academy ceremony, an award for Best Supporting Actor was implemented. This is also only film (up to the time of this writing) to win Best Picture but none of the other awards for which it was nominated.

One of the island girls in this movie, Movita, was Marlon Brando's second wife, and was married to him when he starred in the epic 1962 version of *Mutiny on the Bounty* with Trevor Howard as Captain Bligh. That movie was a resounding flop, and a critical failure as well. It has been more favorably evaluated by film buffs and historians since its initial release.

Despite historical inaccuracies, subsequent remakes and other factors that might disrupt its timelessness, this 1935 MGM *Mutiny on the Bounty* is generally considered the best motion picture treatment of the story. All of the actors offer performances that are somewhere near their best. The Fletcher Christian role was ideal for Gable (he employs just the right combination of toughness and compassion needed) but Laughton's performance is perhaps the most memorable. It's one of Gable's best and most enduring films from the 1930s, behind *Gone with the Wind* and *It Happened One Night*. The characters could have easily gotten lost in the spectacle, but thanks to the actors there is a great balance of action and character development. It is also amazing that this film was as financially successful as it was, considering all the setbacks, accidents and reshoots.

Wife vs. Secretary

Director: Clarence Brown
Screenplay: Norman Krasna, Alice Duer Miller, John Lee Mahin
Story: Faith Baldwin
Producer: Hunt Stromberg
Cinematographer: Ray June
Editor: Frank E. Hull
Cast: Clark Gable, Jean Harlow, Myrna Loy, May Robson, Hobart Cavanaugh, James Stewart, Tom Dugan, Gilbert Emery, Marjorie Gateson, Gloria Holden, Niles Welch, Mary McGregor, Charles Trowbridge, Lucille Ward, John Qualen, Aileen Pringle, William Newell, Harold Minjir, Greta Meyer, Myra Marsh, Margaret Irving, Hilda Howe, Paul Ellis, George Guhl, Holmes Herbert, Frank Elliott, Clay Clement, Maurice Cass, Frederick Burton, Paul Rowan, Phillip Trent, Larry Steers, Nina Quartero, Frank Puglia, Hooper Atchley, Andre Cheron, Guy D'Ennery, Eugene Borden, Sidney Bracey, Tom Herbert, Tom Mahoney, Helen Shipman, Bess Flowers, Beatrice Roberts, Edward LeSaint
Released February 28, 1936
MGM
88 minutes

Wife vs. Secretary is such a delightful film and holds up so nicely in the 21st century, it is bemusing to read that director Clarence Brown was completely dismissive of it, and Clark Gable was as well. Brown stated that he "hated the story and argued over it every inch of the way" and that Gable "wanted to get through it as quickly as possible."[102]

While the movie was being filmed, Brown and the movie were mentioned in the *Los Angeles Times*[103]:

[Brown] now can qualify as the champion worrier in a business where hair turns gray early or disappears. Brown is directing a film with this title: *Wife vs. Secretary*. His cast is headed by Myrna Loy, Jean Harlow and Clark Gable. Myrna Loy in the picture is Gable's wife, Jean Harlow his secretary. The box-office records of all three players are certainly nothing for a director to worry about. Nor is a familiar triangle story of life in an office one to qualify as poor movie material. And yet Brown, admitting this, has found a hazard. "It's this," he says. "Look at that title and you write your own story. I did, and everyone else will. What I'm afraid of is that many people, with their own stories ready-made to fit our title, will be disappointed. We have the old situation, of course, but we are giving it a different twist."

Just one day later, a columnist quoted Brown as reacting negatively to the direction the film industry was going:[104]

Besides being an engineer, a flyer and one of the best-known film directors, Clarence Brown is something of an artistic reactionary. He heaves a sigh now and then for the days of silent pictures. We came upon the sighing Mr. Brown during a lull in the manufacture of an item called *Wife vs. Secretary*.... He said: "I'm not so sure about this screen-art they're talking, about. Looks as though we're getting farther away, all the time, from the only individual art the movies ever had."

In her autobiography, Myrna Loy recalled the film as a fun experience that continued to generate fond memories for her. Of course we cannot gauge just how the film was approached by its director or actors other than based on their anecdotes. But we can see how *Wife vs. Secretary* continues to come off as a delightful romantic comedy.

In Loy's autobiography, she recalled that Jean Harlow begged the MGM brass for a movie role "that didn't require spouting slang and modeling lingerie." Loy continued[105]:

She began to shake that image with *Wife vs. Secretary*. She's really wonderful in the picture and her popularity wasn't diminished one bit. Actually we did kind of a reversal in that picture. Jean, supposedly the other woman, stayed very proper while I had one foot in bed throughout.

The opening scenes are the most risqué in the movie. Linda Stanhope (Loy) and her husband, wealthy magazine publisher Van (Gable), sleep in separate rooms, and they engage in this dialogue the next morning:

VAN: How did you sleep after that man disappeared?
LINDA: Deep, deep, deep.
VAN: He hated to go.
LINDA: I didn't ask him to go.

Recalling this scene in her autobiography, Loy stated that she and Gable were fully aware of what was implied:

[Clark and I] banter, nothing more, but there's just no question about what they've done the night before. Clarence Brown, our director, made it all so subtle, yet, oh, so wonderfully

Jean Harlow and Gable enjoyed working together. They co-starred again in *Wife vs. Secretary* (1936).

suggestive. (In fact, the only vulgarity in the picture is in the breakfast scene, where I discover a diamond bracelet that Clark has hidden in the brook trout I'm about to eat. It didn't seem chic or funny to me—merely messy, typical of Hollywood's misguided notion of upper-class sophistication. I tried to get them to take it out, but they wouldn't. Needless to say, it's the scene everyone remembers, so what do I know?)

Van and Linda are celebrating their third wedding anniversary, and he gives her an expensive diamond bracelet. Jean Harlow plays Helen "Whitey" Wilson, Van's secretary. Van's mother is concerned about their relationship, believing Whitey's beauty is too much of a distraction at the office. Linda dismisses her suspicions, stating that she trusts Van. Meanwhile, Whitey's boyfriend Dave (James Stewart) is jealous of her working relationship with Van, especially situations where she is called away from dinner to work on a project at night.

While Van and Whitey's relationship is strictly business, and there is no romance or even flirting going on, onlookers draw their own conclusions and share them with Linda. Eventually, despite her trust in Van, circumstances arouse her suspicion. At one point he goes away to meet with J.D. Underwood, an important fellow publisher, and Whitey goes along as his secretary. Van is trying to buy Underwood's paper but doing so secretly in order not to arouse the suspicion of a rival publisher. Thus, he cannot reveal many details to anyone, including his wife. Circumstances continue to arouse catty suspicion among Linda's friends, and arguments ensue with Van, who is insulted to think that his wife would doubt him. Another meeting with Underwood, this time in Havana with Whitey along, becomes the catalyst for a potential breakup. Linda phones Van's room and Whitey answers. When Van returns to New York, Linda announces she is leaving him. Lonesome, Van asks Whitey to accompany him to Bermuda as a friend. Even though she has now fallen in love with him, Whitey convinces Linda to take Van back.

The situation of wealthy, privileged people and their affairs in business and life was popular with Depression-era audiences. *Wife vs. Secretary* offered the sort of dream world that was far more popular. And the fact that there is no affair from anyone, no carrying on, allowed suggestive scenes, like the aforementioned opening, to sneak past the censors. On the surface, *Wife vs. Secretary* is a wholesome movie filled with simple misunderstandings that escalate as they become more complicated.

Wife vs. Secretary includes a scene where Van and Whitey admit an attraction for one another. They get drunk, and the possibility of actually engaging in an affair is before them, but they do not succumb completely to temptation. The filmmakers naturally realized that two people as attractive as Gable and Harlow would have a base attraction, and situations could arise, due to their platonic closeness, that would challenge their virtues. The sexual frustration is palpable in this scene. It is very powerful and features solid acting from Gable and Harlow, who continue to exhibit their on-screen chemistry in their fifth movie together.

In an interview with *Hollywood* magazine, Gable revealed that he understood the dynamic between a boss and his secretary[106]: "I've never worked in an office, but just from the way you have to figure these things out for a picture, I'd say that office wives have to be careful. The girl in the office is apt to have a tendency to idealize the guy she's working for. After all, he pays the checks."

James Stewart would soon become an iconic star in his own right, but here he is clearly in support. His supporting role is a significant extension of the Whitey-Van relationship, only from the perspective of her people. Dave is not wealthy like Van, he is a working class sort like Whitey. He cannot give her luxuries. The unpretentious Whitey has no interest in such things. She is content with their working-class status, as they both have jobs that pay comfortably. Traditionalism abounds as Dave insists, "I'll wear the pants!" if they do wed. Stewart was already developing the Everyman qualities that would define much of his later work. In interviews years later, he delighted in recalling that he'd purposely botch the kissing scenes with Harlow, so they would have to do it again.

Moviegoers responded well to *Wife vs. Secretary* and it was held over at many theaters. Critics were pleased as well, *Variety* stating[107]:

> Gable gets a part which might have been tailored to his order and differentiates skillfully between his impulsive love for his wife and his friendly appreciation of his stenographer's merits. Loy gets a part which suits her, but it is Harlow who profits most. She clicks in every scene without going spectacular as to costume.

The film was a huge hit, grossing over four times its production costs. Gable remained dismissive about what he considered a mere formula picture, and Clarence Brown continued to feel it was one of his worst movies.

While it may be formulaic in some regards, *Wife vs. Secretary* manages to turn some of those stereotypes around regarding how the characters behave. Despite their one flirtatious scene, Harlow's character isn't scheming to get Gable away from his wife, and he genuinely loves and is attracted to his wife and isn't interested in engaging in an affair. The title also implies a cattiness between the Loy and Harlow characters that in actuality isn't there. Gable's role as a publisher is not unlike the newspaperman-editor roles that he had already successfully pulled off in previous films.

San Francisco

Director: W.S. Van Dyke
Screenplay: Anita Loos
Story by Robert E. Hopkins
Producers: John Emerson, Bernard Hyman, W.S. Van Dyke
Cinematographer: Oliver T. Marsh
Editor: Tom Held
Cast: Clark Gable, Jeanette MacDonald, Spencer Tracy, Jack Holt, Jesse Ralph, Ted Healy, Shirley Ross, Margaret Irving, Harold Huber, Edgar Kennedy, Al Shean, William Ricciardi, Kenneth Harlan, Roger Imhof, Charles Judels, Jack Baxley, Warren Hymer, Sidney Bracey, Bert Roach, Tommy Bupp, Russell Simpson, Chester Gan, Adrienne D'Ambricourt, John Kelly, Jack Kennedy, Tom Mahoney, Belle Mitchell, Oscar Apfel, Vince Barnett, Vernon Dent, D.W. Griffith, Sonny Bupp, Leonard Kibrick, Jane Barnes, King Baggott, Cy Kendall, Ruth Gillette, Danny Jackson, Fay Helm, Homer Hall, Anthony Jowitt, Frank Mayo, Douglas McPhail, Spec O'Donnell, Jean Acker, Fritzi Brunette, G. Pat Collins, Sherry Hall, Edgar Edwards, Bud Gary, Homer Hall, Flora Finch, Danny Jackson, George Guhl,

Delos Jewkes, Owen Marsh, Harry Myers, Lillian Rich, Dennis O'Keefe, Amber Norman, Carl Stockdale, Madame Sul-Te-Wan, Pat O'Malley, Frank Sheridan, Jason Robards, Myrtle Steadman, Dorothy Vernon, Tudo Williams, Ben Taggart, Myrtle Stedman, Tudor Williams, Douglas Steade, Bill Wolfe, Rosemary Theby, The Highlanders

Songs: "San Francisco," Music: Bronislau Kaper and Walter Jurmann, Lyrics: Gus Kahn; "Would You," Music: Nacio Herb Brown, Lyrics: Arthur Freed; "Happy New Year," Music: Bronislau Kaper and Walter Jurmann, Lyrics: Gus Kahn; "Noontime," Written and Performed by Ted Healy; "Love Me and the World Is Mine," Music: Ernest Ball, Lyrics: Dave Reed, Jr.; "A Heart That's Free," Music: Alfred G. Robyn, Lyrics: Thomas Railey; "The Holy City," Music: Stephen Adams, Lyrics: Frederick Edward Weatherly; "Faust: Air des bijoux" ("The Jewel Song"), Music: Charles Gounod, Libretto by Jules Barbier and Michel Carré; "Faust: Il se fait tard," Music: Charles Gounod, Libretto by Jules Barbier and Michel Carré; "Faust: Anges purs," Music: Charles Gounod, Libretto by Jules Barbier and Michel Carré; "La Traviata: Sempre Libera," Music: Giuseppe Verdi, Libretto by Francesco Maria Piave; "Nearer My God to Thee," Music: Lowell Mason, Lyrics: Sarah F. Adams; "The Battle Hymn of the Republic," Music: William Steffe, Lyrics: Julia Ward Howe (1862)

Released June 26, 1936

MGM

115 minutes

Other studies have stated that, after filming *Mutiny on the Bounty*, Clark Gable went over to Warner Brothers at the request of Marion Davies, to play opposite her in the musical comedy *Cain and Mabel*. That film was withheld from release until September 1936, and *San Francisco* was made and released before the end of June. In fact, it was filmed first. Gable didn't start on *Cain and Mabel* until April 1936 upon completing his scenes for *San Francisco*, which was, and remains, one of Gable's very best films

At 5:12 a.m. on April 18, 1906, an earthquake struck the coast of Northern California. Over 80 percent of San Francisco was destroyed as fires broke out in the aftermath and lasted for several days. More than 3000 people lost their lives—the greatest loss of life from a natural disaster in the state's history. Thirty years after this tragic event, Robert E. Hopkins wrote a story that provided a narrative leading up to the earthquake. It was developed into a screenplay by Anita Loos.

Hopkins had provided topical stories for other MGM movies, including Buster Keaton's last starring role with the studio, *What! No Beer?* (1933). That film, a comedy about Prohibition, co-starred Jimmy Durante, and was immediately newsworthy, thus resulting in a successful box office. Anita Loos had been writing for films since the teens, and had penned the script for the moneymaking Gable–Jean Harlow starrer *Hold Your Man*.

Jeanette MacDonald was impressed with the *San Francisco* screenplay and wanted it to be her next MGM film. She had just scored two huge hits with *Naughty*

Marietta (1935) and *Rose Marie* (1936), the former featuring the song "Oh Sweet Mystery of Life" and the latter including "Indian Love Call." *San Francisco* was a heavier movie that would allow her to give more of a dramatic performance, since her hits up to that point were mainly light musicals.

While she and Nelson Eddy had scored successfully as a team, Eddy was then on a concert tour. Having the clout to choose her co-star, MacDonald wanted Clark Gable.

Gable wanted no part of the production. He realized it would be a vehicle for MacDonald's operatic singing and that would be its focal point. But he was assigned to play the role of "Blackie," a character not too unlike the same-named one he'd portrayed in *Manhattan Melodrama*. To fill a supporting role, MacDonald asked for Spencer Tracy. Tracy had just come over to MGM from Fox and made an impact with *Riff Raff* (1935) opposite Jean Harlow and *Fury* (1936), a powerful drama that he was just completing. Gable and Tracy got along fine and became friends, but Tracy and MacDonald did not get along at all, and avoided each other when they weren't playing a scene together.

Saloon owner "Blackie" Norton (Gable) hires singer Mary Blake (MacDonald) to perform. Despite her classically training, Mary adapts to the popular style of singing and quickly becomes a hit. Blackie's buddy Father Tim (Tracy) is a priest who has long wanted to reform him. Blackie's not a religious man, but he cares about Tim and secretly does things to support his church, including buying a new organ. In his own life, he not only gambles but also runs for the city's Board of Supervisors to help his fellow gamblers protect their crooked interests.

Blackie develops feelings for Mary, and she responds to a point. Being quite pure, she is unsettled by the sexual nature of his intentions. Mary quits the saloon and starts work at an opera house, so Blackie goes there and proposes. Burley (Jack Holt), the opera house owner, has also proposed. Mary realizes that Blackie will want her to leave opera and return to his saloon, but she still chooses him over Burley. As she is about to go on stage for her return performance at the saloon, Father Tim arrives and reacts negatively to her costume, believing it is inappropriate. This leads to a conflict with Blackie, who strikes Tim. Mary, upset, leaves Blackie to return to Burley. She meets with Burley's mother (Jessie Ralph), a wealthy and respected member of society, who approves of her. The mother reveals that she once had a Blackie in her life, but married the more stable Burley Sr.

When the earthquake hits, Blackie frantically searches for Mary. He finds Burley lying dead in a pile of rubble. He later runs into Burley's mother, and must reveal that her son is dead. Blackie finds Father Tim, who tells him Mary is safe and takes him to her. She is in Golden Gate Park, singing hymns to people who have camped there in tents until they are able to return to what's left of their homes. When they are told the fires are out, the people march out of the park with the intention of rebuilding the city.

Despite his misgivings about the role, and his dislike for Jeanette MacDonald, Gable turns in an exceptional performance, using his gritty toughness, his romantic tenderness, his flair for comedy, and his talent for drama. When writers Loos and Hopkins saw some of the rushes, they had a problem with the way W.S. Van Dyke was directing Gable's performance. At one point, Blackie confronts a dancer and says "I thought I told you never to wear this," and violently rips a necklace off her neck. The writers felt that this scene made Blackie look too negative, especially since it came early in the film and helped to establish the character. The producer disagreed at first, but eventually was convinced, so a quick scene was added where Blackie winks at the girl and says, "Watch it next time," which effectively diffuses the intensity of the scene.

MacDonald holds her own playing opposite him in a film that is as much designed for her (she gets above-title billing alongside Gable). MacDonald performs several song numbers, including the title tune, written for this film, and remains an anthem for the city. She is effective as an actress and gets to show off her considerable singing skills, doing both classical and popular songs.

Spencer Tracy had become pretty well-known for playing two-fisted tough guys, and had to shift gears to portray a calm, understanding priest. This was something of a harbinger for what would be one of his greatest roles, Father Flanagan in *Boys Town* (1938); a performance that won him an Oscar. Despite his priestly role, *San Francisco* still found an excuse for Tracy to show off his fighting skills: During a boxing work-out between Blackie and Father Tim, the priest knocks the gambler to the mat. Blackie's reaction indicates that this isn't the first time.

The dynamic between these three are central to the film's narrative. They all love each other at different levels. Mary sees in Father Tim a connection to her own pastor father, now deceased. In a culture of saloons and rowdy audiences, Tim's relaxed and gentle personality is a comfortable counterpoint. Father Tim's relationship with Blackie is more complex. Blackie is established as an atheist ("You don't believe in anything!"), one whose wayward lifestyle gives Tim pause. In one scene, Father Tim explains to Mary how he and Blackie were children together, and that his greatest hope is to bring his old pal around to a cleaner and more responsible way of thinking. Gable's performance is exceptional in the way he conveys his love for Mary, and his genuine love of familial-level friendship for Father Tim. There is never any disrespect, until the conflict about Mary's stage attire.

While he liked Tracy personally, Gable was still a bit unsettled with the actor's great talent. Tracy was already one of the finest actors in movies, despite the limitation in range thus far in his movie career. Father Tim (and his character in *Fury*, released a short time before) were breakout roles. Tracy, meanwhile, admired Gable's rugged manliness and how he could convey his natural charisma so effortlessly and effectively in every role. However, Gable's conflict with MacDonald was on another level entirely. Many biographies claim that Gable would consume a garlic-heavy Italian lunch before intimate scenes with MacDonald, who just about fainted due to his breath.

San Francisco includes many familiar and welcome character performers, including Harold Huber, Edgar Kennedy, Warren Hymer and Charles Judels. Ted

An unimpressed Ted Healy looks on as Gable auditions Jeanette MacDonald in *San Francisco* (1936).

Healy plays Blackie's friend Mat, who helps stage the Paradise shows, and has no ear for Mary's operatic style. Healy had recently broken with the Three Stooges; in *San Francisco* he gives one of his best solo performances.

At one point, Ted Healy, as Mat, looks on with disdain while singer Mary auditions for Blackie. Impressed, Blackie offers her $75 a week. Mary faints, due to not having eaten, but it appears that she is responding to Blackie's offer. "She fainted!" Blackie cries. Mat says, "If you offered me 75 bucks a week, I'd drop dead."

Healy not only gets to be gruff and amusing, he also sings a bit of an original song during a stage sequence. But what is most impressive is that he shows some dramatic chops that he almost never displayed. When he is fatally injured in the earthquake, Mat lies there with Blackie sitting over him, asking if he's okay. Mat is weak but triumphantly claims he'll be good as new in no time. Blackie looks up at the attending nurse, who slowly shakes her head. It's an impressive emotional scene, and Healy does quite well in it.

While the story is involving and the characters are well-drawn and interesting, they lead up to the earthquake sequence, the movie's highlight. This scene is remarkable considering the limited special effects available in 1936. It was the work of

Spencer Tracy and Gable take a coffee break during the earthquake scenes on the *San Francisco* (1936) set.

second unit director John Hoffman, who specialized in creating montage sequences. The collapsing buildings, ground opening up, and fleeing, screaming people all combine in a sequence that remains one of the most impressive scenes in movie history.

The scene starts inside and gradually builds in intensity. Then we travel outside, and while there are a couple of establishing shots showing the devastation on a grander scale, for the most part, the scene is a series of quick edits (people running, buildings crumbling) that gives the impression of chaos without actually showing a whole lot. When the action picks up again after a pause, there are some even more incredible shots, like the ground splitting and the façade of a building sliding off entirely, revealing the interior. Gable seems to be the bridge between the audience and the earthquake, as he stumbles around observing his surroundings, dazed. This incredible scene helped to make *San Francisco* the highest grossing film of 1936, even beating out that year's Oscar winner *The Great Ziegfeld*.

There are a great many crowd sequences, including establishing shots and during the earthquake. While director Van Dyke was quite capable in this department, some of these scenes were filmed by an uncredited D.W. Griffith, who helped establish such visuals with his landmark classics *The Birth of a Nation* (1915) and *Intolerance* (1916).

The visual composition of *San Francisco* is especially impressive. Perhaps the most impressive sequence, other than the earthquake, is a tracking shot of Gable and Tracy walking through the rubble of the streets and into the crowded Golden Gate Park, strewn with tents and all manner of humanity. Van Dyke even cuts to an overhead shot, filling the frame.

San Francisco had two different endings. Originally, it showed the rubble of the earthquake as it panned away from the action and headed toward the END title. The rubble turned to buildings, showing the triumph of the city and its people. This was followed by a montage of shots that included Market Street and the Golden Gate Bridge being constructed. When the film was re-released in 1948, it was decided that those shots were dated, and the film ended with the shot of the buildings and went to the END title. Some TV prints have the original ending, some the re-release one. On DVD, the film has the re-issue ending, with the original ending available as a special feature.

San Francisco was not only a hit, it was well received by the critics. Frank S. Nugent in *The New York Times* stated:

> *San Francisco* is less a single motion picture than an anthology. During its two-hour course it manages to encompass most of the virtues of the operatic film, the romantic, the biographical, the dramatic and the documentary. Astonishingly, it serves all of them abundantly well, truly meriting commendation as a near-perfect illustration of the cinema's inherent and acquired ability to absorb and digest other art forms and convert them into its own sinews.... Primarily, of course, this is the tale of a city, a vigorous story told in splashing melodramatic phrases and with the rich vocabulary of a thoroughly expert cast and one of the shrewdest directors in Hollywood, W.S. Van Dyke.... Mr. Gable, [Jack] Holt, Harold Huber, Ted Healy, Al Shean, Edgar Kennedy and the others were excellent, each in his way, but there must be special mention of another brilliant portrayal by Spencer Tracy, that of Father Mullin, the two-fisted chaplain of a Barbary Coast mission. Mr. Tracy, late of *Fury*, is heading surely toward an award for the finest performances of the year.

Other critics responded with equal favor, as *San Francisco* broke box office records throughout the nation.

Cain and Mabel

Director: Lloyd Bacon
Screenplay: Laird Doyle
Story: H.C. Witwer
Producers: Hal B. Wallis, Jack Warner
Cinematographer: George Barnes
Editor: William Holmes
Cast: Clark Gable, Marion Davies, Allen Jenkins, Roscoe Karns, Walter Catlett, Robert Paige, Hobart Cavanaugh, Ruth Donnelly, Pert Kelton, William Collier Sr., Sammy White, E.E. Clive, Allen Pomeroy, Robert Middlemass, Joseph Crehan,

Charles Teske, Victor Briedis, Arthur Thalasso, George Bruggeman, Robert Eberhardt, Harry Harvey, Marie Prevost, Joe King, Earl Askam, Rosalind Marquis, Hal Neiman, Rose Terrell, William Arnold, William Bailey, Curtis Benton, Billy Coe, John Marsden, Tom McGuire, Spec O'Donnell, Bob Perry, Lee Phelps, Charles Sullivan, Pat West, Bill Archer, Herbert Ashley, Curtis Benson, George Beranger, Jack Bergman, Delos Jewkes, Shep Houghton, Miriam Martin, Jane Wyman, Melba Marshall, Beatrice Gray, Martha Merrill, Victoria Vinton, Sidney Miller, Ralph Dunn, Jerry Fletcher, Dick French, Peter Gowland, Alexander Ikonnikov, Stuart Holmes, Milton Kibbee, Lillian Lawrence, Harry C. Bradley, Georgie Billings, Tex Brodus, George Ovey, Jean Sennett, Earl Tree, Sam Savitsky, Peter Seal, Addison Richards

Songs: "Coney Island," Music: Harry Warren, Lyrics: Al Dubin; "L'amour, toujours, l'amour," Music: Rudolf Friml, Lyrics: Catherine Chisholm Cushing; "Believe Me If All Those Endearing Young Charms," Lyrics: Thomas Moore; "Shadow Waltz," Music: Harry Warren, Lyrics: Al Dubin; "The Rose in Her Hair," Music: Harry Warren, Lyrics: Al Dubin, Italian lyrics: Manuel Emanuel ("Rosa D'Amor"); "I'll Sing You a Thousand Love Songs," Music: Harry Warren, Lyrics: Al Dubin; "Here Comes Chiquita," Music: Harry Warren, Lyrics: Al Dubin

Released September 26, 1936

Warner Brothers

90 minutes

After *San Francisco*, Gable went to Warner Brothers to appear opposite Marion Davies in the low-level musical comedy *Cain and Mabel*. Because he would be playing a prizefighter, Warners wanted him clean-shaven. MGM pointed out that, while *Cain and Mabel* was being filmed, they might need Gable for retakes on *San Francisco*, in which he sports his famous mustache. So Gable completed all *San Francisco* retake work before shaving his mustache and heading to Warners.

Warners had wanted one of its own actors, James Cagney, to play opposite Davies in *Cain and Mabel*. But this was another vanity project for William Randolph Hearst's mistress. As with *Polly of the Circus* four years earlier, Davies wanted Gable as her leading man. And she was accustomed to getting what she wanted. Arrangements were made with Louis B. Mayer and Gable signed the contract to appear.

Cain and Mabel had already been filmed before by Hearst's production company as a silent in 1924 under the title *The Great White Way*. The female lead in that film was Anita Stewart. Hearst wanted to remake it as a talkie with Davies.

Gable was not interested. He had planned one of his coveted hunting trips, feeling he deserved some relaxation before his next job. But Louis B. Mayer overruled him due to Hearst's clout, and Gable had to postpone his trip and begin shooting *Cain and Mabel* on April 15, 1936.

Cain and Mabel was reportedly a box office dud, and also has the reputation of being a weak movie. While not a smash hit, it did make *some* money, and it is a breezy musical comedy with a lot of snappy dialogue. Laird Doyle, one of Warners' wittiest and funniest dialogue writers, provided the script with a lot of laugh-lines that begin

Cain and Mabel (1936)

Marion Davies and Gable teamed once again in the comedy *Cain and Mabel* (1936).

immediately and sustain throughout the film's 90-minute running time. Doyle was killed in a plane crash two months after this movie came out. He was only 29.

The film opens with Mabel slinging hash in a diner, and meeting fast-talking reporter-turned-publicity man Reilly (Roscoe Karns) on the day she gets fired. They cajole their way into a tryout for a musical comedy run by Jake Sherman (Walter Catlett). Because this is a Cosmopolitan production, Davies' character is introduced and developed for the first 20 minutes of the film before Gable is seen. As prizefighter Larry, he has the room beneath hers while she is rehearsing her dance routines. The constant noise keeps him, his manager and his trainer awake—and Larry has a fight the next night. The manager complains to the front desk: "They sound like they're laying carpet with railroad spikes!" The conflict between Larry and Mabel occurs when he goes upstairs to demand they be quiet. Mabel's aunt Mimi (Ruth Donnelly) answers the door:

> LARRY: How am I supposed to sleep?
> MIMI: On the right side, the left side cramps the heart!

When Larry pounds on the door again, Mabel who answers and their conflict begins:

LARRY: I need to get some sleep
MABEL: What am I supposed to do, make you some hot milk?
LARRY: I have to fight tomorrow night!
MABEL: You won't have to wait 'til tomorrow if you keep pestering me!

When Larry fights, he groggily goes through the motions due to the lost night's sleep.

The Gable character is developed quickly, a montage showing that he has risen to the level of champion. However, the boxing commission is unhappy with him. Amusingly enough, Larry has no charisma outside of the ring. This parallels with Mabel starring in a show but having little charisma offstage. It is deemed beneficial for both when Reilly cooks up a romance between the two. Attendance increases at Mabel's show, while Larry gets offers for fights at Madison Square Garden and opportunities to endorse products on the radio for extra money. Larry remains incensed. He believes it makes him seem effete, something that he finds reprehensible. He believes Mabel is planting the stories, and growls, "I'll wring her neck so that the newspapers can't get a word out of her without a corkscrew!" Meanwhile, Mabel believes it is Larry who is responsible for the publicity, so she goes to his hotel, bumps into him in the hall, and douses him with a pitcher of water.

The dialogue is fast and sarcastic, not only from the two leads, but also from wisecracking supporting players Ruth Donnelly (in a part originally set for Mary Boland), Allen Jenkins, Walter Catlett and Roscoe Karns. Jenkins and Donnelly were mainstays in Warner comedies, while Karns had worked effectively with Gable in *It Happened One Night*.

When Larry and Mabel actually do fall in love, the promoters stand to lose everything as the couple plans to go off, marry, and own a garage where Larry will work as lead mechanic. Larry is quite blunt while training for his Madison Square Garden fight:

If I hadn't signed up for this fight, I'd take the title, throw it in the middle of Madison Square Garden and let them scramble for it. And if I win this fight, that's what I'm going to do anyway. I can still hear a bell ringing without trying to take a swing at somebody who isn't there. This pan of mine might not be a work of art. But I can still wear it on the street without someone trying to feed it peanuts. And I plan to keep it that way.

Through a continuous series of conflicts, a lot of witty dialogue, some fun physical comedy, and a fast pace, *Cain and Mabel* is delightfully amusing and holds up well.

During one of the musical numbers that Mabel performs on Broadway, a character imitates the Popeye the Sailor—a Paramount property. And in a dialogue exchange, Mabel makes reference to the Marx Brothers, who were then at MGM. It was unusual for a studio to promote performers or products that were under contract to a rival.

The musical numbers are quite lavish. William Randolph Hearst, who infiltrated in the production even more than usual, demanded that the studio roof be removed, and the sound stage extended 30 feet higher, to make the musical numbers larger and more spectacular. Jack Warner, despite his friendship with Hearst, and the magnate's power, insisted the idea was too expensive. Hearst paid for it himself. It became the tallest soundstage in the world at 94 feet.

The musical numbers can be considered distracting, and much more time is taken with them than any footage of Larry in the boxing ring. But the "Coney Island" number with Sammy White and Davies is fun, and shows off Davies' skill at dancing and using her body as performance art—stiffening up and falling forward to be caught by partner Sammy.

Cain and Mabel is a breezy delight. In the October 1936 *Photoplay*, a critic laid out most of the plot and then added,[108] "Yes, you can guess the ending, but it's so amusing you wouldn't mind it being obvious from the start. Grand laugh lines, tuneful music and a rowdy cast headed by Allen Jenkins and Ruth Donnelly help the stars bring you a very entertaining evening."

Perhaps the film's negative reputation is due to how Orson Welles' *Citizen Kane* (1941) affected Marion Davies' legacy. That film is said to be based on Hearst, and the character played by Dorothy Comingore is said to be based on Davies. As a result, film history often ignored Davies, believing that she was a semi-skilled opportunist. But recent discoveries of her films, especially the silents *The Patsy* and *Show People* (both 1928), have resulted in a reassessment: Davies was a gifted actress. (Welles denied that the *Citizen Kane* character had anything to do with her.)

Perhaps the main issue with *Cain and Mabel* is that the relationship between the two main characters changes from hate to love too quickly. There were times when the idea is more promising than the execution is successful. The music numbers, while quite striking and majestic, don't organically fit in with the rest of the movie—they are too big for this story. Some fans feel that Gable was miscast, not fitting well as a fighter, but both Gable and Davies seem perfectly cast. Gable is great here and has good chemistry with Davies, particularly in the earlier scenes when their characters don't get along. His manly persona provides a good contrast to the theater world that Davies' character inhabits. Romantic comedies that build on hate-love relationships will usually provide ample opportunity for comedy, and both Davies and Gable rise to the occasion

But Gable was not at all pleased with *Cain and Mabel*, believing it to be a Marion Davies picture for which he provided support. Essentially that's true. While his character is important, the narrative revolves around *her*. And while the movie itself is a lot of fun, Gable felt it was not in his best interests. He had a point. While the film is pretty much an amusing trifle on his filmography, it is a highlight among Marion Davies' movies.

It was also her next-to-last film. She made one more and then retired in 1937. She remained with Hearst until his death in 1951. She re-married only weeks after his passing, and remained so until her death ten years later.

Love on the Run

Director: W.S. Van Dyke
Screenplay: John Lee Mahin, Manuel Seff, Gladys Hurlbut
Story: Alan Green, Julian Brodie
Producer: Joseph L. Mankiewicz
Cinematographer: Oliver T. Marsh
Editor: Frank Sullivan
Cast: Clark Gable, Joan Crawford, Franchot Tone, Reginald Owen, Mona Barrie, Ivan Lebedeff, Charles Judels, William Demarest, Donald Meek, Richard Alexander, Duke York, Christian Rub, James Cooke, Martha Mayo, Cyril Ring, Adia Kuznetzoff, Egon Brecher, Alyce Ardell, Gino Corrado, Jimmy Aubrey, Billy Gilbert, Leonid Kinskey, Bert Roach, Frank Puglia, C. Montague Shaw, Douglas Gordon, Adolph Faylauer, Charles Irwin, Margaret Marquis, Otto Fries, Phillips Smalley, Charles Trowbridge, Eleanor Stewart, Norman Ainsley, George Davis, Harry Allen, Gennaro Curci, George Beranger, Bob Corey, James B. Carson, Fred Farrell, Jack Dewees, Elsa Buchanan, Fred Cavens, Frank Du Frane, J. Gunnis Davis, Jack Chefe, Sam Harris, Lilyan Irene, Joe Mack, Payne Johnson, Tom Herbert, E.L. Fisher-Smith, Iris Moore, Viola Moore, Jacques Vanaire, Russ Powell, George Nardelli, John Power, Max Lucke
Released November 20, 1936
MGM
80 minutes

Love on the Run is little more than a lightweight romantic comedy, sustained by the talent of its stars. Accepted by contemporary critics as harmless nonsense, it was nevertheless a popular box office attraction, again due to its stars.

Gable and Franchot Tone play rival newspaper reporters in London to cover a couple of stories which they find dull. A coin flip determines that Mike Anthony (Gable) will cover a socialite's wedding to a prince, and Barney Pells (Tone) will interview an aviator and his wife. The socialite is Sally Parker (Joan Crawford) whom Mike sees running from the church. He decides to follow her and pursue the story but keeps it from Barney. Mike entices Sally and punches the prince, and the two grab a plane and fly to France. When they crash-land, they discover a munitions map that proves that the baron and baroness are spies. Mike wants to track down this story *without* Barney, and also needs to keep Sally from discovering he is a reporter. Barney realizes something must be up and follows them. The conflict between the three of them, and the romance that develops, are all part of the narrative's comic structure. The eventual dangers when the baron captures Mike, then Sally, add tension to the comedy.

Joan Crawford's career was starting to slip at the time this movie was made. She needed a hit, and her last successful productions all featured Gable. The MGM brass decided to re-team the two in a romantic comedy. This is interesting in that back when they made *Possessed*, it was star Joan bolstering newcomer Clark. That's great evidence of how far he had come in his career.

Love on the Run (1936)

Love on the Run is quite obviously inspired by the far superior *It Happened One Night*, containing a few of its elements: Gable as a reporter, Crawford as an heiress, and both of them running away together. Otherwise this movie is completely different, heavier on comedy than romance. What is most impressive at the outset is how Crawford eases into her comic role. Her posthumous legacy among classic film fans is mostly for her work in heavy drama, especially later in her life. *Love on the Run* allows her to display her formidable comic skills and she seems more relaxed doing comedy here than she had previously.

Gable and Tone became friendly when shooting *Mutiny on the Bounty* and appear to be having fun in their unchallenging roles here. Reginald Owen, so evil in *The Call of the Wild*, is nicely cast as the baron, while William Demarest is perfect as the harried editor back in America.

W.S. Van Dyke had a good understanding of comedy and was quite familiar with his stars, having directed all of them frequently. He had a hand in making this sometimes ridiculous story plausible. When Sally and Mike escape in the baron's plane, neither of them knows how to fly. Van Dyke employs some frenetic visual comedy, showing the large plane twisting about and causing comical danger. However, they do manage to get it off the ground, and are flying it easily after a while. At one point, Mike says, "Well, we're either up 2100 feet and going 175 miles an hour or we're up 175 feet and going 2100 miles an hour!" They even manage to crash-land it without causing injury. While fun is more important than logic, this scene is pretty far-fetched. Period audiences didn't seem to mind.

The plane was a Lockheed Model 10E Electra provided by stunt pilot Paul Mantz, the movie's aerial coordinator. That same plane was flown by Amelia Earhart on her ill-fated trip around the world the following year.

There are some dull stretches in *Love on the Run* that disrupt its attempt at comic breeziness, such as a dancing scene with comic actor Donald Meek that perks up a bit as it goes along. And Meek's eccentric characterization is quirky and fun. The scenes of Mike and Sally traipsing across Europe, having various misadventures, forces more comparisons to *It Happened One Night*, but *Love in the Run* doesn't live up to that level at all.

Gable's affair with Crawford was disrupted on the *Dancing Lady* set when she became interested in Franchot Tone and later married him. And, as indicated earlier in the text, Tone and Gable became friendly on the set of *Mutiny on the Bounty*. So, during the shooting of *Love on the Run*, the triangle switched sides again. Crawford and Tone were having marital difficulties and spent a lot of time bickering on the set. Gable and Tone continued to get along fine and spent time playing cards on the set between scenes. The scenes between Gable and Tone were most enjoyable, with their rivalry sometimes friendly and sometimes not, which is established from the very first scene. Their attempts to one-up each other are fun to watch, and both actors had opportunities to be very funny. Their real-life friendship comes through via their chemistry in these scenes.

Love on the Run was shot from August to mid–September 1936. On September

Gable was re-teamed with Joan Crawford as his co-star in *Love on the Run* (1936).

14, the production's last day, producer Irving Thalberg died at the age of 37. The studio closed down, so *Love on the Run* concluded production on September 15. At MGM, Thalberg had established such innovations as story conferences, retakes and sneak previews. He developed the idea of filming literary works. In fact, it was his idea to pair stars for ensured box office, including Gable with Crawford.

Both Gable and Crawford were discovered and developed by Thalberg, and were heartbroken by his passing. Gable volunteered to act as an usher at Thalberg's funeral.

Hollywood trade paper critics were pleased with *Love on the Run* and made no comparison to the superior *It Happened One Night*. The magazine *Hollywood* stated[109]:

Metro's "storm troops" move into the scene again, and as in *Libeled Lady*, they take full control of the situation with a barrage of laughs. Picture Franchot Tone and Clark Gable as rival European correspondents for American newspapers, and Joan Crawford as the million-heiress who hates all reporters. With this premise you have a good start on a rollicking yarn, bound to click regardless of illogical situations. When Gable, suppressing his own identity, helps Joan flee from the rival reporter, an obvious day of reckoning is in the offing. The adventures that follow are funny and fully satisfying. Joan Crawford is given an excellent opportunity to reveal her loveliness as well as have a strong hand in the comedy. Gable's antics are screamingly funny, yet he is hard pressed by Tone throughout the picture.

Modern Screen was also impressed, but acknowledged how far-fetched the movie was[110]:

Here's a merry little item directed in the fast and furious tradition of W.S. Van Dyke and made terrific by the presence of such box office champions as Clark Gable, Joan Crawford and Franchot Tone. The story is an impossible sort of thing, which means that due credit is herewith handed to the scenarists for turning out a script full of comical moments and a generous quota of first-class lines.... The movies continue to portray newspapermen as half clown and half faun, so perhaps Gable and Tone are not to be blamed for falling into pattern. At any rate, they do it well, with the aid, no doubt, of the Van Dyke touch. Joan Crawford unbends surprisingly in her high comedy moments and handles the romantic interludes in her customary manner. Reginald Owen and Mona Barrie sharply define their spy roles, and Ivan Lebedeff is as phony a count as you could ask for. It's good fun for all audiences.

Love on the Run more than tripled its production costs, and gave MGM, Gable and Crawford a hit.

Parnell

Produced and Directed by John M. Stahl
Screenplay: John Van Druten, S.N. Behrman
Based on the play by Elsie T Schuffler
Cinematographer: Karl Freund
Editor: Fredrick Y. Smith
Cast: Clark Gable, Myrna Loy, Edna May Oliver, Edmund Gwenn, Alan Marshal, Donald Crisp, Billie Burke, Berton Churchill, Donald Meek, Montagu Love, Byron Russell, Brandon Tynan, Phyllis Coghlan, Neil Fitzgerald, George Zucco, Halliwell Hobbes, Murray Kinnell, Frank McGlynn Sr., Pat Somerset, Jules

Cowles, King Baggott, Robert Adair, Alec Craig, Dick Elliott, Frank Baker, Otto Fries, Marion Balliou, Randolph Churchill, Pat Flaherty, James Blaine, Thomas Carr, Frank Elliott, Wade Boteler, Lumsden Hare, Ian MacLaren, Olaf Hytten, Godie Mackay, Douglas Gordon, Charles Irwin, J. Farrell MacDonald, Leyland Hodgson, Robert Homans, Jerry Mandy, Joseph North, Frank Mayo, Pat O'Malley, Lee Strasberg, Rita Page, Russell Simpson, Tom Ricketts, Frank O'Connor, Zeffie Tillbury, Clarence Wilson, Yorke Sherwood, Joseph Tozer, Leo McCabe, Harry Myers, Dermott Quinn, Erville Alderson
Released June 4, 1937
MGM
118 minutes

It probably wasn't a good idea to make a movie about Irish politician Charles Stewart Parnell, his affair with Katie O'Shea, and the scandal that destroyed him. The artistic limitations of Hollywood movies during the Production Code era wouldn't allow for much of the real-life story to be depicted, forcing the screenwriters to fictionalize much of it. But the stage play was quite successful so MGM secured the movie rights with the intention of featuring Spencer Tracy in the title role. As early as January 1936, the studio announced it to the press:

> *Parnell*, the story of the uncrowned king of Ireland, which is creating so much talk as a stage play in New York, is intended for Spencer Tracy. Metro-Goldwyn-Mayer handed over the nice little sum of $25,000 for the privilege of putting this story of Ireland's historical fight for home rule on the screen. Anyone who knows anything about Ireland is familiar with the story of Charles Stewart Parnell whose brave fight for Irish freedom made him a real patriot.

However, by the time the film was ready to go into production toward the end of 1936, Clark Gable had replaced Tracy in the title role.

Joan Crawford was announced as the female lead when Tracy was still attached to the project. She remained after Gable was cast, but because of her misgivings about the director, and the fact that her recent costume drama *The Gorgeous Hussy* was a flop, she asked Louis B. Mayer to re-assign her. Mayer swapped Crawford with Myrna Loy, who was to star in *The Last of Mrs. Cheyney*. Crawford was given that role and Loy was cast opposite Gable in *Parnell*. Speaking philosophically, Loy stated in her autobiography: "We were actors, for God's sake. We couldn't be Blackie Norton and Nora Charles all the time."[111]

An ambitious Irish statesman, Parnell (1846–1891) sought to rule his country, but his efforts were thwarted by the scandalous affair he had with the married Katie O'Shea. The film begins in 1880 when Parnell gathers support in the United States for his National Land League. He is jailed upon returning to Ireland, due to his rebellious activities, but with the help of his cronies he runs things from his cell. Enter Captain O'Shea, who refers to Parnell as the "uncrowned king of England" and wants to use him, and his influence, for his own ends. When O'Shea can't get through to Parnell, he sends his wife (Loy) to entice him. She is as captivated by him as he is by her, and their romance ends up disrupting the British Empire.

The first problem Gable had with this film was the need to grow a beard. His mustache was fine for movies set in contemporary times, but men of this period had facial hair, including the historical figure Gable was playing. Gable balked, the studio insisted, and finally a compromise was reached: Gable would sport his usual mustache but also grow sideburns for the role.

Gable's approach to the role was earnest enough, but this was far different from his usual characters. He was noted for being the tough, rugged, charismatic man's man. Parnell was forceful in his beliefs, an aspect Gable could handle, but he also had a sensitivity that Gable tried to explore but was thwarted by his own misgivings. He feared that his fans would not respond well to his acting in a manner that was different than what they'd become accustomed to. Myrna Loy recalled: "He was a man who loved poetry and fine literature, read it, and knew it. He would read poetry to me sometimes during breaks, but he didn't want anyone to know it." Gable had an image to uphold. Parnell wasn't a part of that image.

Still, Gable's performance is good. It just isn't the Clark Gable moviegoers were used to seeing. He is very relaxed in the role, often solemn, and the care in his eyes when he helps a homeless family looks genuine. However, it is difficult to accept the virile-looking Gable as a sick man with a heart condition, one who had to be careful and gentle with himself.

It is interesting to see Gable and Myrna Loy's scenes together. Because we've already seen the two actors work in comfortable roles for *Manhattan Melodrama* and *Wife vs. Secretary*, it is fascinating to see them tackling uncharacteristic roles. Gable's manly charisma is replaced by a character that is soft-spoken, with almost a lilt to his voice. Loy is quiet, measured and refined as an Irish lady of this period might be. Loy told the magazine *Modern Screen* how she prepared for this very different assignment[112]:

> I read 20 books on Parnell and his times. I conferred with the son of Kitty and Willie O'Shea. I wear 15 costumes in the role of Kitty O'Shea. That meant the making of innumerable sketches by Adrian, over which he and I conferred for hours. Materials were tried and approved or rejected. There were 150 fittings. There were the hats, hundreds of hats. There was the jewelry. That had to be just right, not only for the period, but also for me. There were the shoes. I had to practice standing and walking. Kitty O'Shea didn't stand or walk as does the girl of today. When we began to work, I got up at six every morning, as I always do when in production. It takes from two to three hours to dress, get to the studio, have my hair dampened and waved every single morning, get into makeup and costumes. I make myself up. I can't stand having anyone fussing over me. It took me 20 minutes to get into each gown I wore. And then the set and work.

However as hard as she, and Gable, worked, and how much they tried to make their roles believable, the fans weren't buying into it. Loy recalled in her autobiography: "Disgruntled fans wrote to the studio by the thousands—they did that in those days."[113]

Spending a lot of money and a lot of time, MGM was hoping to make *Parnell* a powerful story about a famous person in history and the scandal that befell him. (The director John M. Stahl was best-known for sweeping melodramas like *Imitation of Life* [1934] and *Magnificent Obsession* [1935].) The result was a pretty turgid drama that plodded along and was really quite dull. Studies have usually indicated that the miscasting of Gable was the chief problem, and while that was certainly the reason for the film's failure with period fans, his performance is not bad. It actually did show that he could play this sort of role effectively enough. In Jeanine Basinger's book *The Star Machine*, she explained the problem from her perspective[114]:

> Gable, wearing mutton-chop sideburns and trying to be grand, is stripped of everything that makes him exciting. He plays a noble politician who speechifies, who accepts defeat, and who woos his woman carefully and by the rules, seriously violating his own well-established image. This isn't the Gable people had grown to love. His one big moment of action, in which he socks a fellow politician, is performed almost apologetically and in a highly dignified manner, deliberately and without passion. Gable is supposed to be the guy who kicks down the door to get the girl, the guy who punches his way out of problems, the man's man. As Parnell he is playing a man "who brought reason out of hysteria." Talking reason? That wasn't Gable's style. And the only royalty that Gable represented was King of Hollywood, a man of the people. In *Parnell*, Gable is desexed, all his fires tamped down.

Basinger also felt that this dull drama would have likely failed no matter who played the roles.

Irish politics was not a subject that most 1930s Americans wanted from their movies—and this movie is much heavier on politics than physical action. Some of the best scenes are when Gable and Loy are together, and their relationship is surprisingly playful and flirtatious, sweet and relatable. In one delightful scene, they get lost in the fog and wander around eating hot potatoes. Their dialogue is very entertaining.

For the most part, critics agreed that the film was weak and the leads were miscast despite their earnest portrayals. But at least one review was quite impressed. From the August 1937 issue of *Hollywood* magazine[115]:

> Thanks to the expert and painstaking guidance of director John M. Stahl, MGM's screen version of Parnell has lost none of the fine qualities that marked it a stage success. The picture is an artistic triumph and must be added to the list of outstanding films of the year. It may be criticized on the grounds that, despite its close hewing to history, it lacks the background of violent physical action so long identified with turbulent Irish politics. This criticism, however, is a minor one; for so powerful and compelling is the story as a whole, so free from theatrical tricks, and so completely honest is it from beginning to end that the absence of physical action is forgotten. To Clark Gable for his portrayal of the Irish patriot, Parnell, goes a world of credit. The role was a difficult one if only for the fact that it is a distinct departure from any to which he has been heir to, but the capable Gable presents a genuinely fine and polished performance, as he moves dominant yet restrained and tolerant through his scenes. As Katie O'Shea, …Myrna Loy shares acting honors with Gable. Never in any screen role has she presented a characterization with such emotional intensity and charm. Played in a fog, her love scene with Gable is a memorable one and has seldom been equalled on the screen. *Parnell* is her first costume picture and, we hope, the forerunner of many others. In the supporting cast Edna May Oliver presents a delightful characterization in her role of Katie's elderly aunt. Alan Marshal as the scapegrace husband and Billie Burke

Parnell (1937)

as Katie's simpering sister give particularly fine work. Donald Crisp as a devoted Parnell follower, Montague Love as Gladstone, and George Zucco as an attorney, Brandon Tyron as Old O'Brien, Neil Fitzgerald as Pigott, the forger, Berton Churchill as the Gorman Mahon and others contribute in no small measure to the general all-around excellence of the picture.

Parnell not only lost over half a million dollars at the box office, it went down in history as a notoriously bad movie featuring top stars. Gable would forever cite *Parnell* as the worst movie of his career. It may not be *quite* as awful as its reputation, but it certainly is the weakest of Gable's films of the 1930s. However,

Myrna Loy and Gable in *Parnell* (1937), a notorious flop.

despite its aesthetic limitations, there is a historical aspect to *Parnell* that makes it significant: Gable is one of the truly legendary, iconic stars of vintage Hollywood. His cinematic misfires are few. The single worst film of his career, even of the 1930s, has at least some importance as to the assessment of his talent and growth as an actor.

It is unfortunate that he was so discouraged by the failure of this movie. The movie wasn't right for him, but it goes to show how far his career and the development of his screen persona had come. This role was almost universally recognized by critics and audiences as deviating too far from the sort of character he was known for, which shows how much of an impact his screen persona had made.

Gable told MGM that he no longer wanted to appear in historical dramas. He felt that his attempt to do so in *Parnell* proved to him, and to his fans, that he was best suited for contemporary settings, and the character he had established. MGM responded by casting Gable opposite his pal Jean Harlow in a film that was perfectly suited for his talents. But *Saratoga* was a movie that was fraught with real-life tragedy.

Saratoga

Director: Jack Conway
Screenplay: Anita Loos, Robert E. Hopkins
Producer: Bernard H. Hyman
Cinematographer: Ray June
Editor: Elmo Veron
Cast: Jean Harlow, Clark Gable, Lionel Barrymore, Walter Pidgeon, Frank Morgan, Una Merkel, Cliff Edwards, George Zucco, Jonathan Hale, Hattie McDaniel, Frankie Darro, Henry Stone, Carl Stockdale, Walt Robbins, Gus Reed, Frank McGlynn, Patsy O'Connor, Edgar Dearing, Herbert Ashley, George Chandler, Dudley Dickerson, Ruth Gillette, Margaret Hamilton, Robert Emmett Keane, Sheila Andrews, Walt Robbins, William Carey, Franklyn Ardell, Irene Franklin, Sam Flint, Charley Foy, Jesse Graves, John Hyams, Pat West, Lionel Pape, Si Jenks, Mel Ruick, Grace Saxon, The Four Esquires, Mary Dee
Released July 23, 1937
MGM
84 minutes

Saratoga was an unhappy experience in Clark Gable's film career, because it turned out to be Jean Harlow's last.

Before starting work on *Saratoga*, Harlow—who had been in poor health for some time—had her wisdom teeth extracted. She passed out during the procedure and her heart stopped, resulting in an 18-day hospital stay. The May 3, 1937, *Time* magazine put Harlow on its cover, but used a photo that was a couple of years old. The difference in Jean since that picture had been taken was alarming. Despite her condition, Jean went to work on *Saratoga*. Nobody realized the seriousness of her condition.

Gable stars as enterprising bookie Duke Bradley, who sees an opportunity when the wealthy family of Carol Clayton (Harlow) is about to lose their assets. Carol is set to marry Hartley Madison (Walter Pidgeon), a wealthy man she met while vacationing in England. Lionel Barrymore is Grandpa Clayton, a horse breeder who is losing his stable due to the gambling losses of his son, Carol's father Frank Clayton (Jonathan Hale). Duke prevents the bank from foreclosing and takes over the breeding farm's debts from Carol's broke, ailing father in order to settle the man's massive gambling debts. Frank has a few provisions that Duke must agree to, chiefly to hold up his vow that Carol never become involved in horse racing. After Frank dies, Carol wants Duke to sell Grandpa's stable, but Duke has become fond of the old man and refuses to foreclose. Duke gets his friend Fritzi (Una Merkel) to trick her wealthy husband (Frank Morgan) into making the winning bid on a horse at an auction despite being allergic to them. Hartley, Carol's wealthy fiancé, also buys a horse, Moonray, and asks Grandpa to train him.

While Duke and Carol have a contentious relationship, their attraction to each other is palpable. Carol eventually falls for Duke and dumps Hartley. Hartley

148

responds by hiring a different trainer for Moonray. Duke is upset, because he now loses his gambling leverage with Hartley. But he makes the right bets on the big race and wins enough money to marry Carol.

One day while filming a scene with Walter Pidgeon, Harlow collapsed on the set. She was rushed home. Conway phoned Jean's mother and told her that Jean belonged in a hospital. When the mother refused, it was concluded that she did so due to her Christian Science beliefs, and that is incorrect.

The situation alarmed Gable, so he went to the house and insisted on seeing Jean. He was shocked and saddened by his friend's appearance. She was bloated, and when he bent down to kiss her, she was cold to the touch and her breath reeked of urine due to failed kidney function. He left the house in tears.

When Harlow died, Gable and Lionel Barrymore were doing a scene on the set of *Saratoga*. Upon being given the news, Gable abruptly left the set, walked out of the studio and drove away in his roadster, not speaking to anyone. When the press caught up with him, he said he was too grief-stricken to make a statement. And, for the only time other than the passing of Irving Thalberg, MGM studios closed.

Press reports indicated that although *Saratoga* was 90 percent complete, the studio would take the loss and scrap the existing footage, with plans to reshoot the movie featuring a different actress. An article in the *St. Louis Star and Times* stated: "This film will have to be remade entirely with someone else in the feminine lead, as it had not progressed far enough to show it as it now stands."[116] Louis B. Mayer made the following statement to the *Los Angeles Times*[117]:

> The story *Saratoga* in the form it was photographed up to this time is no more. In accordance with our policy, it was written for two distinct, strong personalities, Clark Gable and Jean Harlow. Jean Harlow has passed on. Therefore, production on the picture will be indefinitely delayed until we can rewrite the story to fit some other feminine personality. All that has been photographed to date, and we were within a week of the picture's completion, will be scrapped.

Both Jean Arthur and Virginia Bruce were considered. What caused the studio to reconsider was the response of moviegoers. A story in *Box Office* stated[118]:

> According to studio officials, a flood of letters from fans has been received urging that the film be released, even in its incomplete state. Mayer and other studio executives are conferring at present to choose one of several steps open to them. It has been reported, but unconfirmed, that the picture will be completed with Mary Dees, Miss Harlow's stand-in, taking over her role for the remaining scenes. In this case, it is believed that one of the Metro actors, possibly Lionel Barrymore, would make a speech to be included in the film explaining the switch in actresses to the audience.

MGM decided to finish the film by using a double in Jean's place. There is a racetrack scene in which Carol never takes the binoculars from her eyes until the race is over. When she does, she turns her back from the camera to speak to others in the

Director Jack Conway, Jean Harlow and Gable on the set of *Saratoga* **(1937). Jean did not live to finish it, which broke Clark's heart.**

scene. Paula Winslowe was hired to mimic Jean's voice in scenes where dialogue was utilized.

Another scene takes place between Carol and her maid Rosetta, played by Hattie McDaniel. Carol's wearing an obtrusively floppy hat and is turned away from the camera. Hattie carries the scene's dialogue. However, several retakes were necessary because Hattie kept bursting into tears due to the loss of her friend Jean.

Even if Harlow had lived to complete this film, it is still perhaps the weakest of the Gable-Harlow collaborations. They didn't have as many opportunities to really play off each other. The structure of *Saratoga* attempts to offer a solid comedy-drama that rests pretty comfortably on the personalities of its stars, not only Harlow and Gable but also Barrymore, Merkel, Pidgeon and Morgan, who can enhance any project.

Saratoga was released on July 23, 1937, just over a month after Harlow's death. It was a box office sensation. In most cities, when Harlow first appeared on screen, the audience burst into cheers and applause. Historically, Harlow's inability to complete *Saratoga* isn't the film's only area of interest. It is fun to see Gable and Hattie McDaniel together in a scene a couple of years prior to *Gone with the Wind*. They became very friendly on the set and frequently teased and joked with each other.

Gable became very fond of Hattie and that continued on the sets of *Gone with the Wind*.

The box office success of *Saratoga* was due to Harlow's death, and because that tragedy made such of an enormous impact, Gable's contribution to the film was overlooked.

Test Pilot

Director: Victor Fleming
Screenplay: Vincent Lawrence, Waldemar Young
Story: Frank Wead
Producer: Louis Lighton
Cinematographer: Ray June
Editor: Tom Held
Cast: Clark Gable, Myrna Loy, Spencer Tracy, Lionel Barrymore, Samuel S. Hinds, Marjorie Main, Ted Pearson, Gloria Holden, Louis Jean Heydt, Virginia Grey, Priscilla Lawson, Claudia Coleman, Arthur Aylesworth, Dudley Clements, Gregory Gaye, Tommy Tucker, Bobby Caldwell, Marilyn Spinner, Ernie Alexander, Nick Copeland, Donald Kerr, Fay Holden, John Mack, Wally Maher, Hooper Atchley, Lester Dorr, Donald Douglas, James Flavin, Forbes Murray, Garry Owen, Steve Pendelton, Hudson Shotwell, Frank Sully, Richard Tucker, Charles Waldron Jr., Ray Walker, Dick Winslow, Dorothy Vaughan, Henry Roquemore, Dix Davis, Billy Engle, Ralph Gilliam, Knowlton Levenick, Martin Spellman, Ken Barton, Lulu Mae Bohrman, Jack Cheatham, Roger Converse, James Donlan, Frank Du Frane, Estelle Etterre, Robert Fiske, Byron Foulger, Otto Fries, Sam Harris, Mary Howard, Brent Sargent, Frank Tomick, Syd Saylor, Tom Rutherford, Alonzo Prince, Dewey Robinson, Tom O'Grady, William H. O'Brien, Claire McDowell, Douglas McPhail, Bert Moorhouse, Richard Kipling, Gladden James, Frank Jaquet, Ken Barton
Released April 12, 1938
MGM
119 minutes

After the debacle of *Parnell*, Gable made sure to round up several upcoming projects that were contemporary stories that matched his established screen persona. He hadn't even finished *Saratoga* when he was assigned to co-star with Myrna Loy and Spencer Tracy in *Test Pilot*. While *Saratoga* was marked by the tragedy of Jean Harlow's death, and has forever been noted as her final film, *Test Pilot* is very much Gable's movie.

Test Pilot was announced by MGM in 1933, when the stars would have been Harlow, Wallace Beery and Gable. But the story for this film was not purchased until January 1936. Frank Wead, who wrote the original story, was an ace pilot himself.

Pilot Jim Lane (Gable) crash-lands on a Kansas farm where he meets Ann Barton (Myrna Loy), who lives there with her parents. While Jim is upset and impatient over his plight, Ann is sardonic and wisecracking, which attracts him. He uses her phone to call his station, then the two of them spend the day going to a ballgame and enjoying each other's company. They fall for each other quickly. Pilot Gunner Morris (Spencer Tracy), Jim's partner and best friend, comes to the farm to get Jim, who then distances himself from Ann. However, when she gets engaged the next night to a longtime beau, Jim is visibly upset. He leaves the next morning but soon returns and puts her in his plane. They get married at a stop on the way back. Jim's cavalier attitude gets him in trouble with his boss (Lionel Barrymore) and he's fired, but he figures he'll be rehired because he is indispensable. He agrees to fly an experimental craft in a race (and wins), while the man sent in his place at his old job is killed, leaving behind a wife and children. Jim tries to mellow and get a steady job testing new aircraft so he can give Ann a home. He and Gunner go on a test flight together but the plane crashes, killing Gunner. Jim then gives up his dangerous occupation and joins the Army Air Corps.

Jim's relationship with Ann, whom he affectionately calls Thursday, is complex because he is a complex character. Upon their first meeting, when his plane crashes on her farm, his anger and impatience over his predicament is somehow soothed by her wisecracks. Her personality softens him. But their relationship extends beyond the parameters of the narrative. When they attend the ballgame, she knows more about the sport than he does, and loudly cheers on her team. Jim immediately notices she "ain't like the other dames" and exhibits the buddy type qualities he gets from friends like Gunner, while also having the attributes of a beautiful and desirable woman.

Jim is pretty much "married" to his work, and any romantic activities are limited to brief flings. (There's a girl futilely waiting for him at the start of the movie.) Gunner has been the one to look after him, keep him out of trouble, and show him the sort of consistent understanding that he doesn't seem to get elsewhere. They understand each other because they are both fliers.

Tracy also plays a complex character, especially in relation to Jim. While Jim is very spirited, gregarious and carefree, Gunner is darker, more cynical, a bit sullen. But his devotion to Jim is such that he sticks by him. After Jim marries Ann, the three are always together. They walk down the street with Ann in the middle, locking arms with each. When the couple buys a house, there is a bedroom for Gunner. Gunner does sometimes project a feeling of being a third wheel, and his tight friendship with Jim is at least partially disrupted. His feelings for Ann are complicated and she recognizes it:

ANN: Gunner, where do you wish I were right now? Back in Kansas sitting on a fence?
GUNNER: Why do you say that?
ANN: Help me make you like me
GUNNER: I do.

Test Pilot (1938)

ANN: Don't wish I were still back on the fence?
GUNNER: Don't expect any day to be any different.

After this exchange, Gunner walks away from the couple. Director Victor Fleming films it in a medium shot, with Tracy in the foreground, while Gable and Loy are in the background. Tracy is walking toward the camera. He stops, turns, waves and continues walking as the picture fades.

The complexity of each central character and their relationships are only part of the drama. Jim's attitude is such that he feels he can blow off a planned assignment to do a test flight with an experimental craft. Boss Lionel Barrymore threatens to fire him, and keeps his word. Jim feels that the company would not survive without him and expects to be called back. Such is his cavalier attitude. However, that extends to his work as a test pilot. When his experimental craft catches fire, he keeps flying until the velocity causes the fire to go out. This is in full view of Ann and Gunner on the ground. Gunner maintains an attitude that has been hardened by experience: "That's nothing. It's nice to have a little fire. You don't know how cold it gets up there! Besides, the guy is made of asbestos!" Ann is upset by this attitude, and tells him so. Gunner pulls no punches in his response:

Why you little fool, who are you talking to? What do you think this game is, anyway? It's death every time you move. It ain't safe to sit in one of them, it ain't even safe to look at one of them. And you married him without giving it a thought.

Tears are visible in Gunner's eyes, but his body is stiff, hardened, as are his feelings from so many experiences. Ann moves closer to him, her own eyes welling up. "Bless you, Gunner," she says. It is at this point that these characters learn to understand each other.

While each of the leads, and supporting player Barrymore, turn in magnificent performances, Gable stands out with some of this finest work. He gets inside Jim Lane and projects a man who uses confidence and a happy-go-lucky demeanor to mask any possible sorrow. When the replacement pilot is killed on the mission that Jim refused, his reaction is to give half the $5000 he won in the race to the flyer's widow. He then gets drunk and refuses to acknowledge what happened, in an effort to handle the tragedy.

The doomed flyer is portrayed by Louis Jean Heydt, who had a career playing tragic figures who invariably got hurt or killed (*Each Dawn I Die, They Made Me a Criminal*, etc.). He was good at projecting amiable, likable, unpretentious types that affect the audience when the tragic scene occurs. There is a scene where we meet his wife and his children. When the plane crashes, the man's wife runs after the ambulance; director Fleming shows this in a long shot that is very effective. He then cuts to a closeup of Gable exhibiting a sad but stern reaction which perfectly matches his screen character. Later, old boss Barrymore tells him, "Let's you and I stop quarrelling. It seems kind of silly." Barrymore says this in a quiet, measured tone, making it that much more effective. And when Jim meets with the widow, Gable makes it clear

Spencer Tracy, Gable and Myrna Loy in their hit film *Test Pilot* (1938).

that he is trying to hide his grief and guilt between a gruff exterior, telling her that at least her husband died doing what he loved. He then makes up a story about them having a bet to explain his gift of half his earnings.

Some studies have claimed that this segment of the film is based on the life and tragic death of actual test pilot Jimmy Collins. Collins had written a book about his exploits, coincidentally called *Test Pilot*, just before his death in 1935. When this movie came out, his widow tried to sue MGM, but a judge ruled against her.

Gunner and Ann bond in their love for, and frustration with, Jim. When he wakes up after a night of drinking, he soberly approaches Ann with remorse. When she is forgiving toward him, he lets her know how amazing she is, and celebrates by drinking more. Ann is philosophical, telling Gunner, "It's easy to be gallant when you're doomed." She often tries to leave, weeping over her tension, wondering how long it will be before Jim is a victim of a tragic crash, because he takes so many chances. She can't connect fully to his cavalier attitude. Gunner, we realize, never could.

The scene where Jim and Gunner go up in a dangerous bomber, filled with sandbags to simulate the weight of the explosives, is among the emotional highlights of a movie that is filled with them. The sandbags come loose as the planes drop, and they crush Gunner. Jim refuses to leave the plane, frantically throwing sandbags out in

Myrna Loy and Gable had been named the Queen and King of Hollywood by the time they were cast in *Test Pilot* **(1938).**

hopes of reaching the wheel and saving them both. He does so in time to crash-land the plane, but Gunner dies in Jim's arms. "Kiss Ann goodbye for me," he says. When Jim gets home, Ann is overcome with grief. "Why wasn't it you?" she sobs, lashing out. "Why don't you die and leave me alone?" Jim turns to leave, stating, "We have no more to talk about, Ann."

In another highlight, Jim bares his anger and frustration to his boss, and Barrymore once again plays it low key, reacting with gentle understanding. He realizes that Jim loves Ann more than the sky, and calls her candidly, telling her just how to handle the situation: "He'll squawk a lot, but you let him and just smile." And that is exactly what each is doing at the end of the film, when Ann brings their baby to the airfield where Jim is teaching young cadets. The scene with Barrymore shows Jim initially angry, but he softens as he listens to Barrymore's advice. He still has a bit of an attitude, but one can tell by his voice and expression and the tears in his eyes that he is sincere in his feelings for Ann.

Spencer Tracy is considered by many to be the actor's actor, and Gable was intimidated by his talent, even though they got along well as friends. Tracy joked to the press that he was going to milk his death scene for 30 minutes, while Gable during one rehearsal muttered, "God damn it, Spence, die already!"

Myrna Loy got on well with both actors. Playing a farm girl instead of a sophisticate, she is called upon to be witty and sarcastic, but also emotionally overwrought. She turns in one of her best performances, and it may be the best of her pairings with Gable. Their playful banter makes it believable that they fell in love over the course of one day, and the montage of them going to the ballgame, making fun of a cheesy romance movie, etc., attracts us to the characters. They demonstrate their stubbornness when Ann reveals that she is engaged to someone else; each is trying to get the other to admit their feelings first. They both continue to hide their true feelings from the other throughout the film; Jim won't admit how important Ann really is to him, and Ann won't admit to him how much his job scares her. This plagues her over time, as she goes from initially not thinking about the dangers of his job to constantly checking to make sure he's still alive.

Some books claim there is a gay subtext to the characters of Jim and Gunner. They are close friends who are there for each other. The intimacy of their relationship is alluded to, but not in a sexual nature—but then during the days of the Production Code, such a thing would not be possible. There are aspects of the nature of Gable and director Fleming that would lead one to conclude that neither would intentionally offer such a subtext. David Bret's book *Clark Gable: Tormented Star* stated[119]:

> Modern-day audiences might perceive ... that if, during their exploits, no suitable females could be found to alleviate the tension, each other's company would suffice. This was clearly the intention of gay screenwriter Waldemar Young, with whom Clark had a ferocious argument over ... dialog between him and Tracy that he wanted toned down. Even his love interest, Myrna Loy is one of the guys, who knows more about baseball than he does.

Such a reaction is completely a matter of perspective on the part of the viewer. Jim absolutely cares for Gunner as a friend, but Gunner's feelings for Jim go a bit deeper. We know that he takes care of Jim when he accompanies Jim on a drinking binge, and at one point he even exclaims that he loves him. At the same time, he never exhibits any jealousy toward Ann for her relationship with Jim, only concern. The three of them definitely have an interestingly close relationship, but it appears that Gunner's main purpose within the narrative is for his death to finally nudge Jim and Ann in the right direction.

The flight scenes, while sometimes using back projection effects, offer some good exciting footage. The second unit director in charge of the flying sequences was Paul Mantz, a top-drawer movie stunt pilot. The actual flying was done by actual test pilot Sammy Wroath.

Just prior to filming *Test Pilot*, Gable and Loy had been named the King and Queen of Hollywood. in a poll of over 20 million fans conducted by 55 newspapers. Tracy had just won an Oscar for *Captains Courageous*. This resulted in *Test Pilot* being one of the biggest box office hits of 1938. It was also nominated for three Oscars: Best Picture, Film Editing and Writing (Original Story). It won none of these. But it did receive critical acclaim, *Photoplay* stating[120]:

> The shrewd combination of rough, soft-eyed Spencer Tracy and rough, glint-eyed Clark Gable with a story of dangerous thrills, makes this one of the most entertaining pictures of the month. Aside from the superb work of Gable, Tracy's flair for sacrificial best friend parts, and Myrna Loy's incomparable wife portrait, the story alone demands your absorbed interest in every reel.... A rousing performance is presented by Barrymore; Gable could not be better cast. Tracy here is not a traitor to the Academy Award he got for *Captains Courageous*, but the part again leaves you feeling sorry for him. The shrieking whine of plane motors will hum in your ears for a long time, but don't miss this.

The *Modern Screen* reviewer raved about the film[121]:

> In a month full of mediocre films, Metro really startled Hollywood preview-goers with one of the year's fastest and most exciting screen dramas—one of those rare pictures which actually lives up to their advance notices. *Test Pilot* has everything: a swell story, a splendid cast, and powerful air stuff which furnishes some of the most breathtaking moments the screen has ever offered.... Gable and Tracy are excellent in their he-man roles, and Myrna Loy is at her charming best. In the supporting cast, Lionel Barrymore deserves praise, as do Tod Pearson, Marjorie Main, Gloria Holden and Louis Jean Heydt.

MGM wanted to continue to build off of Gable and Loy being named the King and Queen of Hollywood, believing they could better market a film featuring the two of them together after this poll attracted nationwide attention. While filming the heavily dramatic *Test Pilot*, Gable and Loy were assigned to a romantic comedy, *Too Hot to Handle*.

Too Hot to Handle

Director: Jack Conway
Screenplay: Lawrence Stallings, John Lee Mahin
Story: Lee Hammond

Producer: Lawrence Weingarten
Cinematographer: Harold Rosson
Editor: Frank Sullivan
Cast: Clark Gable, Myrna Loy, Walter Pidgeon, Walter Connolly, Leo Carrillo, Johnny Hines, Virginia Weidler, Betsy Ross Clarke, Henry Kolker, Marjorie Main, Gregory Gaye, Al Shean, Willie Fung, Lillie Mui, Patsy O'Connor, Josephine Whittell, Barbara Bedford, Luke Chan, John Hamilton, Richard Loo, Chris Pin-Martin, Ray Walker, King Baggot, Ray Cooke, Francis X. Bushman, Jr., Blue Washington, Harry Tyler, Martin Wilkins, George Webb, Monte Vandergrift, Ernest Wilson, Edward Peil Sr., Edwin Stanley, Don Roberts, Franklin Parker, Cyril Ring, Stanley Taylor, Morgan Roberts, Eddie Parker, Charles Sullivan, Jack Richardson, Buster Slaven, Lee Phelps, David Kerman, Roger Moore, Paul Kruger, Ken Nolan, Bud McTaggert, Paul King, Philo McCullough, George Lynn, Ted Oliver, Robert Emmett Keane, Chester Gan, James Flavin, Selmer Jackson, Frank Faylen, Eddie Dunn, Mahlon Hamilton, Natalie Garson, Mimi Doyle, Harry Fleischman, Hal Dawson, Steve Carruthers, Joseph Crehan, Lane Chandler
Released September 16, 1938
MGM
107 minutes

Too Hot to Handle was assigned to Gable and Myrna Loy while they were still working on *Test Pilot*. An earlier treatment of the story (originally called *Let 'Em All Talk*) was considered for Spencer Tracy and Margaret Sullavan. When it was reconsidered for Gable, the script was sent to Marion Davies, who enjoyed working with him. William Randolph Hearst didn't like the script so they passed. When Gable and Loy were named the King and Queen of Hollywood in a 1937 poll, they were chosen as co-stars for the project. There was some thought of Tracy being added to the cast in the role that eventually went to Walter Pidgeon.

Newsreel cameraman Chris Hunter (Gable) works for Gabby MacArthur (Walter Connolly) of the Union Newsreel company. He is stationed in China, trying to get war footage, but nothing is happening, so he tries to stage a scene with villagers and a toy model airplane. He is caught by his chief rival Bill Dennis (Walter Pidgeon), who decides to get even by faking his own scene. Gathering several other newsreel cameramen, Bill arranges for his aviatrix friend Alma Harding (Loy) to swoop in as if she is delivering important supplies and block Chris from filming it. Chris is sneakier than that, and manages to get the shot of Alma's arrival, but his driver gets balled up and causes Alma's plane to crash. Chris rescues her before discovering that it was a prank.

Too Hot to Handle opens by establishing all of the characters in roles and situations that are very familiar for the actors and for the viewer. Chris is sneaky and unscrupulous but in the ruggedly attractive manner that Gable played his characters. Bill Dennis (played by Pidgeon) is the rival who always wants to get the best of Chris but never quite measures up. There is an underlying admiration that both men have for each other. Alma isn't so much a conflict between the men—she clearly prefers

Chris—but despite her own independence and strength, she is still taken by the fast talking and manipulation.

It is interesting that the film deals with aviation, as did the previous Gable-Loy starrer *Test Pilot*. Loy's character Alma seems to be at least loosely based on Amelia Earhart (who went missing the year before), especially since the characters in this film end up going on an equally dangerous expedition.

Much of the film deals with Chris coming up with a series of schemes to attract Alma, including faking that he has destroyed the footage he has taken of her, and that he has been fired. Chris does destroy film in front of Bill, Alma and the other reporters, which impresses them all. But it is a trick; the actual reels are in the hands of his cameraman José Estanza (Leo Carrillo). He then phones his boss Gabby in front of Alma and acts as though he is being fired. Alma, of course, cannot hear the harried and confused Gabby on the other line insisting, "No, no, Chris, I'm not firing you!" She goes to America with Chris to insist he be allowed to keep his job and ends up on the payroll. She wants an expedition to find her brother, who has been missing in the Amazon and presumed dead. They agree but have no intention of doing any such thing. Meanwhile, Bill has gotten the actual footage of Alma's crash and releases it himself, while Chris is left with the actual decoy reels he destroyed.

The various ways in which the two rivals try to dupe each other, and how they understand each other's moves, provides a good portion of the comedy. Each of the men are attractive, sneaky, sly and amusing. Their fast-paced dialogue and various methods cause each to be wryly appealing. Gable and Pidgeon had worked together successfully in *Saratoga*, but that film was so marred by Jean Harlow's illness and death, we didn't get as much of a chance to see them play off of each other as they do in *Too Hot to Handle*. Walter Connolly, so delightful with Gable in *It Happened One Night*, gets to tap into his wonderful skills as a comic supporting actor. The stress and tension of maintaining a competitive newsreel company, dealing with his own rivalries and those among his workers, and also having an unhappy marriage that is coming to its end, are all weighing on him. Connolly plays Gabby in his usual manner: His short, chubby frame flails through his scenes with wonderful comic abandon.

When all of the deceit blows up in the faces of Chris and Bill, and Alma is implicated in the press, they try to make good by hocking their equipment and getting Jose to act like a South American plantation owner willing to finance Alma's Amazon trip. This fools Gabby. An expedition is set up, with Bill, Chris and Jose along. They are approached by a native from a voodoo tribe who produces a watch that belonged to Alma's brother. Bill and Alma travel to the area designated by the native on a floatplane, while Chris and Jose, who do not trust the native, travel with him by boat.

The film's perspective gets a bit more layered here in that it fluctuates between drama and farce. Chris and Jose try to kill the dangerous native, but he gets away. They find the voodoo tribe and see that Alma's brother is with them. The natives have been draining his blood for their rituals and he is now deathly ill. This serious portion of the narrative is augmented by farcical scenes where Chris and Jose use their film equipment to distract and frighten the natives. They project images of forest fires and waterfalls to show they can destroy the area and stop it at will. After being welcomed, things like a cigarette lighter and a hypodermic needle fascinate the natives. Their leader has the medicine man killed and wants Chris to take their place. Pure farce takes over as Chris and Jose don the customary masks and costumes to rule the area and, ultimately, rescue Alma's brother. When Alma and Bill arrive, Chris and Jose remain in charge, but also in costume so they are not recognized. They arrange for Alma to go to her brother unmolested and to take him away. Chris and Jose escape just as the native they thought they had killed returns to the tribe and reveals their identity.

In the 21st century, it is interesting to see a movie about newsreel cameramen and get a peek into that part of history. Gable's scenes where we see him struggling to fake shots for his films are very funny and said to have been staged by silent screen great Buster Keaton. Keaton was working at MGM, punching up some of the studio's comedy productions with his superior comic vision. Even something as simple as a pratfall would be demonstrated by Keaton, who knew how it would look best and hurt least. (Mickey Rooney's excited fall down the stairs in *A Family Affair* is a good example.) Keaton's visual sense was helpful in these scenes, and Gable responded well to the humor inherent in his character.

Too Hot to Handle has all of the elements that make a good, snappy comedy. The dialogue is funny, the lead male characters are appealing in their unscrupulousness, the female lead is strong and attractive, and the supporting cast is delightful. It can be argued that *Too Hot to Handle* is one of the best comedies in which Gable appeared. Unfortunately, audiences disagreed. While they made dramas like *Test Pilot* and *San Francisco* top box office hits, and *It Happened One Night* was still playing neighborhood theaters in successful second runs four years after its release, *Too Hot to Handle* was not a success. It is one of the very few Gable films that didn't generate a handsome profit. In fact, it actually fell about $30,000 short of making its costs back.

Part of the reason why *Too Hot to Handle* wasn't successful can probably be determined by these Letters to the Editor in the February 1939 issue of *Photoplay* magazine[122]:

I never thought I would be writing adverse criticism about Myrna Loy—but here goes! Years ago I wondered when the movie moguls would recognize the ability of lovely, girlish, unaffected Myrna. When she was finally starred I was amazed to see her cast as a sophisticated and rather blasé type. In grooming her for the parts, the studio must have given her an icy veneer. In *Too Hot to Handle*, Myrna wasn't even slightly lukewarm. In one sequence, she says, "How terrible" and shortly afterwards she says, "How wonderful." There was absolutely no change of voice. Her voice rang with insincerity and artificiality…. I'm sorry Myrna has fallen off her pedestal.
—Mrs. McBride Dabbs, Mayesville, South Carolina

I recently saw *Too Hot to Handle* and came away dazed and full of questions I wanted answered. In the first place, I dislike those sophisticated and smart-alecky names which has nothing to do with the content of the picture. Then it was like a four- or five-ringed circus with so much going on in so many quarters of the globe, and such a display of bombing in

Too Hot to Handle (1938)

Gable was a newsreel cameraman in *Too Hot to Handle* (1938) with Myrna Loy.

one hemisphere and native negro dances in the other, with so little continuity to link up the divergence that it left the beholder, at least this one, worried. Besides it seemed to me terribly poor taste to make a laughing matter out of such stark tragedy as the bombing of the poor Chinese...

—Mrs. Herbert Gardner, St. Petersburg, Florida.

The critics were no more impressed. Most agreed with the perspective of Frank Nugent of *The New York Times*: "*Too Hot to Handle* is any one of a dozen fairly entertaining melodramas you might have seen in the last five years. Gable plays Chris Hunter with his customary blend of bluster and blubber. Loy's lady-flier turns in a completely insincere performance." The *Modern Screen* reviewer was also unimpressed and shared the consensus that Loy was underwhelming, but he still figured audiences would like it[123]:

> *Too Hot to Handle* is the first feature-length glorification of the newsreel cameraman and, if some of the exploits of these gallant gentlemen seem slightly incredible, you can blame that condition on the fact that the movies are sometimes guilty of exaggeration for the sake of drama. Up to now no one knew the newsreel business harbored such glamorous characters as Myrna Loy, Clark Gable and Walter Pidgeon, but this trio of expert troupers will make most audiences feel that newsreel people take heroics as a matter of course, disaster and tragedy as part of a day's work. This reviewer doesn't feel that the picture comes up to the recent and somewhat similar *Test Pilot*, but it has action and melodrama and heroics galore, and the majority of people will like it. Gable and Pidgeon are ideally cast, Miss Loy is somewhat less sparkling than usual, and there are fine performances by Leo Carrillo and Walter Connolly in the supporting cast.

Sometimes films that were not terribly well-received in their own time play better at a later date. (Buster Keaton's masterpiece *The General* might be a good example.) When screened for this study, *Too Hot to Handle* came off as a delightful romantic comedy with elements of drama in the narrative and appealing characters; the ending where Alma jumps into the action while Chris is filming a violent shootout is a satisfying conclusion. Alma gets a scratch on her finger, Chris wipes some of the blood on her forehead, and starts filming her as a victim, smiling and winking at her as the picture fades.

Loy is essentially playing a colder and more aloof character as the independent-minded aviatrix. She isn't the farm girl of *Test Pilot* despite the planes and her co-star. She doesn't appear to have been given as much screen time or as compelling, emotional scenes in this film. There was a stretch during the conclusion with the natives where she isn't on screen. Despite being on the lookout for her missing brother, she doesn't have any scenes that are highly dramatic, or highly comedic, in the way that Gable's scenes are. Yet, it is still surprising that more audiences wouldn't flock to see this movie, seeing as how popular Gable and Loy were.

Too Hot to Handle was a fairly expensive production. Cinematographer Harold Rosson's brother, Richard Rosson, joined Clyde De Vinna to do some second until location shooting in Dutch Guiana. However, most of the scenes were shot in Sherwood Forest, California. Shooting ran from May to August 1938. During that time, there was a lot of publicity regarding MGM's acquisition of the rights to Margaret Mitchell's new novel of the South during the Civil War, *Gone with the Wind*. While a search was conducted for the right actress to play the story's lead female character, Scarlett O'Hara, the lead male character of Rhett Butler seemed just right for Gable. After the debacle of *Parnell*, Gable had absolutely no interest at all in doing another

Gable plays a cameraman who stages his own battle scenes in *Too Hot to Handle* (1938).

period piece, and the fact that George Cukor was likely to be the film's director was another problem. Cukor was known to be a "woman's director"; Gable felt that it was not the right project for him based on recent experience, and believed that Cukor would not direct him to his best level, as Cukor worked more comfortably with the ladies in the cast. While these negotiations continued, Gable was cast as the lead in the film version of Robert Sherwood's Pulitzer Prize–winning play *Idiot's Delight*. It is somewhat ironic that while he was balking at how wrongheaded he'd be for the Rhett Butler role, he starred in a film where he plays a song-and-dance man. It is the only movie where he sings and dances.

Idiot's Delight

Director: Clarence Brown
Screenplay: Robert Sherwood (from his play)
Producer: Clarence Brown, Hunt Stromberg
Cinematographer: William Daniels
Editor: Robert Kern
Cast: Clark Gable, Norma Shearer, Edward Arnold, Charles Coburn, Burgess Meredith, Joseph Schildkraut, Peter Willes, Pat Paterson, Laure Hope Crews, Skeets Gallagher, Fritz Feld, Virginia Grey, Virginia Dale, Paula Stone, Bernadene Hayes, Joan Marsh, Lorraine Kruger, Clem Bevans, Frank Faylen, Helen Dickson, William Irving, Frank Orth, Frank M. Thomas, Adolph Millar, Mitchell Lewis, Hobart Cavanaugh, Jimmy Conlin, Joe Yule, Charles Judels, Eddie Gribbon, Emory Parnell, Bernard Suss, Lee Phelps, Francis McDonald, Paul Panzer, Harry Strang, Garry Owen, Claire McDowell, Anna Demetrio, Edward LeSaint, Suzanne Kaaren, Evalyn Knapp, Margaret Bert, Barbara Bedford, Bud Geary, Jack Grey, Gertrude Bennett, Rudolph Myzet (voice only)
Released January 27, 1939
MGM
107 minutes

Robert Sherwood's anti-war play *Idiot's Delight* was a stage hit featuring Alfred Lunt and Lynn Fontanne. It won a Pulitzer Prize for confronting tensions brewing in Europe. Several studios were interested in the film rights, but realized that the Production Code would keep them from presenting a lot of the elements that made it so successful, including the calls for pacifism and the sexuality between the two leads. MGM felt that they could alter it so that it retained its impact and its integrity. They were wrong. *Idiot's Delight* was a generally pedestrian effort and a box office failure.

Gable plays Harry Van, a World War I veteran who returns home to find that his promising stage career is no longer relevant after being interrupted by the war. His agent puts an ad in the trades to announce he is once again available for shows, but all Harry can find is playing straight man to a baggy pants comic in a soft shoe routine, and doing a memory bit with a drunken woman as his partner. While performing in a seedy Omaha venue, he meets acrobat Irene (Norma Shearer), who admits to having been smitten with him for some time. They have a liaison and go their separate

Opposite: **Gable did a song and dance number in *Idiot's Delight* (1939) and came off well. The chorines are unidentified.**

Idiot's Delight (1938)

Gable and an affected Norma Shearer in *Idiot's Delight* (1939).

ways; something that is part of show biz on the road. Years later, Harry is in Europe traveling with a musical act called Les Blondes when their train is prevented from going into Geneva due to the imminent outbreak of war. Among the other stranded people is a Russian diplomat and his countess wife. Harry recognizes that the wife is Irene. She carries on without confirming her identity until the place is bombed at the end of the movie.

Sherwood's original play was set in Italy, so the people of that country were against a movie version. MGM changed its locale to an undisclosed area, where the people spoke Esperanto rather than Italian. Sherwood was hired by the studio to revamp his own play and make it acceptable for the screen. This is when they added the prologue of Harry returning from the war, trying to get back into stage work, etc. They opened up the romantic aspect of the film and played down the political content. Rather than have pacifism be central to the narrative, they assigned it to one unglued character, played by Burgess Meredith. His rants make the other characters feel unsettled, and eventually he is arrested.

It took a great deal of negotiating and rewriting before the play became a screenplay that was acceptable. And even though the script was approved all the way up to Mussolini, the movie was still banned in Italy.

Gable was assigned the lead way back when he was still working on *Test Pilot*. He had misgivings over the prospect of doing a song-and-dance routine, and of playing a role made famous on stage by Alfred Lunt. But he accepted, ready to do his best. Joan Crawford badly wanted to play Irene, but Norma Shearer had inherited late husband Irving Thalberg's MGM stock and had more say in her projects. Shearer liked the idea that she could play a more flamboyantly comic role. At first, she plays a vaude-villian acrobat with the sort of dramatic sincerity that the scenes call for. However, when she shows up as the Russian countess, Shearer gives the character an affected voice, florid gestures, and a manner that is humorously overbearing. She appears to be having a good time devouring the scenery every time she is on screen. Her performance is definitely over the top, likely intentionally so. The Garbo influence is very obvious.

Production began in late October 1938 and the film was ready for release in early 1939. Two endings were shot, one for American audiences and another for European moviegoers. The American version has Harry and Irene discussing future plans in an attempt to ignore the bombing. They talk about doing Harry's old memory act in vaudeville together. In the European version, Irene asks Harry to play the piano while they sing a hymn amidst the noisy bombing. When the bombing subsides, they hold each other with hope for the future of the world.

While moviegoers were dissatisfied with *Idiot's Delight*, critics were often quite accepting. The reviewer for *Hollywood* magazine stated[124]:

> Outstanding among the films of the month, and of the year, for that matter, is *Idiot's Delight*. It has a touch of everything that 1939 audiences want, is brilliantly produced and adapted from the stage play, and, in addition, has a performance which tops anything Clark Gable has done before. Besides being a great play, the picture has some of the most hilariously comic

scenes you'll see in a long while, and anyone who is your true friend will urge you to catch Clark Gable's dance routines, because they alone are worth the price of admission.

While *Idiot's Delight* is not a musical, Gable does play a song-and-dance man, so it was decided to give him a musical number to perform. Gable reportedly rehearsed diligently for his singing and dancing to the number "Putting on the Ritz," and managed to pull it off in one take. Since it ends with the backup dancers carrying him off stage, the number was shot last in case anyone got hurt! This is a fun scene and the highlight of the movie, partly because it's the only song-and-dance number Gable ever did in a film. Watching it, you can see that this definitely isn't in his skill set (he's rather stilted) but he isn't bad and he comes off as very ready and eager to tackle the number. Similar to *Parnell*, this isn't really a role that fits with the kind of characters he does best, and he probably wasn't the right choice for the part, but he turns in a great performance regardless. *Idiot's Delight* is interesting as a portrait of American attitudes about the war just before it really escalated, but outside of that, it's rather dated and tame—likely due to having to adapt the original material to conform to the Production Code.

Idiot's Delight remains a throwaway in the filmographies of Gable, Shearer and director Clarence Brown. Three of Gable's last four films had lost money, just after a poll resulted in his crowning as the King of Hollywood. However, *Test Pilot* was such a major hit, Gable's stardom was unaffected by the losses.

Gone with the Wind

Director: Victor Fleming[125]
Screenplay: Robert Sherwood (from his play)
Producer: David O. Selznick
Cinematographer: Ernest Haller (Technicolor)
Supervising Editor: Hal C. Kern
Cast: Clark Gable, Vivien Leigh, Leslie Howard, Olivia de Havilland, Hattie McDaniel, Thomas Mitchell, Evelyn Keyes, Ann Rutherford, Butterfly McQueen, Barbara O'Neil, George Reeves, Fred Crane, Oscar Polk, Victor Jory, Everett Brown, Howard Hickman, Alicia Rhett, Rand Brooks, Carroll Nye, Laura Hope Crews, Eddie (Rochester) Anderson, Harry Davenport, Leona Roberts, Jane Darwell, Ona Munson, Paul Hurst, Isabel Jewell, Cammie King, Eric Linden, J.M. Kerrigan, Ward Bond, Jackie Moran, Cliff Edwards, Lillian Kemble-Cooper, Yakima Canutt, Marcella Martin, Louis Jean Heydt, Mickey Kuhn, Olin Howland, Irving Bacon, Robert Elliott, William Bakewell, Mary Anderson, Roscoe Ates, Frank Coghlan Jr., Gino Corrado, Blue Washington, John Wray, Tom Tyler, Charles Middleton, Marjorie Reynolds, Jim Corey, James Bush, Dale Van Sickel, Dan White, Dolores Dean, Phillip Trent, Ernest Whitman, Emerson Treacy, Julie Ann Tuck, Zack Williams, Rita Waterhouse, William Stack, Lee Phelps, Terry Shero, Daisy Bufford, Eddy Chandler, Tom Siedel, Naomi Pharr, Ned Davenport, Spencer Quinn,

Scott Seaton, Adrian Morris, John Arledge, Azarene Rogers, Jeanette Noeson, Dawn Dodd, Lee Murray, Dorothy Barrett, Jane Barrett, Si Jenks, Margaret Mann, Tommy Kelly, Martina Cortina, George Meeker, Lola Milliorn, Richard Clucas, Alberto Morin, Ann Bupp, Jerry James, Timothy Lonergon, Alberto Morin, Barbara Lynn, Caren Marsh, Trevor Bardette, Edythe Elliot, Morgan Brown, Peaches Jackson, Chuck Hamilton, Frank Faylen, Kelly Griffin, Lucille Harding, Susan Falligant, Shep Houghton, Jean Heker, Geraldie Fissette, George Hackathorne, Richard Farnsworth, Billy Cook, John Drake, Luke Cosgrove, Yola d'Avril, Lester Dorr, Russell Custer, Kernan Cripps, Wallis Clark, Lennie Bluett, Louise Carter, Eric Alden
Released December 15, 1939[126]
MGM
238 minutes[127]

Gone with the Wind is one of the most significant productions in the history of cinema, maintaining a consistently compelling narrative for nearly four hours. The casting, acting, direction and design are all exceptional. There are some dated qualities, as well as some areas that have become unsettling over time. But in a book discussing Gable's screen work of the 1930s, it is the perfect culmination in that it remains the movie by which his entire screen career is defined.

Entire books have been written about the film, the hundreds of auditions for an actress to play Scarlett O'Hara, the process by which producer David O. Selznick gathered the cast and crew to recreate the novel on the screen, etc. This study will focus on Gable's contribution, which, of course, is significant.

Margaret Mitchell's novel *Gone with the Wind* was released in June 1936, and in July the film rights were acquired by Selznick. He wanted to make it as an independent production for his own studio, but eventually arranged for MGM to release the film so he could cast Gable in the Rhett Butler role. MGM would never have loaned out their top star otherwise. Gable, still smarting from the *Parnell* debacle, didn't want the role. But the public disagreed. Half the country was reading Mitchell's book, and they wrote to the studio stating that it would be ridiculous to cast anyone other than Gable as Rhett. Gable was flattered, but still had serious misgivings about the role in what he realized would be a "women's picture." Selznick hired George Cukor to direct, and Cukor was known for making connections with actresses, guiding them to some of their greatest performances.

Gable was finally convinced to take the role after MGM agreed to award a $50,000 settlement to his wife so she would agree to a divorce; this allowed him to marry Carole Lombard. He and Lombard had worked together in the movie *No Man of Her Own*, but it wasn't until 1936, when they happened to meet at a party, that their romance began.

In August 1938, a deal was worked out where MGM would provide Gable and pay $1,250,000 toward the film's budget in return for half the profits and the distribution rights. Selznick would pay Gable's weekly salary.

Gone with the Wind is set in the early 1860s, just as the Civil War is about to

Gable reads Margaret Mitchell's hit novel *Gone with the Wind*.

commence. The O'Hara family owns and lives at Tara, a Georgia cotton plantation. Scarlett O'Hara (Vivien Leigh) is in love with Ashley Wilkes (Leslie Howard), fiancé of Melanie Hamilton (Olivia de Havilland). The couple announces their plans at a barbecue, where Scarlett first meets Rhett Butler (Gable). They are interrupted by news that war has been declared against the North. The men all react with passion and are eager to enlist, including Melanie's younger brother Charles (Rand Brooks). Scarlett marries Charles before he goes off to war, chiefly to spark jealousy in Ashley. Charles is killed in the war. Scarlett, while still in mourning, stirs up controversy by dancing with Rhett, who works for the Confederacy. Rhett helps Scarlett and Melanie escape the burning city of Atlanta with Melanie's new baby.

When Rhett decides to join the war, Scarlett makes her way back to Tara, which has been pillaged by the Union Army. Her father (Thomas Mitchell) is exhibiting signs of senility, her mother (Barbara O'Neil) has died, and her sisters (Ann Rutherford, Evelyn Keyes) are ailing. The family is helped by two remaining slaves, Mammy (Hattie McDaniel) and Pork (Oscar Polk). Scarlett vows to return Tara to its former beauty.

In an attempt to pay the high taxes on her land, Scarlett basically steals an older, wealthy suitor, Frank (Carroll Nye), from one of her sisters and gets him to marry her so that he will help financially. Frank joins Rhett, Ashley and some others in a raid on a town, and Frank is killed. Shortly after his funeral, Rhett proposes to Scarlett. After Rhett and Scarlett have a child, Bonnie Blue Butler (Cammie King), Scarlett tells Rhett they will now sleep separately. She still longs for Ashley, who feels the same about her, but he refuses to leave Melanie, who is very kind and sweet and does not deserve to be hurt. Melanie even supports Scarlett when Ashley's sister India (Alicia Rhett) gossips about their attraction to each other. When Scarlett returns home, a drunken Rhett, angry about her feelings toward Ashley, forces Scarlett to have sex, carrying his wife up the stairs to their bedroom.

The next morning, a remorseful Rhett tells Scarlett he will agree to a divorce, but she refuses due to the scandal it would cause. Upon Rhett's return from a trip to London, he is told that Scarlett is pregnant. She falls down stairs and suffers a miscarriage. While she recovers, Bonnie Blue is killed when attempting to jump a fence with her pony. Melanie is gravely ill during a second pregnancy. Rhett and Scarlett visit her on her deathbed. After Melanie dies, Scarlett consoles Ashley, and Rhett decides to leave Atlanta forever. The series of heartbreaks have taken an enormous toll, even though he tries to remain stoic. Scarlett realizes it is Rhett she loves, not Ashley, and she pleads with him not to go. Rhett refuses, offering the now classic movie line, "Frankly my dear, I don't give a damn!" He walks off into the fog. Scarlett proclaims her optimism for the future as the movie ends.

Gone with the Wind features a number of outstanding scenes that are beautifully shot, crisply written, and brilliantly acted. This chapter will naturally focus on those featuring Gable.

The Rhett Butler character is introduced to us 20 minutes into the movie, after Scarlett and the characters that make up her family begin to develop. Scarlett is walking up steps with her friend Cathleen, and sees Rhett staring at them from the bottom of the staircase. Gable's ability to convey so much with a single expression is evident here, as he stares intently but with a relaxed pleasing look that is unsettling but not scary. Cathleen describes him to Scarlett (and to us):

> That's Rhett Butler, he's from Charleston. He has a most terrible reputation. He's had to spend most of his time at war because his folks in Charleston won't even speak to him. He was expelled from West Point, he's so fast, and then there's that business about that girl he wouldn't marry.

The viewer is as compelled by that description as Scarlett appears to be. Blushingly, she states, "He looks as if he knows what I look like without my shimmy!"

We learn even more about Rhett Butler when the men get together in a room to discuss the impending War Between the States. After listening to the unbridled passion exhibited by some of the men, Butler speaks up and is challenged by Melanie's brother Charles Hamilton (Rand Brooks):

> BUTLER: I think it's hard winning a war with words, gentlemen.
> HAMILTON: What do you mean, sir?

Gable and Vivien Leigh in *Gone with the Wind* (1939).

BUTLER: I mean, Mr. Hamilton, there's not a cannon factory in the whole South.

HAMILTON: Are you hinting, Mr. Butler, that the Yankees can lick us?

BUTLER: No, I'm not hinting. I'm saying very plainly that the Yankees are better equipped than we. They've got factories, shipyards, coal mines ... and a fleet to bottle up our harbors and starve us to death. All we've got is cotton, and slaves and ... arrogance.

HAMILTON: I refuse to listen to any renegade talk!

BUTLER: Well, I'm sorry if the truth offends you.

HAMILTON: Apologies aren't enough sir. I hear you were turned out of West Point, Mr. Rhett Butler. And that you aren't received in a decent family in Charleston. Not even your own.

BUTLER: I apologize again for all my shortcomings. Mr. Wilkes, Perhaps you won't mind if I walk about and look over your place. I seem to be spoiling everybody's brandy and cigars and ... dreams of victory.

[AFTER BUTLER LEAVES, CHARLES REMAINS ANGRY AND AGGRESSIVE.]

CHARLES: He refused to fight

ASHLEY: No, he just refused to take advantage of you. He's one of the best shots in the country ... He's got steadier hands and a cooler head than yours.

In real life, Rand Brooks was a rugged outdoorsman and didn't like playing such an effete character. When he attended the 50th anniversary reunion of the film, he told the press that he continued to wish he played more of a "macho man." Even the character's death after going off to war was far from heroic: pneumonia after contracting measles.

Gone with the Wind (1939) **was perhaps the most important film in the careers of Gable and Vivien Leigh.**

In Rhett's initial scenes, we see how the character can accommodate Gable's established screen persona quite comfortably. Rhett is aloof, beyond the mainstream parameters of Southern patriotism. He is knowledgeable and unflinching. He has nothing to prove. And he appears to get what he wants, hence his immediate interest in Scarlett.

In the next Rhett-Scarlett encounter, she bursts into a sitting room and throws a vase due to her frustration over her love of Ashley. Rhett rises from a couch where he was lying down and couldn't be seen. "Has the war started?" he asks sarcastically.

Rhett pursues Scarlett at a charity auction. Wearing mourning attire due to her husband Charles' death, Scarlett is not among those being auctioned, but Rhett boldly approaches the stage and loudly announces a high-stakes bid on "Mrs. Charles Hamilton." He is told she is not among those being auctioned. "Yes I am," she insists, and Rhett once again gets what he wants. After they merrily dance a Virginia Reel, they are alone when Rhett tells her: "Some day I want you to say to me the same words I heard you say to Ashley Wilkes: 'I love you.'" A bit later in the movie, his passion is more aggressive:

Open your eyes and look at me. No, I don't think I will kiss you. Although you need kissing badly. That's what's wrong with you. You should be kissed and often and by someone who knows how.

The way the director presents Rhett Butler stands out in some scenes, especially when he rides a horse up to Scarlett's carriage during a crowded street scene with people gathering to find out war casualties. With a lot of action in the background,

Rhett rides in wearing a white suit, Gable almost glowing as he stands out among the dull colors that fill the negative space around him.

This direction was likely the vision of Victor Fleming, who replaced George Cukor during filming. It is sometimes stated in other studies that Gable insisted that Cukor be replaced because he was more of a women's director. Producer Selznick's memos are readily available and there is nothing that suggests that Gable had anything to do with Cukor being replaced. Research indicates that Selznick was unhappy with Cukor's working slowly and providing footage that didn't please the producer. Margaret Mitchell stated:

> George finally told me all about it. He hated [leaving the production] very much, he said, but he could not do otherwise. In effect he said he is an honest craftsman and he cannot do a job unless he knows it is a good job and he feels the present job is not right. For days, he told me he has looked at the rushes and felt he was failing … the things did not click as it should. Gradually he became convinced that the script was the trouble … so George just told David he would not work any longer if the script was not better and he wanted the Sidney Howard script back … [H]e would not let his name go out over a lousy picture … and bull-headed David said "Okay, get out!"

Cukor continued to be contacted by Vivien Leigh and other women in the cast, asking for ideas how to convey this or that while playing their roles. Fleming was not a nurturing director and wanted Leigh to play Scarlett as bitchier and more negative. It was Cukor who guided her into exhibiting a sense of softness and sympathy to make the character more layered.

Naturally Gable had no misgivings about Fleming's direction, as Fleming was both a friend and a favorite filmmaker. Fleming stood back and let Gable play Rhett within the parameters of his screen persona.

While the Civil War is essentially the background, the main portion of the narrative is the romance between Rhett and Scarlett. Rhett does not succumb to her beauty like the other men, he instead recognizes that the two of them are alike. He says as much the first time he admits he is in love with her:

> There's one thing I do know … and that is that I love you, Scarlett. In spite of you and me and the whole silly world going to pieces around us, I love you. Because we're alike. Bad lots, both of us. Selfish and shrewd. But able to look things in the eyes as we call them by their right names.

However, their relationship continues to be complicated. Butler's aloofness and refusal to succumb to Scarlett's haughtiness usually results in her angrily storming off.

When Scarlett desperately needs money to pay Tara's back taxes, she goes to see Rhett, who is in a military jail. She throws herself at him and he responds at first, but when he touches her hands, he feels the roughness, indicating she has been working the fields. She admits her real purpose, and he tells her his money is tied up due to the war. Again she storms off.

Throughout her relationship with Rhett, Ashley Wilkes continues to be a

173

distraction for Scarlett. It continues after Melanie almost dies giving birth to Ashley's child. It is Scarlett who delivers the baby, the doctor too preoccupied with war casualties at a makeshift hospital where hundreds of men are dying. Prissy (Butterfly McQueen), a slave, insists she knows how to deliver a child and has done it often. However, when the time comes, Prissy delivers the memorable line, "I don't know nothin' 'bout birthin' babies!" Scarlett slaps her hard. McQueen recalled in a 1986 interview[128]: "I hated it. The part of Prissy was so backward. I was always whining and complaining. But now I'm very glad I made the film because I make a living off it. I didn't mind being funny, but I didn't like being stupid."

McQueen's career included movies, TV and Broadway. In later years, she made her peace with the film and enjoyed appearing at *Gone with the Wind* events, signing autographs and telling stories to fans.

Rhett maintains a friendship with high-end prostitute Belle Watling (Ona Munson), with whom, it is implied, he has had more than one fling in the past. Belle is a happy presence in Rhett's life, while Scarlett's reaction to Belle indicates she is quite aware of who she is and what she has been. Mammy reacts to Belle's bright red hair, stating, "I ain't never seen hair that color in all my life!" At the end of the scene where Scarlett visits Rhett in jail, as she is angrily leaving, Belle is conveniently arriving. The look Vivien Leigh projects toward Ona Munson, and Munson's response, all non-verbal and only seconds long, is one of the film's many perfect reactive moments.

By far the most challenging scenes that Gable encountered playing Rhett was when he had to cry after the death of Bonnie Blue. On her 100th birthday, Olivia de Havilland recalled in an interview[129]:

> I remember talking to Clark about the scene when he is supposed to cry…. He was worried. You see, he had never cried on the screen before. He thought it was not masculine to cry. He was so worried about it. "I'm just going to have to quit," he told me. I remember I said, "Tears denote strength of character, not weakness. Crying makes you intensely human." He agreed, rehearsed it and it turned out to be one of the most memorable scenes in the movie.[130]

This scene is also one of the reasons why Gable fans single out Rhett as his finest performance. The role has more depth and was far more challenging than the Gable norm, and the actor played it magnificently.

In the final scene, Scarlett realizes it is Rhett she loves, but he has finally had enough of all he's endured. The scene has become movie legend. The line "Frankly my dear, I don't give a damn!" is one of the truly iconic pieces of dialogue in motion picture history. Some believe it is the first time the curse word "damn" is used in a movie (it had been used before in films, even on title cards in some silents). But it culminates the Rhett Butler character, and his relationship with Scarlett, so perfectly it neatly caps the movie before she delivers the final dialogue.

Just as that line culminates the film, *Gone with the Wind* perfectly culminated Clark Gable's films of the 1930s. His career development as examined in this text, from his talkie debut in *The Painted Desert*, is fascinating in the way it evolves from working actor, to successful actor, to movie star, to superstar. *Gone with the Wind*

Gable didn't think he would be able to cry on camera in *Gone with the Wind* (1939) for the scene when his little girl (Cammie King) dies.

was such of an impactful film, Gable became an icon in his own time. In later years, he claimed that whenever his career slowed down, MGM re-released *Gone with the Wind* and suddenly he was in demand again.

Gable's stardom extended beyond the parameters of his acting work. He also stood up for his fellow actors. When he first arrived on the set, he discovered that there were separate bathrooms marked "Whites" and "Colored." He told the MGM brass that he would not work until those signs were removed and it was understood that any bathroom could be used by anyone regardless of their racial heritage.

This is especially significant in that African American rights organizations of the era were unhappy about Margaret Mitchell's book being filmed by MGM. They believed its message about longing for the old ways of the South, including slavery, and presenting slaves as content and satisfied with their status, impeded the advancement of the black race. In the 21st century, many have dismissed the film as racist and, thus, archaic. Even in its time, Hattie McDaniel railed against the organizations that took issue with her working on the film, stating she would rather play a maid for $700 per week than *be* a maid for $7 per week.

Perhaps the argument can be made that the movie is really about the romance of Rhett and Scarlett, and it just happens to be set during the Civil War. And while Prissy is an addle-brained character, Mammy is a leader who bosses around the people for whom she works while exhibiting respect and fierce loyalty. She exhibits qualities of leadership despite her place during the context of the Civil War era. Of the other black actors, Oscar Polk's character shows wisdom and insight, and Everett Brown, as Big Sam, has a scene where he heroically rescues Scarlett. This augments the subservience that is authentic to the Civil War era depicted, but in our more enlightened times, it can still prompt real discussion about how things once were, how they have since improved, and how there's still room for improvement.

Hattie McDaniel became the first black actor to win an Academy Award when she won for *Gone with the Wind*, but she was not allowed to sit at the main table with the movie's other actors; she was seated separately with her escort. Her win was an important benchmark for later actors who could extend beyond stereotyping.

Gable had been fond of McDaniel for years, and really bonded with her as a friend on the set of *Saratoga* where both mourned the death of Jean Harlow. He was among the few white actors who always attended Hattie's Hollywood parties.

However, when it was announced that *Gone with the Wind* was to hold its premiere in Atlanta, which was in the segregated South, it was determined that Hattie, and the other black actors, would not be allowed to attend. Gable was furious, and refused to make the trip. MGM used all manner of discussion, concession, even threats to get him to attend, but Gable stood firm. He stated he would boycott the event unless every African-American member of the cast was allowed to attend if they chose to do so. Hattie McDaniel was the one to talk Gable into attending. She conveyed to him how negative publicity from the movie's leading man could hurt the picture and, therefore, hurt everyone in it. Gable attended the premiere.

Gable and McDaniel were among those who traded practical jokes on the set. Hattie would tell set visitors, within Gable's earshot, that she was his leading lady in the movie. Clark substituted actual gin for water when Hattie took a drink in a scene. Olivia de Havilland got involved as well[131]:

> [T]here is a scene where Melanie is in bed, with a child beside her. Atlanta is in flames, and Rhett is supposed to pick up Melanie and the baby, both wrapped in a comforter, and then bring them down to a carriage. I played some mischief at that time. I had seen a block of cement outside with a steel ring in it. So, I got one of the staff to bring it up to my bedroom, then tied a rope around the ring and wrapped the rope around myself. So when Clark tried to lift me, with the baby, he expected it to be an easy task. Clark ran up to me and tried to lift me and oh, I had such a hearty laugh. Then I explained what I did and he forgave me and we completed the scene!

Gone with the Wind (1939)

Gone with the Wind was a grueling shoot, and jokes like this lightened the atmosphere. The producer and the director let it go.

Beyond Clark Gable, even beyond the acting of anyone in the movie, *Gone with the Wind* is an example of truly brilliant filmmaking. Externals like the costumes and set design, the fires and explosions, the succession of shots, action within the frame, and striking use of Technicolor are all important ingredients that help to make this film an iconic production. When one realizes the limitations of filmmaking technology in 1939, it is even more impressive. Computer graphic effects were certainly not in play when showing the burning of Atlanta or the explosions indicating the approach of Northern soldiers. And the long shot of Scarlett walking through rows and rows of dead and wounded soldiers is a magnificent example of what the French call *mise en scène*, referring to the placing of objects within the frame.

The music also plays a big part in the film's aesthetic success. Composer Max Steiner was only given only three months to compose the score, during a year when he composed music for a dozen different movies. Steiner worked 20-hour shifts to compose three hours of music—the longest film score up to that time.

As far as financial success is concerned, *Gone with the Wind* is the top-grossing movie of all time if the money is adjusted for inflation.

Gone with the Wind won Best Picture at the Academy Awards, and, along with Hattie McDaniel, Vivien Leigh took home an acting award (for Best Actress). Leigh was on screen for two hours, 23 minutes and 32 seconds, making her performance the longest in running time to win a Best Actress Oscar.

Victor Fleming won an Oscar for Best Director. Oscars also were won for Best Cinematography, Best Production Design and Best Film Editing. Gable, though nominated, did not win an Oscar for Best Actor. That was won by Robert Donat for his work in *Goodbye Mr. Chips*. Sidney Howard, who won an Oscar for Best Screenplay, was killed in a car accident in August 1939 while *Gone with the Wind* was in production.

Gable did his best work during the 1930s. And while he continued to make good movies right to the end of his life, his work during this decade clearly shows his development, impact, rise to stardom and ability to deal with his success. Films like *Dance, Fools, Dance, It Happened One Night, Men in White, Mutiny on the Bounty, San Francisco, Test Pilot* and *Gone with the Wind* continue to be the very best representations of his screen career.

3

After the 1930s

As the 1940s began, Clark Gable was truly on top of the world with both his life and career. He managed to obtain a divorce in 1939 and married Carole Lombard. And he had just completed a brilliant decade of film, concluding with one of the most iconic movies in American cinema history.

Gable and Lombard

Gable and Lombard were a perfect match. Their relationship, and marriage, has long been described as one where the personalities, even their differences, meshed.

Gable and Carole Lombard had a truly happy marriage that ended with tragedy.

It had the potential to be one of Hollywood's few truly happy and lasting marriages.

Gable and Lombard had co-starred in the film *No Man of Her Own* (1932). There were no sparks then, each of them married to other people (Lombard was married to actor William Powell). It wasn't until 1936 when the two met at a party that they connected on a friendly, and then romantic, level. Lombard was no longer married to Powell, but Gable was still married to his second wife, Maria Langham. Lombard and Gable's affair was not a secret in Hollywood. She started visiting him on sets, she accompanied him to Jean Harlow's funeral, and she even helped him rehearse his *Idiot's Delight* dance number.

Gable and Lombard were married on March 29, 1939, once Gable's divorce became finalized, and he had a break from filming *Gone with the Wind*. They bought a well-stocked ranch in Encino, California, as Carole was an outdoors type like Clark, accompanying him on the hikes, hunting trips, fishing expeditions and camping trips he so enjoyed. They didn't take anything too seriously, they laughed and teased and joked, and when they weren't together, they delighted in sending each other gag gifts through the mail.

Gable followed *Gone with the Wind* by starring in three features during 1940. *Strange Cargo* reunited him with Joan Crawford (their last movie together). *Boom Town* reunited him with Claudette Colbert and Spencer Tracy, in his last movie featuring either of them. And Gable was a reporter again in *Comrade X*, in which he tries to help beautiful Communist Hedy Lamar leave Moscow. All were hits. Gable continued with such '40s films as *Honky Tonk* with newcomer Lana Turner, *They Met in Bombay* with his friend Rosalind Russell, and *Somewhere I'll Find You* with Turner again. While he was filming the latter, his life was shattered beyond repair: Lombard was killed in a plane crash while on a War Bond tour. Gable immediately flew to the crash site in Nevada and insisted on seeing the wreckage. Guides took him to the dangerous mountainous area, but he was stopped before he got as far as the remains of Carole and the other passengers, including her mother. A hairclip that Gable had given Lombard was found in the wreckage. There were strands of Carole's blonde hair attached to it.

Gable could not return to the ranch. He stayed with friends until after Lombard's funeral. Back at the ranch, his secretary gave him a letter from Carole that had been sent just before she left on her flight. It had not arrived until after her death. His staff reported that Gable's sobs loudly echoed through the house well into the night. Joan Crawford recalled: "Clark was a walking corpse. He had every right to drink during that terrible ordeal, but he kept hitting the bottle. He was in another world and never came back to us."[132]

Gable returned to the set of *Somewhere I'll Find You* a little over a month after Lombard's death, ready to finish the picture. Louis B. Mayer instructed everyone to act as if nothing happened: not tiptoe around Clark, just go about business as usual so as not to upset him. It was a request they could not fulfill. As soon as Gable reported to the set, the cast and crew all stood up and applauded, tears flowing from all of them.

Gable in the Military

Gable was vengeful about his wife's death. Upon completing his work on *Somewhere I'll Find You*, which was another box office hit, he decided to join the Army Air Force. The press reported that he took his military physical in June 1942[133]:

> Mr. Gable, it was learned from a source outside the war department, conferred with Lieutenant General H.H. Arnold, head of the air forces, yesterday. It was understood that Mr. Gable, if he is commissioned, will make movies for the air forces. Lieutenant Jimmy Stewart, another actor in uniform, has been doing this.

Gable enlisted in August 1942 and attended bomber training school in Miami, completing his training in October.

Gable's first military assignment was to make a recruiting film in combat with the Eighth Air Force to recruit aerial gunners. Gable then went to Flexible Gunnery school and took a photography course at Fort George Wright in Washington State. He was promoted to first lieutenant.

On January 27, 1943, Gable reported for training with the 351st Bomb Group

Gable left his movie career, joined the war effort and flew combat missions.

at the Biggs Army Airfield in Texas. He was put in charge of a half dozen men in a movie unit. Gable was promoted to captain because he was unit commander of the outfit.

Gable also saw action during the war, flying five combat missions between May and September 1943. He earned the Air Medal, the Distinguished Flying Cross. On one mission, the aircraft was attacked and one man was killed. This sort of danger upset MGM, and they asked the military to re-assign him to non-combat duty. Gable returned to the States in November 1943 and edited his film footage.

After being promoted to major in 1944, Gable discovered that he was too old to fly any more combat missions, and was disappointed to not be allowed to engage during the attack on Normandy. He requested, and received, a release from active duty in June 1944.

Oddly, none other than Adolf Hitler was a fan of Gable's work. It is rumored that Hitler offered a reward to anyone who could deliver Gable to him unscathed.

Gable's Postwar Comeback

"Gable's back and Garson's got him!" That was the ad line for *Adventure* (1945), Gable's first movie in three years. His co-star was Greer Garson, who had scored mightily in *Mrs. Miniver* (1942), *Random Harvest* (1942), *Madame Curie*

Greer Garson, Thomas Mitchell and Gable in *Adventure* (1945), his comeback film after the war.

(1943), *Mrs. Parkington* (1944) and *The Valley of Decision* (1945). While *Adventure* was a box office hit, the story about a rugged pilot falling for a prim librarian didn't make for a very good movie, even with Joan Blondell and Thomas Mitchell in support.

It was another two years before Gable was in another movie. This time it was *The Hucksters*; a much better film than *Adventure* had been. Gable plays a World War II veteran who returns to the advertising world, only to find it riddled with corruption. He valiantly attempts to maintain success while not losing his integrity.

Gable returned to appearing in movies regularly. He acted in some good films, and remained among the top box office stars, but he was no longer the King of Hollywood. His absence for military duty disrupted his career's momentum. And the death of Carole Lombard impacted him so heavily, he no longer had the sharp edge that permeated his early performances.

Gable was reunited with Lana Turner for *Homecoming*. Some critics called it the worst movie of 1948, but star power made it a hit. Conversely, his military drama *Command Decision* made several Ten Best lists and was a big box office hit, but its production costs were so high, MGM lost money. Gable closed out the 1940s with the gambling drama *Any Number Can Play*, another financial winner. In 1949, he married Sylvia Ashley. The union lasted until 1952.

Gable During the 1950s

While it was hardly his best decade for movies, Gable did have some highlights in his continuing film career during the 1950s. He was no longer the star he had once been, but he was more than just another older actor who still made films. And he remained busy, appearing in an average of two movies per year throughout the decade. *Key to the City* (1950) reunited him with Loretta Young. The race car drama *To Please a Lady* (1950) paired him with Barbara Stanwyck. Real-life race car driver Mario Andretti called it his favorite movie, but money-wise it was a flop.

Gable was ill during the filming of *Across the Wide Missouri* (1951) and unhappy with his performance and his appearance. It was Gable's second color film, after *Gone with the Wind*. *Lone Star* (1952) was noteworthy as the final film appearance of Lionel Barrymore, who was instrumental in Gable coming to Hollywood. *Never Let Me Go* (1953) had Gable as a reporter once again. Gable's other 1953 release, director John Ford's *Mogambo*, was an intriguing remake of *Red Dust*, with Ava Gardner in the Jean Harlow role.

Betrayed (1954) reunited Gable with Lana Turner for the last time. It was the actor's final movie for MGM. He had been under contract there since the early '30s, but his high salary was no longer justified by the box office receipts of his films. Gable was okay with this situation, because filmmaking had changed to where actors could arrange for independent deals that included profit percentages. *Betrayed* tanked at the box office but Gable remained among the top stars of 1954 because *Gone with the*

Gable teamed with Doris Day in the 1958 comedy *Teacher's Pet*.

Wind was re-released to theaters in commemoration of its 15th anniversary. The following year, 1955, Gable married Kay Williams.

Gable's first film as a freelance actor was *Soldier of Fortune* (1955), shot in Hong Kong and released by 20th Century–Fox. Gable was too old for his part in *The Tall Men* (1955), and was doubled in most of the long shots. He created his own production company to produce *The King and Four Queens* (1956), but the stress of such an undertaking was too much for him and he never produced another movie.

In *Band of Angels*, a two-hour saga set in the South during the Civil War, a privileged Southern belle is purchased as property by a wealthy land owner. Critics snarkily labeled the film *Ghost of Gone with the Wind* and it failed miserably.

Gable was again too old for his character in 1958's *Run Silent Run Deep*, in which he co-starred with Burt Lancaster. Don Rickles made his movie debut in this World War II submarine drama, and he amusingly looked back at how Lancaster was very serious about the role, wanting to know the tiniest details, while Gable was more light-hearted. It wasn't an easy shoot for Gable, whose chronic alcoholism and four-pack-a-day smoking habit were catching up to him.

Teacher's Pet (1958) might be Gable's most enjoyable movie of the 1950s. He was cast as an old-school newspaper editor who believes thast learning on the job is superior than learning in a journalism classroom. Doris Day plays a journalism professor whom the much older Gable is struggling to attract, despite their differences.

Gable closed out the 1950s with the drama *But Not for Me*, in which he played a character closer to his own age. Based on the play *Accent on Youth* by Samson Raphaelson, it did well at the box office. Gable was now one of the veteran iconic actors who could still draw moviegoers, but his age, and his health, were making acting more difficult.

The Misfits

Gable filmed his last movies in 1960. Only the first, *It Started in Naples*, was released during his lifetime. He didn't get along well with his much younger co-star, Sophia Loren, and the film was a flop. Gable ended his career with director John Huston's *The Misfits*, from a screenplay by Arthur Miller. It also featured Marilyn Monroe (it was also her last movie), Montgomery Clift, Eli Wallach and Thelma Ritter. Gable was quite good as an aging cowboy, and it was probably the first time he could really use his age and his weathered appearance to benefit the character. Throughout *The Misfits*, he creates a character who has lived, who has been through a lot, and whose choices in life have affected him physically and emotionally. This connects well to Clark Gable's real life.

Production on *The Misfits* was very difficult. The actors dealt with heat that closed in on 110 degrees. Despite his age and health problems, Gable insisted on doing his own stunts. Miller continually revised his script. He was married at the time to Monroe, but the marriage was failing, causing emotional stress for the actress. She engaged in substance abuse during the shoot, and was very erratic, showing up late to the set or not coming in at all. Huston sent her to detox and when she returned, her closeups were shot with a softer focus lens.

Monroe was pleased to be working with Gable, who had been her childhood

Montgomery Clift, Marilyn Monroe and Gable in *The Misfits* (1961), the final film for both Marilyn and Clark.

idol. When she was a kid, Marilyn used to claim that Gable was her father. However, her life was unraveling throughout filming. Despite this, her performance is very good. She claimed to hate both the movie and her performance, but there are some who believe it to be among her best work.

Shooting on *The Misfits* was completed on November 4, 1960. Two days later, Gable suffered a heart attack. He died ten days later, November 16, 1960. He was 59 years old. *The Misfits* was released on February 1, 1961, which would have been his 60th birthday. On March 20, 1961, his only son was born at the same hospital where Gable died. John Clark Gable has had two children, Clark Gable's grandchildren: Kayley (born 1986) and Clark James (1988–2019).

Many insisted the grueling shooting of *The Misfits* led to Gable's death. His widow Kay told Louella Parsons, "It wasn't the physical exertion that killed him. It was the horrible tension, the eternal waiting, waiting, waiting. He waited around forever, for everybody. He'd get so angry that he'd just go ahead and do anything to keep occupied."[134] Gable, however, considered his performance in *The Misfits* to be his finest work, based on the rushes he saw each day.

The Misfits is a good culmination of Gable's screen career, despite the effect it took on him. After several ups and downs since concluding the 1930s with the film by which his career remains defined, Gable ended his career by embracing his age and his myriad of infirmities and presenting himself as a man who had seen it all, done it all, and still had the ability to do more.

Notes

1. Adela St. Johns, *Love, Laughter and Tears* (New York: Doubleday, 1978).

2. "Clark Gable Refuses to Concede Devotion to Stage or Obligation for Its Influence on His Career," *Oakland Times*, June 3, 1934.

3. Adwal Jones, "News Hound Role Not Foreign to Experience of Gable in Chicago." *San Francisco Examiner*, July 10, 1927.

4. Alma Whittaker, "Murder Role Career Climax," *The Los Angeles Times*, June 8, 1930.

5. "Clark Gable Refuses to Concede Devotion to Stage or Obligation for Its Influence on His Career," *Oakland Times*, June 3, 1934.

6. "14-Month-Old Movie Star Dies in Desert Camp," *The Press Democrat* (Santa Rosa, CA), September 12, 1930.

7. "The Screen in Review," *Picture Play Magazine*, June 1931.

8. "The Easiest Way," *New York Daily News*, February 28, 1931.

9. This is not the William Holden who appeared in films like *Stalag 17* and *Network*. That William Holden is no relation and didn't debut in movies until 1939.

10. "Dance Fools Dance," *Brooklyn Times Union*, March 23, 1931.

11. Joan Crawford, *My Way of Life* (New York: Simon and Schuster, 1971).

12. Henry Daughtery, "The Finger Points," *Honolulu Star Bulletin*, October 5, 1931.

13. Irene Thirer, "The Finger Points," *The New York Daily News*, March 27, 1931.

14. Gladys Hall, "Jean and Clark Expose Each Other," *Movie Classic*, May 1936.

15. "Men I Have Loved," *New Movie Magazine*, January 1934.

16. "The Secret Six," *New Movie Magazine*, July 1931.

17. Lyn Tornabene, *Long Live the King* (New York: Dutton, 1976).

18. "A Free Soul," *Photoplay*, July 1931.

19. "'Night Nurse' in Production," *Film Daily*, December 29, 1930.

20. "Directory of Pictures," *Modern Screen*, December 1931.

21. Jane Ellen Wayne, *Stanwyck* (New York: Arbor House, 1983).

22. Jane Ellen Wayne, *Stanwyck* (New York: Arbor House, 1983).

23. Frank Thompson and John Gallagher, *Nothing Sacred: The Cinema of William Wellman* (Asheville, NC: Men with Wings Press, 2018).

24. "Sporting Blood," *San Francisco Examiner*, August 10, 1931.

25. Louella Parsons, "Clark Gable Is Garbo's New Leading Man," *The Los Angeles Times*, May 6, 1931.

26. Louella Parsons, "Movie-go-round," *The Los Angeles Times*, May 10, 1931.

27. Boyd Martin, "Piping the Plays," *Courier Journal* (Louisville, KY), October 17, 1931.

28. Karl Krug, "Show Shops," *Pittsburgh Press*, October 24, 1931.

29. Irene Thirer, "Susan Lenox (Her Fall and Rise) Review," *NY Daily News*, October 25, 1931.

30. Beery actually received one vote less than Fredric March, but back then, if you were within two votes, it was considered a tie.

31. Irene Thirer, "Hell Divers," *New York Daily News*, December 24, 1931.

32. Ben Shylen, "Hell Divers," *Motion Picture Times*, December 29, 1931.

33. "Possessed," *San Francisco Examiner*, November 22, 1931.

34. Some sources claim $850 per week, up from $350, but others claim $2000 per week.

35. John McNulty, "Town Talkies," *The Pittsburgh Press*, March 12, 1932.

36. "Polly of the Circus," *New York Daily News*, March 19, 1932.

37. Patricia Keats, "Clark Gable in Strange Interlude," *Silver Screen*, May 1932.

38. "Strange Interlude," *New York Times*," September 1, 1932.

39. "Strange Interlude," *New York Daily News*, September 3, 1932.

40. "What the Picture Did for Me," *Motion Picture Herald*.

41. "Harlow Sympathetic," *The Los Angeles Times*, July 20, 1932.

42. "Jungle Rubber Plays a Part in 'Red Dust,'" *Times Union* (Brooklyn, NY), October 2, 1932.

43. Robbin Coons, "What Now for Jean Harlow?" *Los Angeles Times*, September 10, 1932.

44. "What the Picture Did for Me," *Motion Picture Herald*, February 1933.

45. Hubbard Keavy, "Refilming 'White Sister' with a Bit of Difference," *Indianapolis Star*, October 9, 1932.

46. Edward Schallert, "Work to Mark Yule Season," *Los Angeles Times*, December 15, 1932.

47. "The White Sister," *Variety*, April 8, 1933.

48. "What the Picture Did for Me," *Motion Picture Herald*, May 1933.

49. Fay M. Jackson, "Dainty Theresa in Gang Film," *The Afro American*, August 28, 1937.

50. "Hold Your Man," *The Los Angeles Times*, July 21, 1933.

51. Louella Parsons, "Night Flight Slated," *Courier-Post*, February 24, 1933.

52. Gwenda Young, *Clarence Brown* (Lexington: University Press of Kentucky, 2018).

53. "Night Flight," *Brooklyn Daily Eagle*, October 10, 1933.

54. Edward Schallert (syndicated column). *Los Angeles Times*, February 18, 1933.

55. "Stars Line Up for New Roles," *The Los Angeles Times*, August 16, 1933.

56. *Transcontinental Bus* was released as *Fugitive Lovers*.

57. "Gable Bus Traveler," *The Los Angeles Times*, October 23, 1933.

58. Frank Capra, *The Name Above the Title* (New York: Macmillan, 1971).

59. Lenore Tobias, "It Happened One Night," *Photoplay*, July 1934.

60. "What the Picture Did for Me," *Motion Picture Herald*, July 1934.

61. Merv Griffin, *From Where I Sit* (New York: Arbor House, 1982).

62. "Clark Gable, Myrna Loy to Be in 'Men in White,'" *The Tampa Tribune*, January 7, 1934.

63. "'Men in White' to be Made into Film with Clark Gable," *Star Tribune*, January 27, 1934.

64. "Clark Gable Refuses to Concede Devotion to Stage or Obligation for Its Influence on His Career," *Oakland Times*, June 3, 1934.

65. "Men in White," *Photoplay*, April 1934.

66. "Clark Gable Will Have More Dramatic Role in New Film," *The Sacramento Bee*, March 1, 1934.

67. Interview with the author—August 2001.

68. Jimmy Butler and Donald Haines were, in fact, killed in the war two days apart—Butler in France on February 18, 1945, and Haines in North Africa on February 20, 1945. Director W.S.

"Woody" Van Dyke committed suicide on February 5, 1943.

69. "Watching Them Make Pictures," *New York Daily News*, March 27, 1934.

70. "New Art Described by Powell," *Star Tribune*, April 5, 1934.

71. "Clark Gable Refuses to Concede Devotion to Stage or Obligation for Its Influence on His Career," *Oakland Times*, June 3, 1934.

72. "Manhattan Melodrama," *Hollywood Reporter*, April 16, 1934.

73. "Clark Gable Model, Patch Pockets, Belt 'N' Etc., Hit Town," *New York Daily News*, July 31, 1934.

74. "On the Set," *Evening Star* (Washington, D.C.), August 5, 1934.

75. Interview with the author, August 2001.

76. Louella Parsons, "Joan Crawford and Gable Will Be Teamed Again," *The San Francisco Examiner*, May 2, 1934.

77. Margaret Landarzuri, *Chained*, TCM.com database.

78. "Chained," *Movie Classic*, October 1934.

79. "Claudette Colbert Sought for Lead," *Courier-Post*, April 13, 1934.

80. "Loretta Young Will Be Starred in 'Forsaking All Others,'" *Morning Post*, May 23, 1934.

81. Louella Parsons, "Forsaking All Others," *Los Angeles Examiner*, January 25, 1935.

82. Joan Crawford, "Hollywood Gossip," *NEA Service*, November 1934.

83. Sidney Skolsky, "Hollywood," *New York Daily News*, October 2, 1934.

84. "What the Picture Did for Me," *Motion Picture Herald*, April 1934.

85. Interview by John Gallagher on July 10, 1977 for a book on Tay Garnett.

86. Rosalind Russell, with Chris Chase, *Life Is a Banquet* (New York: Random House, 1977).

87. "China Seas," *Variety*, August 31, 1935.

88. Louella Parsons, "'Call of the Wild' Will Star Gable," *Los Angeles Times*, November 4, 1934.

89. "Movie Cast Snowbound Filming 'Call of Wild,'" *Courier-Post*, January 18, 1935.

90. Loretta Young interview with John Andrew Gallagher, January 7, 1978, American Film Institute.

91. Jack Oakie, *Jack Oakie's Double Takes* (San Francisco: Strawberry Hill Press, 1980).

92. "Sidney Skolsky's Hollywood," *New York Daily News*, January 8, 1935.

93. "Get Close Up of Film Hero," *Spokane Chronicle*, February 7, 1935.

94. Frank Thompson and John Gallagher, *Nothing Sacred: The Cinema of William Wellman* (Asheville, NC: Men with Wings Press, 2018).

95. Louella Parsons, "Beery Gives Up Role of Skipper of Bounty," *Los Angeles Times*, January 4, 1935.

96. "Real South Seas in 'Mutiny' Film," *New York Daily News*, January 13, 1935.

97. A man is tied to a rope, thrown overboard, and dragged in the water from ship to stern before being brought up. Usually the man died, as he does in the film.

98. "Unusual Weather Delaying Stars in 'Mutiny on Bounty,'" *Indianapolis Star*, June 12, 1935.

99. "Mutiny on the Bounty" (review), *Hollywood*, January 1936.

100. "Mutiny on the Bounty" (review), *Motion Picture Herald*, November 9, 1935.

101. "What the Picture Did for Me," *Motion Picture Herald*, February 1936.

102. Gwenda Young, *Clarence Brown* (Lexington: University Press of Kentucky, 2018).

103. "Hollywood Sights and Sounds," *Los Angeles Times*, January 1, 1936.

104. Paul Harrison, "Hollywood Correspondent," *NEA Service*, January 2, 1936.

105. Myrna Loy, *Being and Becoming* (New York: Knopf, 1987).

106. William Ulman, "Clark Gable Warns Stenos What Happens When Husbands Get Caught in a Triangle," *Hollywood*, April 1936.

107. "Wife vs. Secretary," *Variety*, March 2, 1936.

108. "Cain and Mabel," *Photoplay*, October 1936.

109. "Love on the Run," *Hollywood Magazine*, January 1937.

110. "Love on the Run," *Modern Screen*, February 1937.

111. Myrna Loy, *Being and Becoming* (New York: Knopf, 1987).

112. *Modern Screen Magazine*, August 1937.

113. Myrna Loy, *Being and Becoming* (New York: Knopf, 1987).

114. Jeanne Bassinger, *The Star Machine* (New York: Vintage Books, 2009).

115. Parnell, *Hollywood Magazine*, August 1937.

116. "New Jean Harlow Picture to Be Made Over," *St. Louis Star and Times*, June 8, 1937.

117. "Death Will Cause Discard of Film Nearly Completed," *Los Angeles Times*, June 8, 1937.

118. "No Metro Decision on Saratoga Policy," *Box Office*, June 26, 1937.

119. David Bret, *Clark Gable: Tormented Star* (Boston: DeCapo, 2008).

120. "Test Pilot," *Photoplay*, May 1938.

121. "Test Pilot," *Modern Screen*, July 1938.

122. "Letters to the Editor," *Photoplay*, February 1939.

123. "Too Hot to Handle," *Modern Screen*, October 1938.

124. "Idiot's Delight," *Hollywood Magazine*, April 1939.

125. George Cukor directed some scenes without credit. Sam Wood is said to also have contributed.

126. This is the release of the Atlanta premiere. It premiered in New York on December 19, and in Los Angeles on December 28th. Its wide release was on January 17, 1940.

127. 223 min (1969 re-release) | 234 min (1985 re-release) | 224 min (1994 re-release) | 233 min (1989 re-release) | 226 min (copyright length).

128. "Actress Butterfly McQueen Is Killed in Fiery Accident," *Los Angeles Times*, December 23, 1995.

129. "Clark Gable Almost Went with the Wind: Olivia," *Vintage News*, July 1, 2016.

130. While he never outright sobbed in a movie, Clark Gable did have teary scenes in other films, including *Hold Your Man* and even the recent *Test Pilot*.

131. "Clark Gable Almost Went with the Wind: Olivia," *Vintage News*, July 1, 2016.

132. Jane Ellen Wayne, *Clark Gable: Portrait of a Misfit* (New York: St. Martin's Press, 1993).

133. "Gable Tested for Air Corps," *The Spokesman-Review* (Spokane, WA), June 20, 1942.

134. Warren D. Harris, *Clark Gable: A Biography* (New York: Harmony Books, 2002).

Bibliography

Books

Bassinger, Jeanne. *The Star Machine*. New York: Vintage Books, 2009.

Behlmer, Rudy. *Memo from David O. Selznick*. New York: Grove, 1972.

Bergman, Andrew. *We're in the Money*. New York: New York University Press, 1971.

Bret, David. *Clark Gable: Tormented Star*. Burlington, VT: DeCapo, 2008.

Capra, Frank. *The Name Above the Title*. New York: Macmillan, 1971.

Glatzer, Richard, and John Raeburn, eds. *Frank Capra: The Man and His Films*. Ann Arbor: University of Michigan Press, 1975.

Griffin, Merv. *From Where I Sit*. New York: Arbor House, 1982.

Harris, Warren G. *Clark Gable: A Biography*. New York: Harmony Books, 2002.

Hay, Peter. *MGM: When the Lion Roars*. Atlanta: Turner Publishing, 1991.

Loy, Myrna. *Being and Becoming*. New York: Knopf, 1987.

McBride, Joseph. *Frank Capra: The Catastrophe of Success*. New York: Simon & Schuster, 1992.

Morgan, Michelle. *Carole Lombard: Twentieth Century Star*. Cheltenham, Gloucestershire, UK: History Press, 2017.

Neibaur, James L. *The Essential Mickey Rooney*. Lanham, MD: Rowman and Littlefield, 2016.

Neibaur, James L. *The Jean Harlow Films*. Jefferson, NC: McFarland, 2019.

Oakie, Jack. *Jack Oakie's Double Takes*. San Francisco: Strawberry Hill Press, 1980.

Russell, Rosalind, with Chris Chase. *Life Is a Banquet*. New York: Random House, 1977.

St. Johns, Adela. *Love, Laughter and Tears*. New York: Doubleday, 1978.

Thompson, Frank, and John Gallagher. *Nothing Sacred: The Cinema of William Wellman*. Asheville, NC: Men with Wings Press, 2018.

Tornabene, Lynn. *Long Live the King*. New York: Putnam, 1976.

Wayne, Jane Ellen. *Clark Gable: Portrait of a Misfit*. New York: St. Martin's Press, 1993.

Wayne, Jane Ellen. *Stanwyck*. New York: Arbor House, 1983.

Young, Gwenda. *Clarence Brown*. Lexington: University Press of Kentucky, 2018.

Articles

"Actress Butterfly McQueen Is Killed in Fiery Accident." *Los Angeles Times*, December 23, 1995.

Cameron, Kate. "Gable, Davies Team in Unexciting Film." *New York Daily News*, March 19, 1932.

"Clark Gable Almost Went with the Wind." *Vintage News*, July 1, 2016.

"Clark Gable Model, Patch Pockets, Belt 'N' Etc., Hit Town." *New York Daily News*, July 31, 1934.

"Clark Gable, Myrna Loy to Be in Men in White." *The Tampa Tribune*, January 7, 1934.

"Clark Gable Refuses to Concede Devotion to Stage or Obligation for Its Influence on His Career." *Oakland Times*, June 3, 1934.

"Clark Gable Will Have More Dramatic Role in New Film." *The Sacramento Bee*, March 1, 1934.

"Claudette Colbert Sought for Lead." *Courier-Post*, April 13, 1934.

Coons, Robbin. "What Now for Jean Harlow?" *Los Angeles Times*, September 10, 1932.

Crawford, Joan. "Hollywood Gossip." *NEA Service*, November 1934.

"Death Will Cause Discard of Film Nearly Completed." *Los Angeles Times*, June 8, 1937.

"Directory of Pictures." *Modern Screen*, December 1931.

"14 Month Old Movie Star Dies in Desert Camp." *The Press Democrat* (Santa Rosa, CA), September 12, 1930

"Gable Bus Traveler." *The Los Angeles Times*, October 23, 1933.

"Gable Tested for Air Corps," *The Spokesman-Review* (Spokane, WA), June 20, 1942.

"Get Close Up of Film Hero." *Spokane Chronicle*, February 7, 1935.

Hall, Gladys. "Jean and Clark Expose Each Other." *Movie Classic*, May 1936.

Bibliography

"Harlow Sympathetic." *The Los Angeles Times*, July 20, 1932.

Harrison, Paul. "Hollywood Correspondent." *NEA Service*, January 2, 1936.

"Hollywood Sights and Sounds." *Los Angeles Times*, January 1, 1936.

Jackson, Fay M. "Dainty Theresa in Gang Film." *The Afro American*, August 28, 1937.

Jones, Adwal. "News Hound Role Not Foreign to Experience of Gable in 'Chicago.'" *San Francisco Examiner*, July 10, 1927.

"Jungle Rubber Plays a Part in 'Red Dust.'" *Times Union* (Brooklyn, NY), October 2, 1932.

Keats, Patricia. "Clark Gable in Strange Interlude." *Silver Screen*, May 1932.

Keavy, Hubbard. "Refilming "White Sister" with a Bit of Difference." *Indianapolis Star*, October 9, 1932

Krug, Karl. "Show Shops." *Pittsburgh Press*, October 24, 1931.

Landarzuri, Margaret. *Chained*, TCM.com database.

"Loretta Young Will Be Starred in 'Forsaking All Others.'" *Morning Post*, May 23, 1934.

Martin, Boyd. "Piping the Plays." *Courier Journal* (Louisville, KY), October 17, 1931.

"Men I Have Loved." *New Movie Magazine*, January 1934.

"Men in White to Be Made into Film with Clark Gable." *Star Tribune*, January 27, 1934.

"Movie Cast Snowbound Filming Call of Wild." *Courier-Post*, January 18, 1935.

Myrna Loy interview. *Modern Screen*, August 1937.

"New Art Described by Powell." *Star Tribune*, April 5, 1934.

"New Jean Harlow Picture to Be Made Over." *St Louis Star and Times*, June 8, 1937.

"'Night Nurse in Production.'" *Film Daily*, December 29, 1930.

"No Metro Decision on Saratoga Policy." *Box Office*, June 26, 1937.

"On the Set." *Evening Star* (Washington, D.C.), August 5, 1934.

Parsons, Louella. "Beery Gives Up Role of Skipper of Bounty." *Los Angeles Times*, January 4, 1935.

Parsons, Louella. "Call of the Wild Will Star Gable." *Los Angeles Times*, November 4, 1934.

Parsons, Louella. "Clark Gable is Garbo's New Leading Man" *The Los Angeles Times*, May 6, 1931.

Parsons, Louella. "Joan Crawford and Gable Will Be Teamed Again." *The San Francisco Examiner*, May 2, 1934.

Parsons, Louella. "Movie-go-round." *The Los Angeles Times*, May 10, 1931.

Parsons, Louella. "Night Flight Slated." *Courier-Post*, February 24, 1933.

"Real South Seas in 'Mutiny' Film." *New York Daily News*, January 13, 1935.

Schallert, Edward. Syndicated column, *Los Angeles Times*, February 18, 1933.

Schallert, Edward. "Work to Mark Yule Season." *Los Angeles Times*, December 15, 1932.

Skolsky, Sidney. "Hollywood." *New York Daily News*, January 8, 1935.

Skolsky, Sidney. "Hollywood." *New York Daily News*, October 2, 1934.

Soans, Wood. "Stars Line Up for New Roles." *The Los Angeles Times*, August 16, 1933.

Ulman, William. "Clark Gable Warns Stenos What Happens When Husbands Get Caught in a Triangle." *Hollywood*, April, 1936.

"Unusual Weather Delaying Stars In 'Mutiny on Bounty.'" *Indianapolis Star*, June 12, 1935.

"Watching Them Make Pictures." *New York Daily News*, March 27, 1934.

Whittaker, Alma. "Murder Role Career Climax." *Los Angeles Times*, June 8, 1930.

Reviews

"Cain and Mabel." *Photoplay*, October 1936.

"Chained." *Movie Classic*, October 1934.

"China Seas." *Variety*, August 31, 1935.

"Dance Fools Dance." *Brooklyn Times Union*, March 23, 1931.

"The Easiest Way." *New York Daily News*, February 28, 1931.

"The Finger Points." *Honolulu Star Bulletin*, October 5, 1931.

"The Finger Points." *The New York Daily News*, March 27, 1931.

"Forsaking All Others." *Los Angeles Examiner*, January 25, 1935.

"A Free Soul." *The New York Times*, June 22, 1931.

"A Free Soul," A *Photoplay*, July 1931.

"Hell Divers." *Motion Picture Times*, December 29, 1931.

"Hell Divers." *New York Daily News*, December 24, 1931.

"Hold Your Man." *The Los Angeles Times*, July 21, 1933.

"Idiot's Delight." *Hollywood Magazine*, April 1939.

"It Happened One Night." *Photoplay*, July 1934.

"Letters to the Editor." *Photoplay*, February 1939.

"Love on the Run." *Hollywood Magazine*, January 1937.

"Love on the Run." *Modern Screen*, February 1937.

"Manhattan Melodrama" *Hollywood Reporter*, April 16, 1934.

"Men in White." *Photoplay*, April 1934.

"Mutiny on the Bounty." *Hollywood*, January 1936.

"Mutiny on the Bounty." *Motion Picture Herald*, November 9, 1935.

"Night Flight." *Brooklyn Daily Eagle*, October 10, 1933.

"Painted Desert: The Screen in Review." *Picture Play Magazine,* June 1931.

"Parnell." *Hollywood Magazine*, August 1937.

"Polly of the Circus." *New York Daily News*, March 19, 1932.

"Polly of the Circus." *The Pittsburgh Press*, March 12, 1932.

"Possessed." *San Francisco Examiner*, November 22, 1931.

"San Francisco." *New York Times*, June 27, 1936.

"The Secret Six." *New Movie Magazine*, July 1931.

"Sporting Blood." *San Francisco Examiner*, August 10, 1931.

"Strange Interlude." *New York Daily News*, September 3, 1932.

"Strange Interlude." *New York Times*. September 1, 1932.

"Susan Lenox (Her Fall and Rise)." *NY Daily News*, October 25, 1931.

"Test Pilot." *Modern Screen*, July 1938.

"Test Pilot." *Photoplay*, May 1938.

"Too Hot to Handle." *Modern Screen*, October 1938.

"The White Sister." *Variety*, April 8, 1933.

"Wife vs. Secretary." *Variety*, March 2, 1936.

Trade Magazine Comments

"What the Picture Did for Me." *Motion Picture Herald*, 1931–1939.

Internet

Dear Mr. Gable.

Internet Movie Database.

Turner Classic Movies website

Wikipedia.

Interviews

Tay Garnett with John Gallagher in 1977 for a book.

Loretta Young interview with John Andrew Gallagher, *American Film Institute*, January 7, 1978.

Eugene Jackson, with the author, for a 1985 article.

Mickey Rooney, with the author, for a 2001 article.

Index

Index

Index

197